Journey

In

Grace

11/12/22

٢٢/١٢/١١

FOREWORD BY NEIL DOUGLAS-KLOTZ

author of Revelations of the Aramaic Jesus

Journey

In

Grace

Gems Gathered from a Life on the Path

DAVID L STERLING

Cover design by Anjum Jaleel
Cover image: "The Door to Timeless Grace" – Photograph taken by the author of Shaykh Fadhlalla Haeri's place of prostration

Published independently by the author

ISBN: 978-0-578-27444-7

Published in the United States of America

Your sickness is from you, but you do not perceive it and your remedy is within you, but you do not sense it. You presume you are a small entity, but within you is enfolded the entire Universe. You are indeed the evident book, by whose alphabet's the hidden becomes manifest.

Therefore, you have no need to look beyond yourself. What you seek is within you, if only you reflect.

Imam `Ali (`*Alayhi As-Salaam*)

Table of Contents

Dedication

This book is dedicated to all those seekers who know at the bottom of their heart that there is more to life than what has been on offer: good jobs, education, money, power, politics, women, men. They know that whatever is thrown on the quantitative scale for acquisition is never going to be enough. This book is for the ones who are discovering the true treasure of treasures, the wealth beyond wealth, the source of life and ultimate joy within the core of their being: the Soul within one's heart.

I also specifically dedicate this work to my sons. There is much a father often does not have the opportunity to share with their children. It is my hope that these stories will give them insight into my life and also a view into another way of looking at life's experience and the lessons, teaching and wisdom it contains when you open your heart and see with eyes of the Soul. They are all good men and I am proud of each one of them.

Journey in Grace

Acknowledgements

There have been so many contributors to this work going back many years. They know who they are and my gratitude goes out to all. There are several people who directly contributed to making this book happen, playing an outstanding role in its production. The first of whom is Anjum Jaleel for his relentless encouragement, editing, formatting and being such an inspiring friend. Muna and Abbas Bilgrami for their love and prodding me along to finish this book as well as their editorial advice and suggestions. Dr. Gregory Lipton, who believed deeply in this project, carved out time from his professional schedule to edit and make helpful suggestions to improve the book and its digestibility.

About This Book

This book has been in the making for nearly two decades. As my experiences multiplied over the years, I found myself sharing these experiences in gatherings – big and small – especially among the Sufi community I had been a member of for the better part of four decades. As time passed these stories became a regular feature in our annual gathering. It seemed no matter how many times I would repeat them they never lost their freshness and veracity to touch people's hearts and inspire the mind and imagination of the miraculousness of life and the unique gift of life's experiences we all share.

As time went on the volume of stories grew. It became clear that I needed to do justice to these experiences and share them with a greater audience. This inspiration was confirmed and magnified by Shaykh Fadhlalla Haeri who encouraged me to collect these stories all together and share them widely for the benefit of others that would surely be touched and inspired. It was a struggle for me to corner myself and actually write these stories down. I had been in the habit of "performing" them as is common in the Sufi tradition of oral storytelling. After much reflection I realized my reticence for writing these down was an egoic attachment to performing them, that I had become identified as a persona "Hajj Mustafa – the Sufi Storyteller." It was an ugly but needed realization which led me to put aside storytelling for a while. Overtime, with the grace of God, this inclination dissolved and replaced with a compulsion to share these stories not as an act of self-aggrandizement, but of gifts given to me with the responsibility to pass them on to others. The stories in this book are from my life's experience, but "my life" is a gift of the Life-Giver and the best one can do is get out of the way and be present in the moment as it flows through one. This is what I have attempted to do here in this book and He knows the truth of all things.

I hope you *in-joy* these stories.

Endorsements

I have respected and loved Hajj Mustafa for so many years that I cannot even count them.

The quality that I have enjoyed – and know others do too – is his story-telling ability, which carries considerable meaning and always have an ever-lasting transformational effect on others.

It's a rare situation to have someone who has had most of their life searching, investigating and enjoying meetings with remarkable and enlightened people.

His honesty, truthfulness and courage are the outstanding qualities that will come out in most of what he is conveying in his book.

This book is indeed one of the best ones in our times!

Shaykh Fadhlalla Haeri – An Enlightened Spiritual Master and Author

David Sterling's remarkable stories are a collection of gems that he has spent a life-time threading with the light of his soul.

The reader will journey along with David, connecting one gem to the other eventually to the presence of the Source, where all gems are gathered together in one sparkling message of unity and purpose.

Dr. Adnan al-Adnani – Author of *Lights of Consciousness*

Sterling's remarkable and deeply inspiring account is a real-life *Meetings with Remarkable Men* for the 21st century.

G. A. Lipton, PhD – Author of *Rethinking Ibn `Arabi*

Foreword

"There is an unexplainable alchemy that takes place when there is commitment and sincere seeking to live and be in harmony with the flow of truth as it unfolds in life's everyday occurrences."

Many "spiritual biographies" have appeared in recent years, often by people who were recognized (or who promoted themselves) as saints, masters, *pirs* or divine embodiments of some sort. As human beings, we naturally want to look up to figures that seem far beyond us. Our individual self, our *nafs* in Islamic and Sufi terms, really looks up to our soul (the *ruh*), which is what sees through the self's eyes and creates not only our own "I" but also the appearances we see around us. By only looking for outer heroes, we overlook the real hero within.

Hajj Mustafa never claims to be *anything*. He approaches his many searches and trials with a seemingly indefatigable sense of dry humor and self-deprecation. This is to distinguish the latter from what often appears in such books as an affected sense of modesty, which is really a form self-aggrandizement. The book's absolute, sincere honesty is one of the things that stayed with this reader long after finishing it.

It could be a "pilgrim's progress" except that there is no moralism, or pre-arranged theological arc to the events that unfold before us. It could a *"Candide,"* except that through all of the outrageous twists and turns of fate that the protagonist endures, his heart's compass always directs him to a true "magnetic north," and he is not willing to be satisfied with the mere appearance of what is true. One could easily become discouraged or cynical, especially when those whom one emulates turn out to have serious feet of clay. Here, however, we find an enduring *illa illahu* – "only Reality exists" – as a response to *la ilaha* – "there is no reality."

"Regardless of the many twists and turns and the best of intentions gone awry, in the end there is an arc of ascension that one moves along towards higher consciousness and presence within the everlasting, timelessness of the now."

Despite these short quotes I have pulled out, most of this book is one engaging, remarkable story after another.

From Mustafa's upbringing in an immigrant Jewish family, we follow him through many adventures with Hindu gurus and swamis, a naturist Christian cult, Rainbow people, Hopi elders, the Fourth Way school, and finally with various and sundry Sufi teachers, many of whom were largely unknown in the West during their lifetime. He travels around the world, from the USA to Europe, Saudi Arabia, Libya, Morocco, South Africa, Pakistan and back to the USA. Often, there is much crisscrossing, back and forth, like the movements of the knight across the chess board.

About half of the book follows what his main mentor Shaykh Fadhlalla Haeri calls the "arrow of time." Viewed through the eyes of our individual self, life unfolds as "one thing after another." It's the story of a journey, step by step. We are most often impacted by our past as we try to re-create pleasant moments we have experienced or avoid re-creating unpleasant ones. If wisely reflected upon, past experiences knock some rough edges off our *nafs* and prick enough holes in it to allow light to shine through. Then we begin to experience the soul's freedom rather than the self's false emulation of it.

> *"Life is full of lessons. Some come to us like a fragrant breeze, others like being hit by a train. There is no doubt that if one is sincere to God and to themselves, then the lessons of life will come in a way like the breezes. But when one is thick and without fear of consequences, then the lessons are knocking louder at the door."*

At a certain point, if we have the grace to follow the light that comes through the heart from either pain or love, we can not only *seek*, but stop seeking and *find* (as the Jesus in the Gospel of Thomas recommends). Then life is no longer "one thing after another," but a series of moments in which one witnesses blessing in whatever arises. Then one "marvels," again in the words of Jesus in Thomas. A step-by-step Newtonian line – cause inevitably leading to effect – turns into a quantum field from which particles of unexpected happenings suddenly appear and disappear.

Likewise, about half way through, Hajj Mustafa's book switches from the "arrow" of a straightforward story into a retelling of illuminated moments with various beings and events that demonstrate, as one of my Hindu friends likes to sing, "God is real."

Make no mistake. There are many remarkable meetings in this book. Some you may find miraculous or unbelievable. But this just shows that, despite the hypnosis imposed on us by an increasingly individualistic (selfie) and materialistic (selfish) way of living, an illusion supported by both social and non-social media, there is a secret life beyond and underneath everything we claim to know, especially about what is "possible."

The story here is not only about the existence of miracles, but also about the existence of ordinary people who are receptive to them. It's a two-way street in the neighborhood of the appearances with which we surround our selves (again our *nafs*) both individually and collectively as a humanity.

As Hajj Mustafa says after one of his extraordinary meetings:

> *"It is my hope in sharing these few stories about this great being, that whomever reads them will be blessed with a realization that there is more to our lives and this world than meets the outer senses. That, at any given moment, there is more influence by the unseen than what we experience in the seen world. What we often see is only the shadow-show of a play whose breadth and length are immeasurable. That the action of Angels, prayers and Decrees are more relevant, and that Allah is forever in charge."*

My only caution would be this: If after reading *Journey in Grace*, you were to go out and try to re-create Hajj Mustafa's experiences, you would be doing him, and even more yourself, a disservice. Have your own experiences, which can be equally remarkable. You need only open that remarkable place in your heart through which the soul's eyes can witness life through your own.

Dr. Neil Douglas-Klotz (Saadi Shakur Chishti), Fife, Scotland

Introduction

"I was a Treasure hidden
Wanting-loving to be known,
I created to be loved and be known".
— Sacred Tradition

There is only one story behind every story.

There is One Being behind all beings.

There is only One Originator, whose will and life force manifests all forms and gives rise to sentience within time and space.

The Originator, being Itself not subject to time and space, stirred with love and wanting to be known burst into the infinite forms of the universal effulgence.

Out of timelessness the first moment in time was born, its physics, inconceivable and incalculable by any scientific measure. Each and every atom, particle and wave of energy expanded in all directions, destined with the decree of the original intention, to be loved and known.

"To be known" is synonymous with consciousness, while "love" is the universal glue that connects all life in a seamless manner devoid of fault or fracture.

> *Existence contains every conceivable and imaginable creation and combination of forms and energies. Everything that exists connects and relates to everything else within space-time and beyond.*
>
> — Shaykh Fadhlalla Haeri (from Witnessing Perfection).

At the core and essence of every human there is the representative of the Absolute.

That representation has been given many names: *Ruh*, Soul, *Atma, Nefeesh* and Spirit. This "Soul" contains the original blueprint from which the limited or conditional self emerges. The material world is an appearance perceived by conditioned consciousness that expresses the meaning and purpose of life.

We are essentially a Soul or Spirit, caught within space and time, experiencing itself as a body and mind that gives rise to an illusion of being separate from that very Soul.

Everyone potentially has conscious access to the Soul, our true and authentic Self.

The challenge and purpose of human life is to *dis*-cover and willfully align to Soul and

Peace as Oneself.

> *O humankind! Be careful of your duty to your Lord Who created you from a single soul....*

— Qur'an 4:1

Just as energy and matter are bound to each other, constantly echoing their seamless connections between the material and non-material, that dynamic matrix underlies all manifestly discernable realities reflected throughout the universe.

Our lives mirror the Big Bang.

Look at the moment the female egg – the ovum – when the sperm pierces through the outer cells, it instantly locks out any other sperm from entering, declaring that the two have now become one. It immediately begins to multiply, through all the stages of evolution until the two genes become one singular message, producing a unique representative of God.

> *The Big Bang was not the beginning. There was something before the Big Bang and that something is what we will have in our future.*

— Sir Roger Penrose

On this earth, through time this guided preprogrammed evolutionary patterning, produced humankind, gifted with self-awareness and consciousness, hereto giving humanity the potential to *re*-cognize the Original Source and purpose of the universe.

From the moment we are born we are caught in a process of discovery. At first, we are driven by the instinct to survive and later, as we become self-aware, we transition from base animal instincts to ego centered motivations. This is a natural consequence of developing relationships with parents, siblings, friends, education, religion, etc. It is through experiencing multiplicity that the ego-self assumes that it contains the locus of consciousness, limited and conditional as it were and identifies itself as separate from that which it is experiencing. Ultimately the ego-centered life disappoints. This too is a process of the original intention. Whatever we believe or experience or identify with has no lasting consequence.

Everything is vanishing, except the face of the Lord, Owner of Majesty and Honor.

— Qur'an 55:27

The Sufi Way to seek and realize this knowledge is through Love. The Sufi sees the world as a complete and cohesive holistic panorama of signs, each reflecting back to the heart and mind of the seeker – another piece of the puzzle that leads to the realization of the wholeness of all things. That there is no separation between you and what you see and experience. When this is embraced wholly, Love embraces you. No one can give you or take away what has always been with you at the very core of your being.

For the one gifted with higher consciousness, in itself an attribute of spiritual intelligence, he or she recognizes these patterns and seeks to invest their attention on what is truly reliable and consistently leads to real joy, love and certainty.

— Shaykh Fadhlalla Haeri

The relative self, or conditioned self, is an emanation or echo of the Absolute, its form and unique expression are designed to realize the illusion of separation from its origin, returning through yielding its imagined will, to the Ever-Constant Spirit within: Allah, the One and Only.

The potential to perceive our interconnectedness to the universe has never been as advantageous to humanity as a whole as it is in this moment and time.

There is a confluence of new discoveries and tools that are influencing the evolution of higher consciousness impacting the collective awareness of humankind.

Today, in our news feeds and notifications a day does not go by that we hear about climate change or see a new photograph from the James Webb telescope. The first reminds us of our seamless connection to the earth and the collective and individual accountability of our actions. The latter is a devastating perceptive leap out of our small and seemingly insignificant lives into realizing that we are part of a magnificent vast effulgence of Life itself.

The stories in this book are offered as a means to reflect on the clear and obvious meaningful nature of life.

The landscape of my life has been full of experiences that have been part of a personal evolutionary process towards awakening to its rich meaningful content. The world and how we experience it is perfectly designed for each one of us to read and reflect on what is being communicated in every perfect moment.

We are all the same in this way. One underlying, ever-constant life-giving light is at the core and nature of our being. The only difference is the outer shell and conditioning: the individual self-architecture that creates the lens by which we see, experience and identify with as a separate self.

Each one of us is at the threshold of awakening to *dis*-cover the true and ever-constant within. This worldly experience is nothing other than an alchemist's pot in which all the basic elements have been brought together by The Master Alchemist in a process of transmutation revealing the pure gold that lies in hidden potential to be *dis*-covered.

> *Lasting fulfillment can only be achieved when the perfection of every moment is seen and realized. The rational mind relates to the world of cause and effect and guides us to physical survival and well-being. The heart and soul is what distinguishes humanity and enable us to relate to the unseen and the worlds beyond time and space. This earth is God's nursery where every creation evolves to the highest level of its consciousness within its soul's capacity.*

— Shaykh Fadhlalla Haeri

The formula is clear. True lasting fulfillment can only be realized by putting aside one's own ego-centered agenda through aligning with the ever-present Soul. The nature of that Soul is beyond time and space. When you willfully put aside the acquired self, that which has always been present (Soul) becomes known. This is what being present in the moment means.

David L Sterling
(aka Hajj Mustafa)
Istanbul, Turkey 2022

A Brief Family History

My Parents Fleeing Poland to Russia During the War

My parents fled Poland just after the German invasion of September 1, 1939. They headed east, towards the Russian-controlled areas. Along with my mother, two of her brothers also fled, leaving behind my grandparents and ten of her brothers and sisters. My grandparents had thought that the Germans would respect the civilian population of Jews, and that staying behind would be prudent to protect their homes and properties. It did not go the way they thought. My entire mother's family, grandparents and extended family were either killed or sent to concentration camps to eventually perish.

The Russian authorities arranged traveling papers for my parents and directed them to go to Central Asia, where the people of Tashkent and Samarkand had generously offered to welcome them and provide shelter from the war.

My parents joined a group of over eighty travelers, all setting out on foot to Tashkent. It took nearly two months to cover the four-thousand-kilometer journey. Along the way, they relied on the good graces of towns and villages, as well as Russian Army barracks, where they were given leftover food and used clothing.

In Tashkent

Upon arriving in Tashkent, they were warmly greeted by the Muslim-Jewish Support groups. The travelers were given new clothes and assigned to volunteer families throughout Tashkent. My parents stayed with a small family who worked in a Russian owned Tea factory. Eventually, both my mother and father worked in the Tea factory for the duration of the war.

I always joked that I probably became Muslim after a *Wali* (Saintly Being) of Allah in Tashkent saw my mother and looked to the heavens, hands raised and prayed: "*May her first born be a Muslim.*"

Group Portrait of Jewish Refugees in Samarkand in Front of Tamarlane's Tomb
(1942 - 1946)

Courtesy of United States Holocaust Memorial Museum

My parents often retold the hardships they had to go through to reach Central Asia, detailing how they survived with each day bringing uncertainty, unsure whether they would make it to their destination or not, and, when they arrived, what they would find.

My mother and father showed humility and gratefulness that they were able to make it through the hardships of the journey.

It reminds me of the verses in the Qur'an:

In the name of the All-Encompassing, Eternal Source

Whose First and Foremost nature is unfathomable Mercy.

Who manifests a taste and echo of His Mercy within the limitation and relative, conditioned consciousness of the human heart and mind?

Have we not opened up your heart and lifted away any burden that may have weighed heavy upon your back?

Raising you high in remembrance of that which all things are predicated.

Behold the true nature: that within every difficulty, there is ease; surely, with every difficulty there IS ease!

So, when you are relieved from distress, hold steadfast to this certainty and turn towards that which sustains you in Love.

Qur'an's Chapter 94, *Surah Ash-Sharh*

— **Interpretation by author**

The seeds of one thing are always present in the other. The Yin and Yang symbol so eloquently displays this reality. One has the seed (potential) of the other within it. They dance in harmony with each other.

War is Over

The war ended on September 2, 1945. My parents returned to their homes in Pinsk, Poland, only to find everyone in their families dead and their properties taken away. Like the majority of Jews displaced in Europe, all were in shock and uncertain of what was to become of them; there was no going "home."

Immediately after hostilities ceased, Zionist organizations were set up throughout Europe, especially in major cities and towns, offering a way forward to most of the Jewish refugees. They would provide money, support, and boat tickets to either New York or Tel Aviv. My parents signed on with the group for New York.

Growing Up in Brooklyn, New York

I was born in New York in an island neighborhood, uniquely placed, in that it was a gathering point for post-holocaust refugees, trying to heal and regain themselves after the brutal ravages of World War Two.

It was here that I was adopted by aunts and uncles, grandfathers and grandmothers, not of blood, but of the common need of circumstance in which we all found ourselves to rebuild the families and communities lost in the war.

My first language was Yiddish and, as far as I knew, everyone was Jewish.

Later, I learned there were the "goys," strangers, aliens, that I would hear about on occasion, but it wasn't until I attended public school that I had any exposure to these "outsiders."

The door of our home/apartment was always open and there was a steady stream of visitors, cakes and cookies and the constant stench of cigarettes. The conversations were like anyone might find when people get together: so and so is marrying this one and that "Yankle" (a Yiddish generic term to mean "so and so") is a womanizer, etc. But inevitably the conversations would turn towards the war, recanting the loss of family, mothers, fathers, brothers, sisters and aunts, some not even knowing where their graves were, or in some cases not knowing if they were truly dead or not. Laughter often changed to tears, then to anger. Silence would follow in desperation, as there was nothing to do but face the loss and uncertainty and hold out hope. For most, hope was a faint glimmer which they did not allow themselves to seriously consider. Many felt guilty about surviving the war, so many of their mothers, fathers, sisters and brothers had perished senselessly. I often heard my parents' friends shout out in despairing guilt, "Why me, why I survived and they did not!"

Growing up in Brooklyn, New York, as a first-generation post-holocaust child, I felt obliged to take on the persona of a victim and the responsibility to always "remember" what "they" did to us. It was like an alter ego that we carried around, leering in the background as a dual identity.

On the one hand we were first generation Americans, happily and gratefully growing up in the USA, with all its privileges and opportunities and, on the other hand, imprinted within our hearts and minds, we were not the same as those around us. We were always reminded that what happened to us in Europe could happen again, even here in America.

Hitler, and the Germans in general, were cursed regularly in our homes. I can remember how as a child my brothers and sister and I would lie in bed at night and imagine countless ways in which we would kill and torture Hitler and his generals if they should fall into our hands.

We had little exposure to "gentiles." We attended public school in a Jewish neighborhood, attended "*Shul*" religious study after school six days a week and lived in an apartment building with nearly 100% Jewish European refugees.

My father sold buttons on the street to make ends meet and my mother worked in a sweatshop sewing garments.

When I was not attending public school, mostly on weekends and holidays, my father would take me to where he set up his vending table, on the sidewalks of midtown Manhattan.

His preferred location was near Broadway and 42nd street. All day long he would hawk his buttons: "Two for a quarter, come and get it!" His plea blended into a cacophony of calls from the hundreds of street vendors, selling anything from ladies' bras, to walking sticks, dill pickles and snake oil.

In the winter months, he would leave early in the morning to do his best to locate himself near several old oil barrels, strategically positioned on the streets. They were filled with wood from broken pallets and shipping boxes, whatever would burn, so we could stay warm on the cold winter streets of New York. It was very hard for him. I had much respect for his tenacity, diligence and the sacrifices he made to support us. My mother worked in a "sweatshop," spending 12 hours a day in a dimly lit, poorly ventilated room, working piecework in an assembly line. I could never repay what they did for my siblings and me.

Thankfully, my father was an entrepreneurial type. He saved his money and, after a few years, opened a ladies' dry goods store in Harlem. Life was still a struggle, so after a few years my uncle in California invited us. He had touted California as a state flowing with milk and honey. He didn't realize how prophetic he was, when my father's first job upon arriving in Sacramento was delivering milk.

Moving to California

Sacramento did not work out for my family. There were no other Jewish families besides my uncle's, so we moved to Los Angeles.

Los Angeles was not like New York at all.

Our island-neighborhood we had so enjoyed and in which we felt protected was gone. We were now at the edge of "manifest destiny" and there was nowhere else to go but into the sea.

LA had a large Jewish community with Synagogues and Kosher shops and restaurants. Many of my parents' friends from New York had moved there, and there were many others from the "old country" as well. Our family was doing much better. My father worked as a shoe store manager for Karl's Shoes and my mother worked for Rudi Gernreich, a famous clothes designer. Rudi invented the first topless bathing suit; my mother had the infamous role of sewing the original prototype.

Initial Spiritual Encounters

My First "Goy" Friend – Exposure to Meditation

One day I saw our neighbor sitting in the shared garden of our apartment complex. His legs were folded one over the other, which later I came to know as a yogic position for meditation. His eyes were closed but I sensed that he was very awake and inward looking. I found this inward looking to be intriguing. I slowly snuck up to him to observe him from close up.

I clearly felt contentment shining from his face and emanating from his being.

It drew me like a moth to a flame. Upon opening his eyes, his hand also opened and revealed a flower held delicately cupped within his palm. He gestured to me to come closer and said, while handing me the flower: "the entire universe is contained in that flower, but that we could truly perceive it, surely it would lift the veil of separation from our minds and hearts, and we would experience the interconnectedness of all things".

My eyes and then my heart fell upon the flower. It opened its secret voice. I saw the swirling pattern and intelligent design. It urged me on, diving past the outer architecture and revealed the mirror echo of the universal patterning, evident throughout creation. My body tingled; my mind became excited yet still, expanding into a new way to see the world. From that day forward nothing was the same.

I was stunned with the whole experience, and especially with the depth and character of my new goy-friend. Up until that point, I did not consider that any Goy could have anything of a profound nature to offer. The idea of veiled perception and flowers that mirrored profound meaning turned my world upside down.

This happened three days after my Bar mitzvah. I had just become a full man in the Jewish traditions and a member of the congregation. I had felt proud and ready to take up the mantle of the next generation of Jews. All that was swept aside like a Tibetan mandala, which, once completed, is blown away by the invocation-filled breath by the Lamas who originally constructed it. The mandala of my life up to that point vanished.

My goy friend, Tom, took me on as a guru would a disciple, teaching me to meditate as prescribed by the Maharishi Mahesh Yogi (the same Guru the Beatles followed), and introduced me to incense, the Beatles, Marijuana, and friends of his in the music and entertainment industry.

One of his friends was Paul Mazursky, a Hollywood producer and director. The introduction was in the context of babysitting his children. I developed a good reputation as a reliable babysitter with other Hollywood personalities like Leonard Nimoy, Bernie Hamilton, William Shatner, and others.

My mother complained that I was keeping too close a company with the "Goyim" (plural of Goy). She argued that I was losing my "Yiddishkayt" (Jewish identity) and that it would lead me to ruin. Little did she know that all the actors mentioned above were Jewish.

This led me to question myself, my faith, my culture and my beliefs into which I had been brought up, and which I had held and accepted all my life. It was arrogant, in my mind, after meeting "others", that "my people" were the "chosen people" and that somehow the rest were of a lower caste.

As time moved on, I became certain that truth, as I knew it, was not 'the' Truth. In fact, the whole idea of an "ultimate" truth did not enter my thoughts until I came face to face with the lies and illusions of which I now became aware and started to question. I began to question everything.

"Nine rules of life: Don't analyze. Don't complain. Don't compare yourself to others. Don't expect things to be done for you. Don't expect perfection in the relative. Look at the knowledge aspect daily. Own the movement. Be present in the Now.

"Problems are all in your head. Hold yourself together."

— Maharishi Mahesh Yogi

My Spiritual Realization

Building within me was a sense of disconnectedness. Little by little, and sometimes like a landslide, the world I knew and defined myself through was crumbling. What kept me going was a deep sense of "knowing" that there is a "center," a place within that is "real," reliable and sacred. By this time, I had met many people who "lived" by another drumbeat. They all had the same thing in common, a look that shone from their eyes, as though they were "seeing" beyond, seeing more. I soon calibrated to this shining and became obsessed about being in their company and seeking out a way to be like them.

This realization was the catalyst that urged me on and helped with the pain and suffering and feelings of loss and hopelessness. I now knew that the answer was "out there, somewhere," and set out on a quest to find where I could plug into it.

I was 17 years old.

At the core of every human being resides a spark of The Eternal. It is known as the *Ruh* (Spirit, Soul). Its shadow is the relative self, conditioned self. It is the challenge and task underpinning the purpose of human life to dis-cover and willfully align to that soul and, through the process of constantly referring to its presence, live more in harmony and Peace with oneself.

There is no doubt that we exist in an interconnected Universe. Each one of us has the potential to awaken and recognize this within the evolving plot of our individual lives.

Most of us can point to times and circumstances where felicity fell upon us. There are many stories of people with incurable cancer suddenly going into remission. Wasn't there a moment in your life that you thought you might die and you were saved? You may have had no money, about to be evicted onto the streets, then, out of nowhere, help came.

These types of experiences abound and touch everyone's life.

There is only One Reality, One Light that resides at the core of every perceivable thing. It is the Source of all and is "The hidden Treasure" within the heart of every human being. God speaks to His creation through the creational effulgence. Everything is His speech! When we awaken to His Presence, only then can we "read" with inner sight the boundless signs of His manifest Guidance and Mercy.

So it was that at the age of 17, feeling restless, yet hopeful, in the concrete desert of Los Angeles, help came.

"Be Here Now."

Be Here Now

Around this time, I discovered the book *Be Here Now* by Ram Das (Dr. Richard Albert). It became my "bible" and constant companion. When I was confused and needed answers, I turned to this book, opening it like one would consult an oracle. It never failed to provide me with an inspirational and satisfying answer to contemplate. *Be Here Now* contains many wisdom stories about past and living spiritual guides and masters. The main theme put forth in this book is that through the millennium there was, and remains, one constant unchanging reality, that this world and all that it contains cannot fill the yearning within the heart for that, which is everlasting. The crucible of sickness, old age and death hangs over us all. This non-negotiable reality drives us to ask if there's more beyond this existence.

The other main theme of *Be Here Now* is that answers to these questions are already within us but it takes a change in consciousness to be open to discovering them. This was the most intriguing theme for me, in that it postulated the potential to discover a "path" or discipline that could be followed to lead one to a higher state of being, i.e., higher consciousness.

> *"Everything changes once we identify with being the witness to the story, instead of the actor in it."*

> — Ram Das

Paramahansa Yogananda

Los Angeles in the late sixties and early seventies was overflowing with Gurus from many different traditions and nationalities. Los Angeles was also the home of the Self Realization Fellowship, founded by Paramahansa Yogananda.

On August 20, 1950, Yogananda also formally opened Shrine Lake, coinciding with the thirtieth anniversary of Paramahansa Yogananda's work in America. Shrine Lake was born out of a vision to enshrine and acknowledge that all religions emerged from One Source. The lake covered 10 acres and was shaped like a heart. It had pathways around its circumference, each spaced evenly along the lake. There were small buildings at the end of each path, each dedicated to a different religion or teaching. Visitors could enter these spots and remain for meditation and prayer. At the crown of the Lake, Yogananda designed the Golden Lotus Archway as a "wall-less temple." The top of the temple featured a large golden lotus flower. In India the lotus flower is a symbol of divine unfoldment – the awakening of the soul to its infinite potential. Underneath the archway, Yogananda dedicated a portion of Gandhi's ashes, encased in a brass and silver coffer, where it was enshrined in a thousand-year-old stone sarcophagus from China.

Shrine Lake became my place of refuge. Its grounds were like an oasis from the tumult of the world. It was like entering the eye of a hurricane, a place of respite. The good energy of its precincts was palpable. Whenever I was struggling, I would come and sit under the "Wall-less Temple" and be at peace. Nearly every time I visited Shrine Lake I would meet another sojourner, whether walking on the circular path or sitting in meditation, there always was someone "waiting" for me to commune with. These meetings were priceless and encouraged me, lifting my state and resolve.

When opening descends upon us, it is so necessary to have others that are like-minded, like-hearted to reflect and to mirror what is within your heart and mind. It is a symbiotic process that helps with doubts and further expands your knowledge and vision.

The Guru

During this time in Los Angeles while walking on Santa Monica Blvd. and La Brea Ave., I came across a new shop that had opened. It was like no shop I had ever seen before. Looking through the large wood framed display windows there were rows of men and women sitting on carpets facing the back of the store. They were of mixed age, many dressed like hippies, some wearing saffron robes, lots of jeans and Levi jackets. Incense was pouring out the door from what appeared to be a religious altar of some type. At the center back of the room there was a raised area, set with cushions and a man sitting there with his eyes closed, long hair draped down over his shoulders. He was wearing a white Indian kurta shirt; prayer beads fell around his neck and his hands were in a meditative *mudra*. He spoke into a microphone that was attached to a junction box with several leads that led to earphones. This was how most were listening to the man sitting on the platform.

I was transfixed, staring into the shop, and wondering what was going on. In that very moment the man opened his eyes, which immediately landed on me and with an elegant gesture called me in to sit down. I was ushered in by one of the male acolytes and a headset was placed upon my ears. The man was introduced to me as Franklin Jones, (later changing his name many times to Bubba Free Jon, then Da Free Jon, finally settling as Adi Da), and began to chant the Hindu *mantra* of "OM". Within moments I was swept into another state of consciousness. My body felt as though it were melting away; there was a feeling in my heart of overflowing love. My mind raced to provide explanations, thoughts riding on fear that I may "lose" myself in the midst of a disappearing body, at least that is the way my mind tried to "frame" the experience. I could not take my eyes off

Baba Free Jon. He looked at me as though he knew exactly what was happening to me. I took strength from his glance and went with the flow. I remained there for about an hour. The session was over and soon turned into an opportunity to socialize with the other meditators. Baba Free Jon walked among the folks for a short time. Before leaving he came over to me giving me a warm embrace and invited me to come again. As we separated from the embrace he said, "If I love you, God loves you."

Initially I was deeply moved by the teacher's words, as they were reassuring and made me feel special. It also unleashed a torrent of thoughts and emotions in contemplating the meaning of his statement. Was he "God"? Did God inform him in some prophetic way that the Almighty acknowledged His Love synonymous with God's Love? Was I being played? Having been brought up in New York with a modicum of street savvy, I felt that although the Guru might have been sincere, it felt like it was accompanied with an errant agenda. Nevertheless, I returned for many nights to the "meditation shop," sometimes the Guru was there and when he was not, we would listen to prerecorded talks. My visits there expanded my mind as well as introduced me to the ideas and concepts of Vedanta teachings. On one cold and rainy night, I made my way to the meditation and found the shop closed, lights off and locked. There was a small sign on the door accompanied with a phone number that said:

"Gate Gate Pāragate Pārasamgate Bodhi Svāhā"
Gone, gone, gone beyond, gone beyond, beyond, Hail the goer, beyond even conceiving of a place beyond which you can go, beyond.

That was the last time I had any contact with Baba Free Jon's group until many years later after moving to the San Francisco Bay Area.

"Be Consciousness (Itself) – Contemplate Consciousness (Itself) – Transcend Everything in Consciousness (Itself)"

— Adi Da (AKA: Baba Free Jon)

Life Goes on in Los Angeles – Jiddu Krishnamurti

My job as babysitter continued to grow. I was baby-sitting almost every weekend and sometimes after school. On one of these weekends Paul Mazursky asked me to bring my sister along to help with looking after several families' children. They were taking me to the Self-Realization Fellowship to hear a talk presented by a special guest speaker, Jiddu Krishnamurti.

The SRF had organized a special meet and greet after the talk as well. The audience was filled with Hollywood actors, movers, and shakers as well as several devotees from the SRF.

My sister and I were looking after the children in the hallway behind the theater room, but I stood near the swinging doors peering through a wide crack, where the doors separated. Someone had taken the stage and began the introduction of Krishnamurti.

He then asked the speaker to come out on the stage. As Krishnamurti walked out on the stage, the entire audience broke out in loud applause, some even cheering. I could see the shadow of utter pity come over the face of Krishnamurti. He stopped halfway, turned back, and left the stage. The master of ceremonies asked everyone to be quiet and patient as he went after KM.

After some time, the MC emerged and explained to the audience that the way he was lauded by the people present he did not believe to be appropriate, and that anyone present would benefit from his talk. Nevertheless, Krishnamurti was convinced to return to the stage with hope that after being reminded of projecting their self-aggrandizement, they would review and reflect on their behavior and get serious.

Krishnamurti returned to the stage and began his talk with a reprimand, underscoring the urgent requirement to let go of identification with one's persona, career, and status in the world. He admonished the actors in the audience pointing out that their welcoming him on the stage was as if he were beginning a performance. He smiled after saying this with a glimmer of light from his eyes. "We are all actors in this life," he said, "but behind the façade is the One and Only actor, and it is to that we must awaken." Krishnamurti emphasized that awakening begins and ends in being present, in the ever-lasting now and we should not be distracted by the ever-shifting sands of ephemeral life.

> *"Without comprehending the present, which is rooted in the past, you will have no understanding. The present misery of [humanity] is understood when through the door of the present, [They are] able to be aware of the causes that have produced it. You cannot brush aside the present in trying to understand the past, but only through awareness of the present does the past begin to unfold itself. …. The present is of the highest importance; the present, however tragic and painful, is the only door to reality…. The present is the only time for understanding, for it extends into yesterday and into tomorrow. The present is the whole of time; in the seed of the present are the past and the future; the past is the present and the future is the present. The present is the eternal, the timeless… Look only to the present, neither to the past nor to the future, for love is the present, the timeless."*

— Jiddu Krishnamurti

I was deeply touched by the majesty, humility and abandonment Krishnamurti displayed in the mirror of my heart. His small frame was eclipsed by the immensity of his being and perennial message. At the time I could not fully comprehend what I had just witnessed, but the "taste" of this moment remained with me as I later came across the same emanations from other teachers and masters.

It reminds me now of chapter 108 in the Qur'an, Surah *al-Kawthar*:

> *We have truly given abundance to you [Prophet]—*
>
> *so, pray to your Lord and make your sacrifice to Him alone—*
>
> *it is the one who hates you who has been cut off.*

Krishanmurti was given abundance; he remained steadfast in his being and committed to it in every moment. Many could not fathom him and remained with their opinions, but he was filled with the eternal drink, while others, drunk with that which has no sustainability, constancy, or durability, were met with ruin.

Leaving Los Angeles

On my eighteenth birthday I was ready to make a move out of Los Angeles and begin my quest to find a person, a community, and a teaching that would lift me from the mires of my pain and conflict raging within me.

It was very hard for my parents to understand when I tried to explain to them what was going on with me and why I had to leave Los Angeles, leaving them to find my way. My father, however, was less concerned and I noticed his near approval of what I was proposing. On a sunny LA morning both my parents drove me to the Hollywood freeway entrance on Highland Blvd., where, after giving me $20.00, dropped me off to hitchhike going north. They waited until a car pulled over and I disappeared from their sight.

On the Road

The car that pulled over was a panel truck. There were three people sitting in the front. They asked me where I was going? I answered north. They opened the back doors and there were several hitchhikers already inside, sitting on a foam mattress that covered the entire back of the van. The windows were tinted and, when the door closed, it was almost pitch black. My fellow travelers were from all over the US, and all were heading to northern California and some as far as British Columbia. I immediately felt comradely with everyone sensing we were all the same, seeking answers.

The rocking of the van, combined with not having slept very much the night before, caused me to readily fall asleep.

It must have been several hours that I was out, at least I felt that way as I began to wake up. The van was still, and all my fellow travelers were gone. In the distance I heard voices of people, young and old, accompanied with the sound of splashing water. I could see through the cracks in the window tint, trees lit with sunlight and glittering dust particles sparkled around me. I opened the back doors of the van, and as they swung wide, it revealed a beautiful shining lake or reservoir. The van was pulled right up to the edge. As my eyes adjusted to the bright light, I was stunned to see the entire lake filled with several dozen people, frolicking in the water, all naked as the day they were born.

At a Lake

Within moments of emerging from the van a man enthusiastically approached me. He welcomed me and suggested I come out of the van, get naked and join the fun. Although I was all for people who found this a rewarding and maybe freeing experience, I had a strong sense of modesty and self-preservation. I thanked him for the invitation, but I told him that I needed to get back on the road towards my destination. He explained that the lake was far from the nearest road and that it would soon be dark. He suggested I at least remain for the night and take off in the morning. He continued to press me to join them; my resistance began to wear down. I felt conflicted and found myself in a labyrinth of self-doubting thoughts. So, giving in to the old saying, "when in Rome do as the Romans do," I found a tree, leaned my backpack against it (containing all my belongings), pegged my clothes to a broken branch, shoes at the foot of the tree and quickly slid into the lake up to my navel to minimize exposure.

The people were all very nice. We played Marco Polo, and other such games. Some had set up a pool volleyball set, everyone was naked, but it was pretty much like a suburban pool party in any middle-class neighborhood.

The sun was beginning to set in the forest. A caller standing on the perimeter of the lake called out an announcement that it was time to get out of the water. Without question, everyone began to exit the lake. I found this to be odd, in that there was not the slightest expression of dissent, just total uniformity in their response.

I stealthily came out of the lake and went towards the tree where I had stashed my clothes and other belongings. When I arrived at the tree a tsunami of anxiety swept over me as I could see no backpack or the clothes I was wearing, only my shoes left at the foot of the tree. I panicked. I saw the man who had initially invited me to the water. I asked him where my clothes and backpack were. He manically laughed and said: "You do not need your clothes anymore. You were born in God's image, and today you will reclaim your natural state." Panic turned into anger, and I insisted that my belongings be returned to me immediately. He said: "Come with us to our village and we will see about getting your belongings back." It was now dark, only a worn footpath was discernible going through the forest. Everyone walked single file down the path. I had been given a Mexican blanket to throw over my shoulders as the temperature dropped with the setting sun.

Christian Cult

We walked for about half an hour. I could hear other voices coming from the distance ahead. There was a clearing in the forest. The clearing was a circular line with huts, teepees and converted school buses. In the center, was a large geodesic dome. It had triangular windows cut out in a symmetric pattern around the sides. I peered through the windows and saw that the entire space was jammed up with people. All naked, of course! I was ushered in and asked to sit down. In the middle of the dome there was a raised platform. At the center of the platform was a large, man-sized wooden cross. Standing in front of the cross, a man with a bullhorn was speaking out, requesting people to come forward and testify their experience with Jesus that day.

Several people, young and old, came to share their stories; the whole time, the people in the room became more agitated and excited, some started swaying, others jumping up and down, many shouting out spontaneously, some with words of praise, while some began speaking in indiscernible tongues.

As the number of witnesses died down, there was a long pause. The man with the bullhorn began to talk. He said: "There is someone amongst us that has not witnessed, someone who does not believe." I started to look around the room like most others were doing; I had no idea that he was talking about me. He ordered that I be brought to the platform. Two men approached me. They each grabbed one arm and lifted me off the ground and brought me to the platform. I was now standing, naked in more ways than one, under the wooden cross. The man with the bullhorn began speaking to me gently at first. He asked me, in a firm, commanding way to accept Jesus Christ as my savior. I desperately struggled to answer, my mind caught in a vortex of circling thoughts and anxiety. I answered, "Although I respect your beliefs, I am but a visitor here and, …" Well, before I could finish my sentence, he yelled into the bullhorn, "These are the words of Satan! Satan be gone! Satan be gone! His tone grew more aggressive, and he asked me again to accept Jesus Christ as my savior. Feeling like whatever, I say now would be useless, I held out hope and tried again to explain myself just as before, but he cut me off and began shouting again. Without warning, the two men that brought me up to the stage pulled my legs from underneath me and laid me down flat on my back at the foot of the cross. I looked up at the cross looming over me, like a tombstone. The crowd that filled the dome rushed forward, towards me-- men, women and even children, all vigorously slapping my body with their hands like a relentless torrential hive of stinging hornets. At my head was the man with the bullhorn at my ear, shouting over and over again: "Satan, be gone! Accept Jesus Christ as your savior!" This went on and on, my body burning, my mind overwhelmed, until finally, I desperately shouted out, "Jesus Christ, save me!" In that instant the brutal ritual ceased. The dome was now silent. I was brought to my feet and congratulated by the bullhorn man and the two thugs that delivered me to the stage. In an Orwellian mind-hive fashion, all the attendees in the room lined up to welcome me to the fold with a hug. There was palpable relief in their eyes after I had finally been saved.

If they only knew!

I was told that I would remain with one of their families, living in their tent until I had been initiated in their community ways, worship, and customs.

Needless to say, I was in a state of shock. From the moment I was lifted from the stage, I felt a deep sense of loss. I didn't know who I was any more. My mind entertained the idea that maybe this is what I was looking for, maybe Jesus in my own way.

The next day, I was brought to the leader of this group whom they all referred to as the head apostle. His tent was the biggest with the most accommodations – there was an electric generator, a real bed and plenty of food visible in the pantry. He introduced himself as The Hand of Christ on earth. Sitting with him were 12 other men. I later learned these were representative of the 12 apostles of Christ. They read me the "riot act" as it were, and said that he was the absolute leader and demanded full fealty. He said that I would be given tasks to maintain the village and after some time I would be provided with a house and a wife that would be chosen for me. The Hand of Christ was charismatic, well spoken with a commanding personality. He looked and sounded like Charlton Heston, who played the role of Moses in the movie, *The Ten Commandments*.

After a few days, I started to return to my senses and made plans to escape. This was easier said than done, in that they always had someone with me, to keep an eye on me.

Fleeing From the Christian Cult

On the fourth night it was a new moon. Everyone was asleep in the tent. I had my shoes, nothing else, and fled into the forest in the pitch black of night.

I ran for my life. The forest was pitch black, only the light of the stars and the sliver of the moon to guide my steps. I prayed the whole time that I would find a way out, fearing that I may just go deeper into the forest that merged with a national park of millions of acres.

After about an hour I picked up the sound of a motor. I followed the sound until up ahead I could see a small light through the trees, rocking back and forth. As I approached closer, I could make out that there was a clearing up ahead and a man on a small old tractor was plowing a field. This was in the middle of night, so it seemed odd, but nevertheless I ran towards the man, naked, hoping that he would help me. He stopped the tractor after hearing me yelling out, but as soon as he saw me, he jumped from the tractor and started running away. I noticed that he was Mexican from his dress and Spanish music playing from a transistor radio from the tractor. I again beseeched him in Spanish, shouting "please, please! In the name of God, please!" Thank God, he stopped running and cautiously approached me. I explained as much as I could with limited Spanish, hand, and body language, hoping to communicate with him. I was overjoyed when he broke out laughing and exclaimed in Spanish "Oh! The loco Christian camp, they cause so much trouble for us." I asked him to help me get out of the forest. To at least guide me to the nearest highway, so I could continue my journey. He thankfully agreed. In a wooden box attached to the back of the tractor he pulled out an old, tattered pair of overalls. He gave them to me to cover my naked body. I cannot adequately describe the sense of gratitude for these clothes. Putting them on after being naked for about five days was like draping myself in the finest linens and silk. I broke into tears.

As we headed out of the forest at an even click of about five miles per hour, we arrived at the coastal Highway 1. Along the way, he told me about the field where we met, it was a Marijuana crop, hidden deep in the forest. He was cultivating it for a dealer in Eugene, Oregon.

He dropped me off at Highway 1 where, somewhere in the forest, was that turn off where I had been kidnapped. Many years later I was passing through this same area and inquired about the Christian Cult. There were many stories, and all ended in disaster.

Arriving at the highway, I stuck my thumb out and the first car that came along pulled over. The driver asked me where I was going. I said anywhere but here; he opened the door and let me in. The driver whom I will from now on refer to only by his first name was Peter. He became a lifelong friend not just to me, but also to the rest of my family.

The First Rainbow Family Gathering

In the summer of 1972, I was visiting Vancouver, Canada.

Vancouver was another hub for spiritual seekers. Most of the Gurus and teachers that established centers in California also had centers in Vancouver. One of these centers was the International Society for Krishna Consciousness, known colloquially, as the Hare Krishna movement, or Hare Krishnas, founded in the US, by A. C. Bhakti Vedanta Swami.

I had always been attracted to the chanting of the Hare Krishnas. I admired their courage and tenacity, boldly exposing themselves to the public on street corners, plazas, and airports throughout the country. Although, they sometimes came off as "Indian Style" Jesus freaks, over the top proselytizing using the same arguments, promising to "save" your soul and end of the world scenarios, yet, when they chanted the Hare Krishna mantra, I witnessed upon them a shining abandonment into a bliss that transcended all rhetoric.

One day in Vancouver, I saw a large group of them, chanting and dancing, expressing in a deep celebratory way, their love of God. I entered their circle, chanting with them. I lost track of time. The chanting and dancing took over my mind and body. My awareness became delocalized, and I felt as though I'd become bodiless, swirling like a band of energy in the infinite circle of Shiva himself. When the leader of the Hare Krishna troop called out to stop, its effect upon me was like when I was a child sleeping in my bed and felt as though I was taken up into the heavens and slammed back into my bed with a shuddering sensation, being thrust awake. Many readers may recall this happening to them, as a child.

I was invited to come to the Ashram for dinner, more chanting and talk about the Hare Krishna movement. That night, I decided to join the movement. The next day they invited me to be initiated as a lay member with the idea that in the near future I would become a fulltime devotee. I remained with them, daily chanting, studying and being trained in their ways and what was expected of me in promoting the movement.

The idea of being involved and promoting the movement and their almost fanatic energy regarding this matter was the only question I had. Collecting funds, selling books and convincing others to join had an almost predatory feel. It was that in the end that precipitated my leaving the Ashram and taking another path that came my way.

There was a part of Vancouver called "Gastown", where there were many new age shops, restaurants, bookstores, and lots of hippies hanging out.

The Hare Krishna was there regularly; it was a fertile ground for recruiting new devotees. I joined them on one of these recruitment missions. We were chanting in Maple Tree Square, surrounded by many onlookers, some stoned hippies joining in as well and some not so savory types that shouted obscenities. In the midst of the tumult, I noticed a group of young people sitting in a circle holding hands, their eyes closed and from what I could make out also chanting.

Rainbow Pilgrims

Intrigued, I went over to have a closer look. They were indeed chanting the mantra OM. I sat down with them in the circle and chanted along with them. The young man on my right, pointed out that in the middle of the circle was a tambourine. It had some cash and coins in it. He explained that they were all preparing to go to the first Rainbow Gathering taking place on Table Mountain in Granby, Colorado. The mountain has been a place of pilgrimage by most of the Native American Tribes west of the Mississippi.

The gathering was being touted as a meeting of the tribes so to speak; hippies, spiritual communities, teachers, Gurus, and Native Americans, especially from the Hopi Nation, were planning to attend. He went on that the gathering was to commemorate and hail in the New Age of Peace and Love predicted in Hopi tradition.

There is a Hopi prophecy that states, on the last day of the gathering, a white buffalo would appear as a sign marking the beginning of a new millennium of brotherhood among all people.

The tambourine had been placed at the center of the circle to collect enough money to take the group to the gathering.

By this point I had come to a dead end with the Hare Krishna. I enjoyed the chanting, the vegetarian food, and exotic clothes, but I could not get over the political agenda that seemed to overshadow what I had initially been attracted to.

I remained in the circle with the Rainbow Pilgrims. I closed my eyes and joined in the chanting; hours passed; the warmth of day replaced by the cold air sweeping in from the coast. Little by little, each member in the circle opened his or her eyes. Joy and tears spread through the circle as we all realized that tambourine was not only overflowing with money, but someone placed a large hand-woven basket next to the tambourine and it too was filled with cash, caught in this miraculous moment, I asked to join them on their journey. They took me in wholeheartedly and I was off to the mountains with my new, New Age family.

There were approximately 20 of us. We loaded into the school bus that was converted to a hippie style mobile home, and we were off to Colorado.

Table Mountain, Granby, Colorado

It took us about three days to get to Granby. As we approached the town, the traffic swelled with hundreds of hippie-converted school buses, VW vans and a host of creative mobile homes converging on the small town of Granby. All in all, there were well over 20,000 people that came to attend the gathering.

The hike up to the top of Table Mountain takes about 2-3 hours from the trailhead. In order to bring all the needed equipment, kitchen gear, food and utensils, portable shelters and many other items up the mountain, a human chain was formed consisting of hundreds of volunteers to pass everything up the mountain hand to hand. It was a magnificent feat of human cooperation.

Camps were being set up along the circumference of a wide meadow that lay beneath the summit of Table Mountain. Kitchens were built in lean-to style using fallen wood and branches. Latrines were dug and spread out strategically, to make them accessible to everyone staying along the meadows edge. Each kitchen was given a name after the group that set it up. There was the Holy Order of Man's kitchen, The Hare Krishna kitchen, The Love Family kitchen, others like, Orthodox Jewish Group, Rastafarians, Native Americans, Sufis, Hindus, Buddhists, Wavy Gravy and many more. There was a childcare area as well as medical triage tents and communication.

Each day would begin with a gathering on the meadow. Everyone attending formed concentric circles around a center point. The daily meetings would begin with an invocation given by a representative of each group attending the gathering.

These meetings were always chaired by an indigenous chief or healer who would set the context of the gathering, always sharing the Hopi vision that brought this particular gathering to Table Mountain.

During the days and nights of the gathering people would share their experience, their teachings, and their hearts with others promoting and exemplifying the common purpose of life. It promulgated the idea that although we come from different backgrounds, races, and creeds, we were all the same ultimately in fulfilling our purpose in this life.

Hopi Prophecy – A White Buffalo

According to Hopi tradition, a White Buffalo would appear at the gathering as a sign and signal that the New Age of Peace and enlightenment was born.

On the last night of the gathering it snowed. The meadow and the north face of Table Mountain were covered in snow. Sometime in late morning there were cheers and tears echoing through the campsites. People were running to the meadow to witness the White Buffalo that was clearly visible from the meadow.

In the course of the morning, as the snow melted off the mountain face, it left behind the silhouette of a White Buffalo, carved from the snow left behind.

Joy and jubilation flowed through the people of the gathering. All of us shared a deep sense of gratitude and joy that we were honored to witness the fulfilling of the Hopi Prophecy.

I regrouped with the Vancouver folks, whom I had originally traveled with to the gathering. They invited me to join them on a new adventure. One of the men had a family claim on a goldmine in Alaska. He put forth the idea that we all travel there together, sharing the expenses along the way and take part in mining for gold. After this gathering I was up for anything. We all had similar experiences, openings of heart and mind; it bonded us together like a new-minted family. Mining for gold together sounded perfect.

Although our plan was to eventually go to Alaska, we decided as a group to make our way there in a roundabout way. We were all touched by the Hopi Prophecies and instead of heading northwest we first traveled south to visit The Lama Foundation (The name "Lama" comes from "la lama" which means "mud" in Portuguese) and later westward to visit the Hopis in their ancestral town of Oraibi.

Oraibi was founded sometime before the year 1100 AD, making it possibly the oldest continuously inhabited settlement within the United States.

The Hopis do not ordinarily mingle with outsiders. They are very private and shun exposure to "Indian Curious" tourists. We were fortunately invited by one of their tribal members to visit them.

The Hopi People in Oraibi

Arriving at the Hopi village we were escorted to the meeting area where visitors were given a tour of the museum and a walk about through the village. There were "traditional" homes set up to get an idea how Hopi day-to-day life was lived. The tour lasted for about an hour. Part of the way through the tour, we were greeted by one of the Hopi elders whom we met at the Rainbow Gathering. He escorted us out of the tour area and welcomed us to his home. We were invited to remain for the night. This was a rare opportunity; as a rule, they did not allow non-Hopis to remain in the village overnight. We were even more fortunate in that the Hopi villagers were going to perform their traditional rain dance. There had been a drought for some months. Several "Snake" dancers came from outlying areas to perform the ritual, although in the past "outsiders" were allowed to witness the Snake Dance, but it had long become forbidden, with few exceptions. Our host insisted we stay, and he generously referred to us as Hopi Rainbow Brothers and Sisters.

Before the midday sun the dancers gathered in Kachina costumes. They marched in single file and formed a circle around the head shaman. Many were holding snakes, others lizards and water grasses and plants. The sky was almost blue-white like the bright burning flame of a welder's torch. There wasn't a cloud in the sky. Their dance became more intense, and in a rhythmic scale the energy ratcheted up to a point where I felt not only the dancers were losing themselves in the cacophony of sound and movement, but also that we were all drawn into the vortex of the energy they summoned. At the crescendo of the dance, droplets of water began to wisp in on the breeze descending from above us. The sky darkened as a layer of clouds formed on the horizon. We all stared into the sky, stunned by the awesome appearance of rain clouds, followed by bursts of thunder and lighting. Many of the people burst into tears, some in laughter, and the elders just nodded their heads in humility.

We stayed up most of the night, sitting in the rain around a fire. Everyone was touched with gratitude after witnessing no less than a miracle.

The Fourth Way School

The Lama Foundation

We arrived at the Lama Foundation[1] and were warmly welcomed by one of the founding members, Steve Durkee (Shaykh Nooruddeen).

We remained at Lama for a few days. It was like a spiritual pit stop. It was an oasis of overflowing and generous hearts. The high desert air, good wholesome food and spending time in the domed meditation building all contributed to recharging us, making us ready for the road ahead.

The Alpha Guru on Board

Before we departed from Lama, we picked up another member, joining us for the journey ahead. He had just returned from living in an Ashram in India and was staying at Lama. He wore a white lungi and kurta shirt, most of the time with Ruska beads, bracelets, and toe rings. His hair was long, and he looked like a European version of Satya Sai Baba. At first, he was personable and generally easy to get along with, but later he slowly manipulated his way to becoming the Guru of the bus. He never spared his need to share how much more experience he had in meditation and spiritual practices, berating, and often condescending to others on the bus.

Most at first resisted his psychic bullying, but soon he became the alpha male in our group. I mention this here because it was these dynamics that led to my expulsion from the bus. I was framed as a rebellious self and judged that I would eventually cause more trouble, so while traveling through Eugene, Oregon, on our way to Alaska, I was asked to leave.

I had "street wisdom" growing up in a rough neighborhood of Brooklyn, New York. From an early age, I could tell if someone was trying to "game" me or make themselves out to be something they're not, in this case an advanced spiritual being, all along prosecuting a selfish, egoic agenda. I was on his blacklist from the very beginning when I was

---

[1] Lama Foundation was founded in 1967 by Steve (Shaykh Nooruddeen), Barbara Durkee, (Shaykha Asha Greer) and Jonathan Altman, whose work with the psychedelic art community, USCO in New York, led to the intention, and eventual creation of the community in Lama, New Mexico. Excerpt from www.lamafoundation.org.

critical of his claim to take leadership of our group in the name of his "spiritual" experience. Last, but not least in terms of proof of his ulterior motives, was his hitting on all the girls in our group, having his way with them, one after another. I also made myself clear to him that I felt that was an abuse of his status as the acknowledged leader. Finally, he requested that for a period of ten days, we would all be required to practice Manu, the Hindu practice of silence. However, he could talk to us, but we could not talk back. At this point I refused; hence, I was labeled to be a disrupter and asked to leave.

Fourth Way School at Eugene, Oregon

I stepped off the bus, backpack and sleeping bag in tow. Just as I was gaining my bearings, I noticed a man holding a water hose, spraying his lawn. I approached him and asked if there were any youth hostels or places I could stay until I figured out what I was going to do next. He answered me with a big jovial smile that I could stay in his commune house, just behind him. I took him up on the offer and moved into an attic space in the eaves of the roof. There was just enough room to lay out my sleeping bag as well as a place for my clothes.

The house was full of fellow travelers, all searching, most not knowing for what, but compelled away from wherever they came to find answers and experiences that would quench their inner hunger for more possibilities than what they had before.

The man who invited me to stay was Jessie, a large and generous being; when being hugged by him you vanished into a loving and reassuring embrace. I discovered that the house had core groups that were followers of a man by the name of Jerry Patterson who was coming to the house soon. Everyone was very excited about his imminent arrival. I was told that he was a Sufi and a teacher in the Fourth Way School. I had not had any exposure to Sufism or the Fourth Way School at this point.

There was an ebb and flow of visitors; some stayed for extended periods of time, many just overnight as they continued on their journey. The house was maintained by the donations contributed by the main members of the house. Although there were few funds to go around, there was always food in the kitchen and hot coffee brewing throughout the day.

Some members of the community would go "dumpster diving" and collect delicacies, like specialty cheeses, milk, vegetables, and many other perishable items.[2]

> *Here's some "food" for thought: The United States is the global leader in food waste, with Americans discarding nearly 40 million tons of food every year. That's 80 billion pounds of food and equates to more than $161 billion, approximately 219 pounds of waste per person and 30-40 percent of the US food supply. The average American family throws away over $1,600 dollars' worth of fruits and vegetables per year.*

Eugene was another hub for seekers. Young people from all over the country congregated in and around Eugene. Beside the "naked Christians" I had encountered, there were other alternative Christian groups, Sufis, Buddhists, etc., kind of like a mini version of the Bay Area, the main difference was that Oregon was better suited to establish living communities, as there was so much open land as well as reasonable rural rents and property costs.

Jessie had invited me to stay on at the commune and I was happy to do so. I felt at ease with everyone in the house, especially because the emphasis of the house leaned towards spirituality without ritual impediment or restriction. We all had an idea of The Universality of which all religions and paths were The Source.

After some weeks, I started a Hot Cider and Oxtail soup stand at the local weekend flea market. My booth was a popular stop at the market, especially on the many cold and rainy days that predominate in Eugene. It earned enough funds for me to remain at the house and become a more significant contributor to the house's finances.

The Fourth Way Sufi Teacher

Within weeks of my arrival, "The Teacher" Jerry Patterson and his wife arrived. From the moment they arrived, the whole energy of the house shifted. They were given the attic room. It felt like a magnetic pole/vortex had appeared and all things pointed in that direction from that moment on.

---

[2] In those days grocers threw out "sell by date" items into open dumpsters. It was so common that the poor and needy regularly visited their local dumpsters and some shop owners would separate the perishables in boxes and buckets to make it easier for folks to pick them up to take home.

My first meeting with Jerry was something I had never experienced. He was handsome and charismatic. He chain-smoked Lucky Strike cigarettes and sat most of the time in a half lotus position. His presence was full of self-confidence and in his eyes was a disarming stare that solicited immediate affection. I had met several Gurus and teachers before him, but none who were as relatable in a cultural sense as Jerry. He was very American, although clearly, he took up all the air in the room, when you were in his presence. I had no past experience to guide me in that moment. I was prepared by his followers, living in the house, with a pre-planted expectation of who he was. I was impressed with an overwhelming sense that he knew something I didn't, and I wanted to discover what that was. From that day forward I was his student.

In the beginning, he would lend me books to read, the first being the writings of Hazrat Inayat Khan. He also insisted that I read books by George Gurdjieff and Peter Ouspensky. He characterized himself as a Fourth Way teacher as well as an adherent to Sufism and a follower of Meher Baba.

Gurdjieff and Ouspensky – The Enneagram

This was the beginning for me to engage on a discernible path. The teachings of Gurdjieff and Ouspensky gripped me like no other. The position of humankind as a reflection of higher and cascading levels of existence were new and compelling. There were three main teachings that I gleaned from their discoveries.

The first is that humankind is imbued with and predicated upon The Original Source of the Universe. Second, that we are asleep, living a "mechanical life" structured by our up-bringing i.e., our conditioning. Third, throughout humanity's history there have been those who, by awakening to the reality of higher conscious being, discovered ways and means to become self-aware and liberated from the confines of relative consciousness.

The first method was to "observe" oneself. The practice of observing myself and becoming familiar with mechanical behavior was an (inner) eye opener for me. Whether I was sitting, standing or lying down, we were guided to be aware of our thoughts and motivations.

Jerry constantly reminded us to be present, awake and in constant observance. In this way, he was very useful. He encouraged the idea that being present and observing oneself can transform to a higher state of being. As part of the Gurdjieff/Ouspensky teaching, there is an ancient tool, called the Enneagram. It attempts to depict the construct or matrix of existence encompassing both the microcosmic experience of a single relative consciousness as well as the macrocosmic view of the greater universe. Tones and notes were ascribed to the different stations on the matrix grid to represent potential stations of consciousness. Its overall form is a metaphor of the dynamic play of energetic movement. The archives of the Naqshbandi Sufi order of Dagestan claim to provide an account of a meeting between Gurdjieff and Shaykh Sharafuddin Daghestani in which the secret of the nine points was transmitted to Gurdjieff.

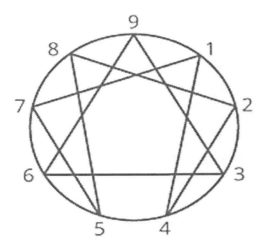

The Enneagram was very useful to me as a mirror. It reflected a basic pattern that applied to all human beings. In its deepest mirroring, it awakened within me a clarity that comes from recognizing the cosmic nature, and interconnectedness of all things, but also as an individual mirror of one's patterning and essence. The Enneagram's utility as an externalizing map, expanded my mind, drawing me towards seeing myself as a hologram of the Universe and a potential for the dissolution or attachment to "my" individuality, into the All-Encompassing, Eternal Reality.

This assessment came to me many years later. At the time I was exposed to this teaching, I was encouraged and compelled by my inner desire to find answers to essential questions about God and my place in the scheme of things. I wanted answers and a way out from my suffering mind, burdened with anxiety and the fear and pain that accompany it when you are relentlessly gripped by its heavy yoke.

Self-Observation

As time went on, self-observation had a profound effect upon me. Over time, I became aware of being present in the moment and a budding awareness and knowledge of what motivates me. I became acutely aware of the dynamics of attraction and repulsion, as applied to the physics of the universe and echoed within.

Without awareness and observing the self, there is no potential access to understanding the self, let alone knowing the self.

It is the most difficult thing to witness the self as an observer and what motivates it to action. The real gift of this practice is the observer begins to have a monitoring presence within. If you are fortunate, a shift takes place in your consciousness to where the observer's presence is more active and accessible – it is already "there." In this way, when an errant thought or stray energy begins to motivate desire within you, you are present to potentially intervene between that signal and your actions.

Our Eugene house outgrew its usefulness. There were two main factions occupying the house, one was Jerry's people and the other an ever-changing wave of hitchhikers and accidental "seekers" who stayed for a while and moved on. Jessie had gone to the Bay Area in California to visit friends. He was also scouting out for Jerry a new place for us as a group to resettle. We shortly heard back from Jessie that there was a house in Albany with a small group of his friends that would welcome us to move in. After a brief period, we moved to the house on Stannage Street, which eventually became our "Spiritual Commune."

There were about forty people living together in two small houses next door to each other. The backyard connected us; we took down the dividing fence and built a small out-building to hold the overflow of people. Everyone in the house was, to some degree or another, connected to a spiritual teaching. There was Jerry's group, which I was a part of, and there were others strictly connected to the Gurdjieff Fourth Way School, as well as New Age Christians, Buddhists, Hindus, and Hasidic Jews. Everyone chipped in for the rent and one person a day would buy the food for that day as well as cook the evening meal. You can imagine what the after-dinner conversation was like with the diverse group we had. Coffee and Reefers (marijuana cigarettes) would flow into the early morning hours as we sat around contemplating the Universe and the many ways to understand what life was really all about. The conversations often became quite animated. The Christians, as New Age as they were, could not get around the exclusive requirement to accept the Godhead of Jesus; although they did acknowledge the Buddha and other teachers, one could not pretend not to feel the air of supremacy of Jesus as "The Truth and the Way." The Buddhists mostly remained quiet, courageously practicing, not minding the content of the conversation or, in other words, having no mind at all. The Gurdjieff people believed wholeheartedly that they had the ultimate distillation of "The All and the Everything," teaching of every teacher that came to humankind. The Mystic Jews often remained on the sidelines of the conversation. They had their own special mandate with Yahweh. Then, there were the Gurus, Jerry and others who usually had the final say when we ended with the sunrise beaming through the kitchen windows. No one had the right answer and any attempt to claim they did was ignored and usually signaled the end of the conversation.

The Way of Muhammad – Through the Buddha

There were several Tibetan Lamas that made the Bay Area their residence. One very prominent Tibetan Lama was Tarthang Tulku Rinpoche.

There are four main schools of Tibetan Buddhism, the Nyingma, Kagyu, Sakya and the Gelug. Tarthang Tulku from the Nyingma Institute was in Berkeley in 1972, along with Dharma Press. The institute's main activities were teaching meditation and accepting live-in students that took vows according to Nyingma traditions. The Dharma Press published and printed books mostly related to Buddhist traditions, but also general books on spirituality. Within the arm of the publishing house there was the Tibetan Aid Project or TAP.

TAP was an outreach project to connect Tibetan refugees with American pen pals; its hope was to set up a support network for both the refugees and Americans interested in learning, Tibetan Buddhism and culture.

I volunteered to help in organizing and facilitating connections between US citizens and Tibetans. Part of my job was to help in the Press from time to time, folding, stacking, and reading through potential manuscripts.

I had also become very interested in Tibetan Buddhism as a practice and attended many of the meditation sessions at the Nyingma Institute of Tibetan Buddhism. Tarthang Tulku would often come to visit me in my small office; it helped foster a closer relationship. I once invited him to our commune and he accepted the invitation, coming with an entourage that included his wife, Nazli Nour. The entire commune, including invited guests greeted him in traditional Tibetan fashion, exchanging white scarves that each would place upon the other.

My office was basically a glass enclosure, sharing the same room with a printing press, the walls of which only slightly muffled the rhythmic and shifting sounds of the press when it was printing, especially the hydraulic sounds when sheets and pages changed direction. I could also see the comings and goings of clients working on their publications. On one particular day, I noticed a strange group of young men entering the print room. They were all dressed in European style suits, and some three-piece suits, appeared to be wing tips, with colorful ties around their necks. Also adorned upon their necks were large wooden prayer beads and, upon their heads, green turbans, with the slight edge of a white cloth just showing across their upper forehead. There was an air of nobility about them and I could see that their interaction with each other signaled self-awareness and obvious deference to each other, especially to an older one among them. It was a fleeting moment, full of content that left an indelible impression on me.

The Way of Muhammad, by Shaykh Abdalqadir as-Sufi

Several weeks had passed since the encounter with this group. They had contracted Dharma Press to print their book, *The Way of Muhammad.*[3] I did not often see any books that came fresh off the press, but on this day, *The Way of Muhammad* landed on my desk, placed there with a note saying, "You might be interested in this." It was the early morning when I opened to the first page with these words:

> *"There is only one method by which you can approach the Sufic sciences and that is to start, tabula rasa, by putting away the whole world-picture and value structure, which has formed you until now and which is completely the result of your social and historical imprinting, which you share with millions of others, whatever particular individuality you may imagine you have over and against those millions of others. You have an idea of how things are, and how you are, how things should be and how you should be. Interposed between you and reality is a functioning, fluctuating conceptualization of existence that, mingled with your personal emotional responses to events and personality, make up what you think is both 'you' and 'your world'."*

> *"Non-realities that have now crystallized in people's imagination as having some kind of dynamic actuality like history or class or individuality have to be set aside."*

— *The Way of Muhammad*, by Shaykh Abdalqadir as-Sufi, Diwan Press 1975

---

[3] It is customary to say, Peace Be Upon Him (PBUH), when the name of the Prophet Muhammad is mentioned. In this book, PBUH will not be written beside his name each time his blessed name is mentioned – it will be implied and the readers are encouraged to say it in their hearts.

As I read these words the room around me faded in detail, the sounds of the press moved miles away and my mind both thrilled and feared in the profundity of truth. My heart was racing as I was being drawn in by words and meanings that echoed within me. I was reading outwardly what was already printed within me.

The morning sped by page after page, reflecting and revealing to my mind and heart a clarity of meaning that I had never experienced to this depth. By the late afternoon I had nearly finished reading the entire book.

As I put the book down, Tarthang Tulku entered my office. We exchanged formal greetings, but this time he did not default to what had become a more informal friendly exchange. He pointed to the book, asking me what I thought of it. Nervously, seeing that he was already displaying disdain for the book, I answered that I enjoyed reading it. I also noted to him that these Sufis were clearly people of great spirituality and that I was looking forward to reading the final pages. At this point disdain turned into anger, as he picked up the book and tossed it in the rubbish bin, next to my desk. He exclaimed, "These people are murderers of Buddhists," dismissing what had been my experience of the book's content. He ordered me not to read anymore. Feeling very insecure, but compelled to respond, I defended the writings in the book and further commented that the writer had a deep understanding of the human condition.

Tarthang, known for his bursts of anger and frustration, slammed a bamboo staff on my desk, almost shattering the glass top and rebuked me for answering him back. He then called for the Press manager to come into the room and asked that I be escorted out of the building and not to come back until I changed my attitude.

I was crushed. I had deep respect for Tarthang – he, after all, was my meditation teacher, and I considered him my main spiritual guide at that time. I was escorted down the loading dock and noticed that the "Sufi Guys" had pulled up to load their freshly printed books. I walked by them, tears flowing from my eyes. I felt compelled to reach out to them in some way. I remembered the Muslim greeting, wishing peace upon them, so as I walked away, I shouted out to them, making a fist in the air, "*As Salaam alaykum*" (Peace be upon you).

I walked to my car, still in shock and emotionally upset. I got into my car, and I looked at a small photograph taped to my windshield of Meher Baba. He was lovingly smiling. His smile cooled my heart and calmed me down. I looked past the photo and saw the elder of the Sufi guys walking towards me. He came to my window signing to roll it down. His eyes piercing with compassion and empathy, I could not help but be touched deeply by his presence. He answered, *"wa alaykum Salaam"* (Peace be upon you too). His glance turned to the picture of Meher Baba on the windscreen, he reached into his suit pocket, where a handkerchief would be and pulled out the very same picture of Meher Baba and said: "you cannot follow this man, he left no path." He asked me to get out of the car. I stepped onto the street, feeling fragile as it was; he questioned me why I greeted them in the Muslim tradition. I explained what had happened, how I read their book and the Lama's reaction.

Completely unexpectedly, he grabbed my shoulder with one hand and with the other started to pound my chest repeating over and over again, "You are a Muslim, wake up!" After several thumps on my chest and his repeated call to wake up, I burst into tears. He stopped and embraced me and asked me to leave my car there and come with them to their center in Berkeley. I was clay in his hands at that point and went along.

My First *Salaat* at a *Za`wiya*

We arrived at their center, which they called the *"Za`wiya"* (a Sufi center). Sunset was approaching. Upon entering the house, a beautiful melodious, Muslim call to prayer was being made coming from the large living room. It was covered in oriental carpets, cushioned seats and pillows straddled the parameter of the walls and incense wafted through the house like a gentle mist caressing over the coastal hills of the bay.

There were many people scurrying about, but the same awareness that I had noticed before was evident, making the space seem much larger and accommodating than it appeared. If this space had agitated unaware people trying to negotiate it there would be chaos. There were men and women, practicing special awareness with each other; it was almost celestial, like the dance of planets and galaxies. The lines for prayer formed, and I was invited to join, between Hajj Abdul Aziz, the man who pounded my chest, and another member of the community. With hands raised, I turned like everyone else towards *Qiblah* (the Ka`ba in Mecca) and exclaimed *"Allahu Akbar!"* (God is great!) resting my hands at my sides, while the leader of the prayer recited. This was my first experience in *Salah* (or *Salaat*), Muslim prayer. There was an immediate familiarity in it. I recalled how during Yom Kippur the Levite members of our congregation used to prostrate. Also, in Tibetan tradition, full prostration was part of the Buddhist way. I also remembered a life-changing moment some years before; walking in a dense redwood forest of Northern California, I had come to a clearing, the sun beaming in through the trees reminiscent of

40

sunlight pouring into the floor of Saint John's Cathedral in New York. In the middle of the clearing was a dwarf albino Redwood tree. Yes! A dwarf albino Redwood tree! It stood on a rise, as though it were upon an altar or pedestal.

The brightest light beam found the tree and illuminated it making it glow as though from inside itself. The moment transformed into a metaphor reflecting celestial meaning. That meaning descended into my heart, with majestic force, and all I could do was prostrate onto the ground.

I re-lived that moment as we knelt, bowed and placed our foreheads upon the ground in complete surrender and acknowledgment of the divine.

Singing the *Diwan* / Meal Together

After the sunset prayer the men and women broke into two circles. I was again placed next to Hajj Abdul Aziz with Abdullah on my right. After reciting Surah *al-Fatiha*[4] the *Sama`* (Sufi ceremony performed as *dhikr*) began with the recitation of the *Diwan*,[5] a collection of songs, *Qasidas* (odes, praising God), as commonly referred to, and contained the teaching of the Sufi path through the inspirations of Shaykh Muhammad ibn al Habib.

I was immediately swept up into the beauty of the recitation performed in Andalusia style. Everyone in the room sang the refrain, while more experienced singers recited the poetry itself. I could feel the energy in the room rise as the meanings flowed deep into the hearts of the reciters. Hajj Abdul Aziz informed me that tonight was *Laylat ul Fuqara* (Night of the Wayfarers) and encouraged me to stay through, then immediately after we would have dinner.

The *Laylat ul Fuqara* began with everyone sitting, knee to knee, together in two circles on the floor, one for women and the other for men. A young man moved around the inner edge of the circle sprinkling rose water into everyone's hands, splashing it onto their faces. When it was my turn, I copied what I witnessed and what others did. When I splashed the rose water on my face, I understood: It was like an ablution, casting off the crust and dust of the world, from the heart and mind.

---

[4] "The Opening" – The first *surah* (chapter) of the Qur'an.
[5] See also, "Path to Light: The Haydari Handbook", published by Zahra Publications, which contains many of these odes.

With eyes closed, looking inward, many present began to sway, and I could see they were reflecting and internalizing the meanings of the *Diwan* as they sang.

The atmosphere of the room was filled with both beauty and majesty. The ancient melodies wafted over our ears delivering the majestic message contained in the *Diwan* of Shaykh Muhammad ibn al-Habib. I was in the circle of a dream yet to come, taking my place, as the world faded without concern over the horizon.

The man who had struck my chest earlier, Abdul Aziz, was sitting next to me. He would occasionally glance over at me, his face not only shone with light, but his smile also embraced me, signaling me that he was happy I was there.

At the end of the *dhikr*, everyone remained sitting in place. Indian and Persian printed sheets were passed out and spread out as a tablecloth; it was like one would do at a picnic, but indoors. Food in large platters came quickly from the kitchen, including salads, garnishes and rice. There were no individual plates or silverware.

The same young man that had sprinkled everyone in the *dhikr* (remembrance of God) with rosewater was again in the middle of the circle, standing on the tablecloth with another jug and bowl along with a towel thrown over his shoulder. He moved from one person to the next pouring warm water into each and everyone's hands, wiping them dry with his shoulder towel.

No one touched the food until it was all served, and then with a hardy voice, Hajj Abdul Azizi called out, *"Bismillah"* (In the name of Allah!). Everyone sitting shoulder to shoulder began to eat, using only their right hands without fork or spoon. The company was delightful, people from all over the world, sitting together in fraternity, acknowledging the One from which they and all things emerged.

Although I was very inclined towards this path, I could not bring myself to officially join them. Over the next few weeks, I visited the *Za'wiya* and got to know several of the people well. All were very kind to me. At some point they informed me that they were packing up and returning to England, where most of them lived in a place called Bristol Gardens. Hajj Abdul Aziz Redpath left an indelible impression on me. He was strong and sometimes over the top dramatic, but one could only see his good intention to share what he knew was the best for those he met. Hajj Abdul Aziz invited me to embrace Islam. I could not; although I was deeply affected by the *fuqara* and their practice, I still held a strong belief in the New Age narrative. I framed my belief that all religious traditions, mystic paths, and teachers, were all correct within the limitations of their belief system. I could not join any one particular path but believed in all of them and lived my path, taking knowledge and wisdom from all of them respectively.

It would be several years before I came across the *Fuqara* again. This story is told later in the book.

The Institute for the Study of Human Knowledge (ISHK)

One day I was walking down University Avenue, in Berkeley, towards the food Co-op, and I saw a young lady sitting on the street surrounded by pots, pans and various restaurant equipment. She had a sign written out on a cardboard box that read, "Going out of business, selling kitchen equipment, all offers will be considered".

I noticed that she was clearly upset. I sat down next to her on the sidewalk. In those days sitting on the street wasn't unusual, especially in Berkeley. One would often find street corner gatherings playing music, chanting or just passing sacrament between them. I inquired about her situation. She pointed to the restaurant behind her and said that she had tried to sustain a juice and sandwich bar next door to the Co-op, but it failed. She was selling off the equipment to pay off her final bills and debt. While she was explaining to me her circumstance, I felt from within my gut, a compulsion to make her an offer. I could hardly articulate what I had in mind due to the level of excitement I felt. I could almost "know" what the answer would be before posing the question.

I proposed that she gave me the restaurant, equipment and all, and I would give her $200 as a good faith offer and promised the balance in six weeks. She burst into tears, throwing her arms around me and exclaimed, "Let's do it!"

It was still early afternoon when I rushed back to the Berkeley Spiritual commune (ISHK) to tell all my friends what had happened. Everyone was delighted; a party of them came to the shop to see it.

That evening, we redesigned the interior as well as the color scheme and signage on the front window. I started re-working her menu with the group, brainstorming what new and creative food combinations we could come up with. Within a few days the store was set up with new colors, new seating and a new name of the business painted on the front window of the shop, Abe's Juice & Sandwich Bar.

Abe's Juice & Sandwich Bar

From the very first day we opened, we had a line waiting out the door. Our fresh squeezed juices and protein shakes, sandwiches and soups were the talk of the street. We were the first ones to use bread commercially produced by the Black Muslim Bakery. I formulated several soy and nut spreads for the sandwiches as well as what went into the soups and salads. In those days workers were only allotted 15-20 minutes for a lunch break. There was already a growing consciousness in Berkeley for "healthy" foods. We offered a "fast food" healthy meal that appealed to the style of working and business people in the area.

Within six weeks we made enough money to pay the previous owner off what we owed and then some. Over time, several of our commune friends worked in the shop as well. It put us in a position sometime later to buy the two homes we lived in with the financial contribution of two other members of the commune. It was also made possible by the generosity and kindness of our landlord, who made it easy to make the purchase.

Who Will Feed a Man of Allah? (Encounter with Sayed Jamarani)

One crisp and breezy fall morning, as I was just opening up the restaurant, a man appeared in its doorway and shouted several times, in a heavy Persian accent:

"Who will feed a man of Allah?" "Who will feed a man of Allah?"

As I waved him in, I answered, yes, welcome, come in and have a seat.

We often fed the homeless or "street people." At that time, it was expected in Berkeley that the local businesses would contribute and feed street people, it was part of the "counterculture" ethos to do so.

He entered my shop as a vision out of the tales of Scheherazade. He was dressed in a long grey Arab style robe, a flowing green turban wrapped around his head. Draped across his chest, several strands of prayer beads surrounded his neck. In his left hand was a *kashkul*, a begging bowl shaped like a gourd, but his was made from a thin hand beaten metal with carved ornamentations on its underbelly. There were small chains attached at each of its elongated ends that were extended from his shoulder fixed onto a leather pad holding them in place. In his right hand was a staff, longer than his own length, and tied to the end of his staff was a cloth sack, in which I later discovered he carried all his worldly possessions. His shoes were worn leather sandals barely held together by frayed twine.

I had seen many travelers come through Berkeley, but this being was clearly different.

He entered my restaurant with an air of humble nobility, his eyes lowered, hands crossed around his waist. When he looked up at me for the first time there was the sparkle of genuine gratitude and appreciation.

I welcomed him to sit at a table near the counter and retreated to the preparation area to make him some food. When he entered my shop, it was like a beam of light pouring through a stained-glass window, bringing with it the presence of the sacred. I felt as though both of us were experiencing the same thing as neither of us entered into a conversation, not asking a name or purpose for being here. We were imbued with the presence of the moment and its overwhelming sense of beauty. It wasn't until sometime later that morning that we started to converse.

In broken English he introduced himself as *Sayed Jamarani*, from Iran. He explained that he was a *dervish*, traveling throughout the world. He professed his total trust in God to provide him with provision. It was a means to develop absolute dependence upon the Divine. He saw the means of that provision to be agents of the divine will. He also said that traveling in this way helped to purify himself from bad habits, the worst habit he explained was not seeing the hand of God in everything that comes our way.

I was profoundly moved by his story and sincere resolve, abandoning the comfort and familiarity of his own home and language and having the courage to roam a foreign land and maintain his commitment and composure. I looked forward to talking to him and hearing what no doubt was a compendium of tales and experiences.

The store was unusually busy that day and I did not have much time to chat with him. He sat there most of the day, eating, reading, and dozing off. Every once in a while, he would turn and look at me. His eyes and smile were infectious. They beamed directly into my heart a sense of warmth, love, and gratitude. I sometimes lowered my eyes when turning to look towards him as I started to feel undeserving of such purity and sincerity, but also his glance unveiled my hidden cynicism and sense of cultural superiority.

It was nearly closing time. I informed the dervish that we would be closing soon. He curiously did not respond in any way, it almost felt like he was ignoring me as irreverent.

After a few moments he stood up in the shop, bowl and staff in hand like earlier, and he shouted out: "Where will a man of Allah sleep tonight?"

I took him home.

There was a sunroom off the living room at my home. There was no one living in it at the time, so I made up a floor futon for him and he retired for the evening. I could hear him chanting throughout the night.

Sayed Jamarani remained as my guest for nearly one year. He rarely came out of his room except two to three times per day. On one occasion, when I was about to leave my home to go out, he met me at the front door holding a magnificent, illustrated book containing the collected works of the Sufi poet Hafiz of Shiraz. He said some prayers over me then, in a most dramatic fashion, licked his right forefinger, waved it in the air, ending with his finger pointing straight up while exclaiming, "*Bismillah er Rahman er Raheem*", (in the Name of God, the all-Merciful, the all-Compassionate). Then he opened the book with that very finger and read from the right-hand page whatever poem or story his eyes happened to fall upon.

He did this regularly.

If the poem or story was of a positive nature, he would allow me to leave my house, if not, he would refuse to let me leave until he had repeated this divining process ending up with something positive.

Other times, he would come out to bathe and perform the ritual preparation for prayer. At these times, he would dart out of the sunroom, not looking at anyone and return as soon as his ablutions were concluded.

On several occasions, he would come out to find me to share tea with him in the sunroom. The first time I was invited into his room I was astonished to find that he had a portable single gas burner on which he would prepare his Iranian tea. In his room, there was nothing but that burner, a prayer rug facing Mecca and a single change of clothes that he washed when he bathed. At these rare meetings, he would take the time to share stories with me that contained wisdom teaching. He also would read from the Qur'an and in broken English relate the meaning to me. It was the same when the conversation turned towards the poems and writing of Hafiz. Although I could not fully understand or comprehend what the dervish was trying to impart to me, just his being, his love, taught my heart and mind lessons and reflections beyond the need for words. This alchemy worked. I especially realized its influence on me after he left our home. He left a part of himself with me, a connection through love that is beyond reproach.

One day, after many months, he called me in for tea. This time it was different. I could feel a sense of finality, as though the very air and atmosphere in the room was speaking, recognizing that it was time to move on.

It was but a few days after that that he appeared one morning, packed, and looking just like the first time I saw him. In his best form he shouted out: *"Who will help a dervish return to his home?"* I drove him that morning to the airport, purchasing a single one-way ticket to Tehran.

Before he departed, he gave me three gifts. The first was a carnelian ring inscribed with the name of the Prophet of Islam, and his family. It said Muhammad, Ali, Fatima, and Hassan and Hussein.

The second gift was cloth calligraphy with the singular name of Allah written upon it in green ink. He instructed me to place the flag over the cash register at my business. He said that it would wave blessings upon my store and attract those who will come to help me when I need it.

The third gift was what he had left of his Iranian tea. He said when I was to drink it, I was to pray for him.

That was the last I saw of Sayed Jamarani.

Sayed Jamarani's Allah Flag

Stannage Street Spiritual Commune

Although Tarthang Tulku and I did not see eye-to-eye in the past, his visits to our spiritual center in Berkeley became more frequent and we reconciled our relationship. We both enjoyed each other's company and left the past behind us and eventually formed a warm and cordial relationship.

Due to Tarthang Tulku's visits to our home our commune grew in reputation as a spiritual hub to visit and meet other like-minded/hearted people.

Through the course of several years, 1972-1976, we were hosts for visiting teachers and Gurus, often holding sessions of talks and meditation. The list of visitors included, Rabbi Zalman Schachter, Ajarya Warwick, Lama Kunga Rinpoche, Dr. Hamid Alger, Mursheed Hassan Al-Moumani, as well as many local personalities like Country Joe (of Country Joe & the Fish), Wavy Gravy (of "The Farm"), and Jerry Brown (Governor of California).

Swami Muktananda

In April of 1974 the word on the "spiritual street" was that Swami Muktananda was coming to the Bay Area for a visit. A two-day retreat somewhere in Oakland, California was being organized for him. Some of my contacts learned when he was arriving at San Francisco Airport. We found out just a few hours before his arrival time and we set out to San Francisco to meet him and welcome him to the Bay Area. I had read his first book, "Play of Consciousness: A Spiritual Autobiography," where he goes into detail about his own experiences with *Shaktipat*. The whole idea of being "opened" or "Cracked open" by proximity to or contact with an enlightened being was intriguing.

Shaktipat (Sanskrit, from *Shakti* "psychic" energy and *pāta*, "to fall"), refers in Hinduism to the transmission, of spiritual energy, from one person to another. It is considered an act of grace.

There were hundreds of people lining up at the terminal where Swami Muktananda would be arriving. His devotees had brought a golden chair, hand-carved with deities and divas and draped with floral patterns, as well as bundles of flowers strewn around the concourse. People were chanting as the plane pulled up to the hangar.

The ornamental throne had been placed near the passenger exit doors. When the Guru emerged from the gangway, he took his seat in the chair, smiling and waving, at all the mostly young devotees who lovingly had come to welcome him. In his left hand he held a wand made of Peacock feathers. One by one, devotees came forward and knelt before the Swami, placing their heads at his feet. Upon each one, the Guru caressed the wand of feathers on their heads. Many swooned; others went into a trance-like state. There were some, however, who yelled out different mantras and collapsed onto the floor motionless, as though they passed out.

I was witnessing *Shaktipat*.

As the crowd moved forward, my proximity to him grew closer. I felt both excited and held some trepidation. The compulsion of the mind trying to "understand" what it was witnessing was futilely in full gear. I had never seen anything like this before, but I was willing and trusting enough to surrender to the palpable grace of the moment.

In line third down from having the Peacock feather wand fall upon my head, my thoughts went silent. It was my turn now. I looked into the Swami's eyes; they were like portals of light beckoning me from this world into another realm of overflowing love. The feathers came upon my head and, for a moment, I was erased from existence. As I returned, I struggled to recall my name and where and why I was there in the first place. The sounds of the concourse grew louder; someone hugged me and stood me up from where I collapsed on the floor. He smiled, assuring that all was good. I snapped back as I saw the backside of the ornamental chair being carried through the concourse, people chanting and singing Bhajans, while Muktananda waved his Peacock wand at everyone along the way.

After some days, I visited Swami Muktananda at his ashram in the Oakland Hills. It was always filled with people, meditating, levitating, and jumping in and out of *Shaktipat*. Although I saw the Swami several times and attended his weekend retreat, he never personally addressed me. The experience at the airport was more than enough to confirm within me a recognition that what I was seeking was within me, and that even the most enlightened Guru could only reflect or mirror the potential that each one of us has within.

A few years later, there were many not so enlightened stories that emerged about the Swami. There was alleged sexual abuse, profiteering on the good graces of others' charity and alleged gluttony for power.

After many years of exposure and personal experience of Gurus, teachers, and their lieutenants, it became clear to me that without accountability, rooted in Prophetic teaching, it was inevitable for the emergence of patterns of abuse. A pattern of abuse still manifests itself even when there is claim to adherence to established religions and paths. This is accomplished by twisting the meanings of religious tradition to justify and expedite selfish agendas. These patterns have common themes, shared across all those teachers who claimed to be of one path or another. It did not matter if they were Hindu, Buddhist, Christian, Jew, Muslim, Sufi and beyond. Sexual abuse, misappropriation of funds, self-aggrandizement, and claims of being beyond accountability, i.e., being God itself, gave self-appointed license to do anything their half-baked persona desired, even sometimes with good intentions.

So, the question remains: how can I explain and reconcile the "opening" experience I had with Swami Muktananda?

There is a story that offers a perspective on this phenomenon, drawn from Tibetan Buddhist tradition.

The Buddha's Teeth

There once was a wealthy Tibetan trader living with his old and ailing mother in the provincial city of Xigaze. Every year the trader would travel to the capital city of Lhasa that was located on the famous Silk Trade Route that connected the Far East to the West. He would bring back silks, threads and various sundries to offer in his village shop.

When the time grew near to his yearly pilgrimage to Lhasa, his mother would request him to bring something from the holy city, something she could put on her altar to adore and worship. He always agreed, but never took her request seriously enough to make it a priority, so each year he returned without fulfilling his mother's request.

His mother had grown very old and frail and hardly left her home. The trader was leaving again for his journey to Lhasa. Before he left his mother asked again for some relic, something that would help her in worship. He agreed, but again, he started his journey home without fulfilling his mother's request. When, along the way, he remembered and relented his forgetfulness, he saw in the road ahead a dead decrepit dog, far along in decomposing its body. He noticed the whiteness of his teeth and, with a blade he kept under his waist belt, he carved the teeth out and placed them in a silk bag. When he returned home, his mother asked her son if he had brought something for her. The son displayed excitement and handed her the silk bag with the dog's teeth. He said that he had brought her the holiest of gifts. He went on that it was out of the favor of the gods and goddesses that she was honored to be gifted the teeth of the Buddha himself.

His mother, overjoyed, praised her son, and thanked the gods and goddesses for bestowing this precious gift. She placed the Buddha's teeth on her altar of worship, bowing and making full body prostrations towards the holy teeth of the Buddha. She would stay in deep contemplation and meditation inspired from the Buddha's presence on her altar. Friends and family would visit her and see the teeth; most commented how she was so at peace. Overtime, she became the go-to in the village for advice on both minor family issues as well as that of a deeper spiritual nature. When she died, her face was lit with light. A place on a nearby hill was built in honor of her and a silver encased box was custom-built to hold her ashes and the Buddha's teeth. It became a popular place of pilgrimage for the sick and frail. Many stories over the years of miraculous healing and spiritual opening were reported.

Shaykh Hassan al-Moumani ar-Rafa`i

By the winter of 1976 I had become a regular at most of the new age/spiritual gatherings that were taking place in California in and around the Bay Area.

California had become a Mecca for visiting gurus and teachers from all over the world. It was a dynamic time, in which the force of societal patterns and habits were disrupted, questioned, and loosened their hold to an evolutionary groundswell of spiritual inquiry. Who am I? Where am I? What is death? Is this world all there is?

In a matter of a few years, I had the opportunity to have personal encounters with teachers like Chogyam Trungpa Rinpoche, Kalu Rinpoche, Shaykh Sulayman Dede and His Holiness, the Karmapa Lama of Tibet, and many more.

But no encounter, up until that point, would have a more profound effect upon my life, than meeting Shaykh Hassan al-Moumani ar-Rafa`i.

Shaykh Hassan, or Murshid Hassan, as he liked to be called, was of Syrian/Lebanese background, living in Nablus, in the West Bank of Occupied Palestine.

Murshid Hassan was a well-known Sufi mystic in Nablus. In the courtyard of his center, he had a grave dug for himself. Once the grave was finished, he moved into his burial spot with the intention to remain in it, without a set time, in *"Khalwa."*

The translation of *Khalwa* from Arabic is seclusion or separation, but it has a further meaning in Sufi terminology.

Khalwa is the act of total self-abandonment, in desire for the Divine All-Encompassing Presence. While in complete seclusion, eating and sleeping little, the Sufi continuously repeats the name of God as the highest form of remembrance of God meditation.

Day and night, year after year, Murshid Hassan meditated and practiced the invocation of the *"ismul afrad"* repeating the singular name of Allah, repeatedly, with every breath.

Coming Out of the Grave

One day, while deep within his meditation, he heard a voice calling him to leave his retreat and visit America.

Murshid Hassan recalled to me how the voice came like a command. It came through him like a bolt of lightning. After emerging from his grave, he told me that he was in a very fragile state. It took him several weeks before he could tell the difference between a dog and a tree.

After some time, Murshid Hassan was mingling with his family, friends and students.

On one occasion, he took a bus ride to visit some friends. As his heart-full eyes scanned the people sitting on the bus, he noticed a woman, clearly not a local, sitting by herself. Murshid Hassan said he was drawn to her, knowing that he was about to meet his destiny.

In broken English, Arabic, and lots of hand-signing, they introduced each other. The young lady was Benefsha, an early student of Sufi Sam; she was in Israel to attend a Sufi gathering in Jerusalem. Benefsha and Murshid Hassan immediately recognized that this meeting was no ordinary event. In time, their meeting would lead to inviting Murshid Hassan to America.

In 1976 Murshid came to the US under the auspices of the Sufi Ruhaniat International of which Sufi Sam was the founder. Benefsha organized Murshid's tours, meeting other Sufi groups, as well as linked spiritual organizations.

It was the spring of 1976; I was invited to attend a Circle of *dhikr* at the home of a friend of mine who was a student of Sam Lewis or Sufi Sam, as he was commonly known.

Meeting Murshid Hassan

My first connection was made with Murshid Hassan while attending the *dhikr*.

He tossed an unlit cigarette at me. When it hit me, he laughed and offered to light it for me. I came close to him, and we greeted each other in the customary way, '*as salaam alaykum*.'

He repeated it again and again, requesting me to follow him in repeating it. I felt like a child learning their first words; as I repeated them over and over again, a big grin grew bigger and bigger on Murshid's face. He suddenly grabbed me and pulled me towards him in a warm embrace saying over and over again, "*inshallah enta Muslim*" (God willing, you are a Muslim).

I was immediately taken by the Shaykh's presence and manner. I felt a strong attraction to his being, and for the next few months, followed him wherever he went. Whenever I entered a venue where he was, I would customarily sit towards the back. He would always call me up front to sit near him. Over time, I grew very fond of Murshid and looked forward to seeing him as much as possible. I felt in his presence an alignment to the Soul taking hold within me.

One evening, several months after meeting Murshid Hassan, I received a call from my friend who had originally introduced me to Murshid. He was clearly upset on the phone. He said that Murshid Hassan had stormed out of his home and demanded that he be brought from Marin to my home in the East Bay. No sooner had he said this to me, I heard a car pulling up in front of my home followed by a loud knock at the door. It was Murshid Hassan. He had asked one of his followers to bring him over to our commune.

Murshid Hassan came into my living room, sat down on the floor, and said with utter authority, announcing that I was his host from now on, and that I was his only sincere *mureed* (student of a Sufi teacher). He went on to pronounce that all the others that had been hosting him were the followers of the *Shaytan* (Satan).

Although we were all taken aback by his arrival, the idea of having Murshid right in our home was more than I could hope for and, later as I shall elaborate, more than I had bargained for.

He soon established a routine of evening gatherings in our living room with all house members attending. He would tell stories and sing songs from a collection of *diwans*, some were penned by him, and others were the works of famous Sufis from around the world. He would sit until late in the evening, drinking tea and smoking cigarettes. He smoked about seven to ten packs a day and his tea was more like sugar syrup. Within a very short time I found myself translating what he recited or spoke from Arabic to English. To this day, I cannot explain how this happened. I did not speak Arabic. I only knew a few words, but whenever I sat next to him, I was gifted with the ability to translate for Murshid.

Murshid Hassan remained in my home for nearly a year. At that time, he initiated me in the *Rifa`i Tariqah* (School/Sufi Order) and declared me to be his *khalifa* (successor) in the United States.

One early morning, while most of us were asleep, we were awakened by the sound of chopping and the crackling of a fire. When I went to see what was happening, I found that Murshid had taken all the furniture out of the living room and was having it chopped to bits and put on a bonfire. I was surprised, to say the least. When I questioned Murshid about his actions, he laughed in his inimitable way and said that it was better that we all sat on the floor from now on. I accepted the idea and we saved only the cushions and pillows from the couch and chairs to sit on.

Murshid Hassan held *dhikrs* every week and sometimes several times a week. During the *dhikr* he would play cymbals and have a huge drum counting out the rhythm and the speed of the *dhikr*. He taught me to play the drum and cymbals and all the *dhikrs* that these instruments accompanied.

Towards the end of Murshid's stay at my home he had become interested in one of the young women at our house. He wanted to marry her, and he did. Maryam left with Murshid and bore him several children. I had intended to visit Murshid and Maryam in Nablus in the near future, but destiny overrode our plan and God's plan came to be.

The last time I saw Murshid Hassan was at the ramp of a jet plane bound for Israel. His very last words to me were, *"lazim ta'araf Islam"* ("You must come to know Islam").

In one of many intimate moments with Murshid Hassan, he related to me how he had tried his best to introduce Islam to all whom he met. In the beginning, he insisted that people embrace Islam, but he soon realized that he had to take another tack with those around him. He figured he should rather introduce the practices of *dhikr* and meditation to them first, in the hope that people would get a taste of the ecstasy and bliss of what's possible from these practices, and then move on to the completion of the path in the house of Islam. He had thought that little by little, those around him would give up their old ways and become Muslim.

He said that the greatest gift he could impart to others was the love of the Prophet Muhammad and submission to the *Deen* (Life transaction/Religion) of Islam.

Murshid Hassan never returned to the States again. He remained in his *za`wiya* until his death in the late Eighties. His American wife returned after his death with several of their children. His works and memoirs remain with her and have not, to my knowledge, been published to this day.

The Dream

I dreamt one night that I was in the hallways of a great school. It was an ancient institution made from hand-carved stones and with long arched hallways. Standing in the middle of one of these hallways was Murshid Hassan, clanging away on his cymbals and chanting over and over again a litany of *wazifas*[6] and names of Allah. Suddenly, on the opposite side of the hallway, I saw another figure: a man dressed in a long black robe, wearing a green turban with a large *tasbih* (prayer beads) around his neck. His presence was so overwhelming that, in my dream, I collapsed at his feet in tears. He reached down and pulled me up by my arms and requested me to look into his face. When I looked, his face began to change over and over again into various faces of men, each with nobility and light in their eyes. I asked who he was, and he replied that he was the father of all the Shaykhs, saints, Sufis and it was time for me to follow him.

I hesitated and turned to look at Murshid Hassan standing at the other side of the hallway. When our eyes met, he smiled and waved an approving gesture, to go on and take the hand that is being offered. He then turned and disappeared down the hall. I turned to the Shaykh in the green turban and followed him. As I turned to follow him, I awoke.

---

[6] *Wazifa* (lit. 'to employ'), is the repeated invocation of some words, usually from the Qur'an, or verses or *suarah*(s) of the Qur'an in order to manifest something, e.g., ease in a difficult situation, for a wish to come true, etc.

Initiation of Our Commune into the Rafa`i Sufi Path

Murshid Hassan left an indelible mark upon our commune; he shook the very foundation and structure of our home to its core. Jerry, who had been the leading figure, became less involved in the activities of the house.

Murshid had informally accepted about half the people living in our commune as his students and he requested them to follow me. Before he left our home, we gathered in the main room. He had Randy Scott and I sit together in the middle of a circle of our members. He then recited from a collection of litanies from a book of the Rafa`i Sufi Path.

He sat in front of me and asked me to repeat several formulas; after each formula, he would blow his breath into my mouth. He did the same with Randy Scott. He then explained to all present that both of us were initiated into the Rafa`i Path and that I was his *khalifa* and Randy Scott was his *mureed*. He asked those present to obey and support me in establishing the *dhikr* and the Rafa`i Path.

As per Murshid's instructions, we established a regular circle of *dhikr* in our home. Word got out in the community at large, often filling our house to capacity, many became regular attendees at our gatherings.

Rabbi Zalman Schacther had met Murshid in Boulder, Colorado on one of Murshid's sponsored visits with the Sufi Ruhaniat International. He grew very fond of Murshid, later telling me how he saw him as one of his teachers. The Rabbi heard about our connection and gatherings to Murshid, so while visiting the Bay Area, he joined us for a night of *dhikr* and contemplation. After the formal *dhikr*, he gave a short talk, mostly underscoring the connection that all human beings share and especially the wealth of "Brokha" (Hebrew same as Baraka or Blessings) that are accessible in the company of the Friends of Allah or Asheem (In God's name).

The Return of the *Fuqara*

It was late afternoon in the winter of 1976; the low angle of the sun sprayed a rainbow of light as it passed through the faceted crystals hanging in the window of my shop. The beams of light danced across my eyes yielding, to the thrill, of witnessing, the mystery of colors, and a metaphor of the One Light, behind many colors.

It was nearly five in the afternoon and time to close for the day. I was sweeping out the shop, scooping the last remnants of dust and particles while standing at the front door. I saw a familiar group of men coming down the street towards me. I stopped and watched to see if they were, in fact, who I thought they were, dressed in long sleeved shirts, ties and wing-toed shoes, green turbans on their heads and prayer beads, rocking back and forth as they moved closer towards me. They were about to pass me, I prepared to greet them with Salaams, but before the words could pass my lips, they all stopped in front of my shop, looking beyond me at the calligraphy of the name of Allah flying above my cash area – the one that Sayid Jamarani gave me and asked me to place it just where it was. One of them spoke out and asked me if I was a Muslim. I answered, no. He then, without hesitation, said, that if I was not Muslim, I should not have that calligraphy in my shop. They were definitely the *fuqara* of Shaykh Abdalqadir as-Sufi. I invited them into my shop and served them some fresh squeezed juice. I mentioned Hajj Abdul Aziz to them and the circumstances under which we had met some years back. One of these *fuqara* recalled being told the story and invited me to visit them in Monterey California, where their center was. The invitation was to attend a wedding of one of their members. I was delighted to meet them again. I felt as though I had a bit more in common with them after meeting Murshid. I was looking forward to comparing notes as it were.

After closing the shop that evening, I headed over to the Mediterranean Café on Telegraph Avenue.

The Mohawk on a Mission

I used to frequent this Mediterranean Café before and after opening and closing my shop. They had the best espresso coffee in Berkeley. Its clientele was an eclectic lot, intellectuals, philosophers, seekers, Go players, political activists and die-hard caffeine addicts. The interior of the café was composed of a large first floor strewn with wooden chairs and tables. Above the main room, was a mezzanine floor that protruded over half of the ground floor. Different groups carved each area of the cafe out. Everyone felt comfortable to mingle and join in on conversations of their particular interest. I indulged in a game of Go from time to time. This evening I was tired, needing a double shot of espresso to see me through the rest of the night. With my espresso in hand, I headed out the café door. Once outside, I noticed a man sitting on a cloth in the street in front of the café. He was dressed in an aboriginal Indian tunic, his hair combed back in a ponytail, with a feather, and beads waving behind his head. As I walked by him, I greeted him and he greeted me back, and, gesturing with his hands to come closer, he asked if I would spend a moment with him. I obliged and sat down next to him on his blanket right there in the street.

After some small talk he asked me if I knew of any spiritual groups where he could meet with their leaders, and he explained that he had some questions that needed to be answered.

I knew many spiritual teachers in the Bay Area, and I could easily introduce him to many from the Sufi traditions, Buddhists, and new-age Christians and more.

He explained to me that he was a Mohawk Indian warrior, on a mission given to him by the Council of Elders of the Hopi Indians. His mission was to travel around the world to seek the "new prophet" that was foretold by ancient Hopi traditions. He had been given ten secret questions to be asked and answered, and if all ten questions were answered according to Hopi prophecy, that would qualify that person as either the Hopi Prophet or their representative. He shared with me that he had already encountered several spiritual leaders, some answered a few of the questions right, but none to this point answered all ten successfully. I asked him if this new prophet had a name? He said he has many names, but one that stood out in his mind was "the severer of heads."

I asked him if he had a place to stay that night and he said that God provides him every night with a place, but he didn't know where he would be that night. So, I invited him to come and stay at my communal house in Berkeley. The Mohawk explained that he could not sleep inside a building as part of several conditions and vows he took pertaining to his mission. He also informed us that he could only eat meats that had been killed in the traditional Hopi way. Thankfully, we were mostly vegetarian. The Mohawk Warrior remained in the backyard of our home for many days. Our destinies were linked. It wasn't until weeks later that we discovered how linked they were.

The next day was as usual; off to the shop via the Mediterranean Café, but this morning, and most mornings to follow, were tinted with a sense that a change in my life was coming. It was as though forces behind the obvious were focusing me through a confluence of meetings and events that would predicate a major shift in my life. In the days to come I was beset by a sense of uneasiness, rising from my gut and spreading throughout my body and mind.

The Unraveling

I felt as though I was being pushed towards a cliff, to a leap of overwhelming inevitability. These feelings were there when I awoke and when I slept. It was now 10 days before I was to visit the *fuqara* in Monterey.

For the next ten days, images of Murshid Hassan and Sayid Jamarani filled my thoughts. Their presence in my life brought a measure of contrast to reflect upon. These were men of depth and knowledge. In their light, I felt bereft, without real knowledge, just a pretender, and a novice seeker at best.

One weekend morning, while having my afternoon coffee at the Café, I ran out the door to the Shambhala Bookstore directly across the street from the Med. I stood at the front door and shouted out, "Are there any Sufis here?" At the back of the shop, sitting on the floor next to the Sufi section of the bookstore was a thin figure of a man, beads around his neck and his finger in the air, signaling me to come on over. He answered, "I am a Sufi now, what do you want?" This was the beginning of a lifelong friendship with Hajj Abdul Quddus Hitchcock. We had a brief meeting in which he handed me a card with an address on it. He said, "This is our Sufi Center, please come to see us tonight at 8PM."

The Sufi Center house was in the flats, as they were locally known, in Berkeley, bordering the city of Oakland. It was a run-down neighborhood, lots of abandoned cars and trashed out streets. I found the entrance to the home and knocked at the door. A young African-American man dressed in a white robe was counting his prayers on the beads that slowly circled through his fingers. He acknowledged that they were expecting me. I was invited into a large room, yet unfinished, the drywall missing from parts of the ceiling and off the walls. In the middle of the room was a post supporting the ceiling. A pillow was set under it and above it a poster with the name of Allah. It wasn't just the common type of calligraphy, but the one used by the Alawiyya-Darqawi Path of Sufism.

I was asked to remain there until Hajj Abdul Quddus would come to see me. I waited there for some time, many cups of tea, with my patience running thin; finally, I got up and headed for the door to leave. As I rose from the pillow, Hajj Abdul Quddus entered the room and invited me to sit down. He spoke to me for some time, in a very loving, but strong manner, compelling me to consider embracing Islam. At that point I was not in any state to decide. I was still processing the experiences I had had with Murshid Hassan and Sayid Jamarani. I was genuinely interested, but not ready to take a leap of faith. In any case, I was put off by the manner I was spoken to and the purposely choreographed stage, making Sufism and Islam appear mysterious. It was all too contrived. I insisted on leaving and told him that if I were interested, I'd get in touch.

It would be many years later that Hajj Abdul Quddus and I would meet again. When we did, we had a good laugh about that first meeting.

It was only five days before meeting the *fuqara* in Monterey.

Shaykh Suleiman Dede

Photo Provided by Shems Friedlander

I had heard that Reshad Feild was visiting the Bay Area, and that he had brought with him his Shaykh from Turkey. There was an open meeting planned in San Francisco to introduce the Shaykh and hear him speak. It was to take place in a small hall in a community center in the downtown section of San Francisco. I had just read his recent publication, "The Last Barrier." His story of discovery and the serendipitous unfolding of his path was very inspiring to me. It communicated hope that with strong intent, felicity can smile upon you.

The room was filled to the brim; there was an overflow onto the staircase leading to the room. Sitting, framed by three large Victorian Bay windows, Shaykh Suleiman Dede sat flanked by Reshad Field and, on the other side, his son Jallal'uddin. Dressed in a tweed coat, handkerchief folded perfectly into the jacket's breast pocket, his eyes sparkled like the desert sky in the darkness of the night. He scanned the room taking in each person, smiling, and greeting them, beaming with warmth and love, disarming everyone, making all present feel at home.

He spoke through an interpreter, underscoring the need to discover our seamless connection to God. That separation from the divine is an illusion and its remedy is to practice remembrance (*Dhikr*) of God. He invited anyone interested in the path of remembrance to join under the tent of the Mevlana Path, which is based on the teachings of Jalal ud-Din Rumi. There were several people from the gathering that stepped forward, kissing his hand, signaling that they were ready and willing to be accepted by the Shaykh.

The Shaykh laid his hands on the heads of these few, welcoming them into the Mevlana Sufi Order.

After some time, the Shaykh got up to leave, the crowd parted, making an opening for the Shaykh to pass from the front of the room to the rear, where the exit door was. I was standing by the exit door, my heart leaped with anticipation, with the idea that I might greet him personally, as he passed to exit the room.

Just a moment away from exiting, he turned to the crowd of people in the room and said that he would remember all of them in his prayers, the lovely ladies and men. He then turned right to me, face-to-face, and said: "I will especially remember the men with beards." He smiled at my beardless face, took my hand with both of his and said, "I'll remember you too, but grow a beard." From that day forward I let my beard grow and, to this day, I have never been without it.

A Dream the Night Before Visiting Monterey

I found myself standing in what appeared to be a big city set somewhere in the future. All the buildings shone as though they were made out of mirror or metal; they appeared multiplied in each other's reflection.

People were walking in all directions, as would be indicative of any day in the life of a city dweller. Suddenly, the ground began to shake and panic stricken, people scattered in all directions, but there was nowhere to run. With each moment the shaking became stronger and stronger. The mirrored glass from the building began to pop out of the frames, shattering into razor sharp shards, raining down on the people below. People continued running aimlessly seeking shelter, but little was to be found. The ground heaved up and cracked so wide open, entire buildings plunged into the gaping mouth of the earth. Fire and smoke loomed up blocking out the sun until darkness fell everywhere and upon everything.

I was present as a witness. I was there in body with no ability to move. My eyes fixed, looking just ahead of me, when a priest appeared. In his hand, he held a mask covering his face. The mask had a smile painted on it. From behind the mask a voice spoke, and it said: "Come with me to the church, you will be saved there." I was unable to move or answer, and the priest ran into a large building that appeared to be a church. Thousands of people were pouring into it. I could see the priest standing on a balcony of the building urging them on, telling them to hurry. I saw the building swell to capacity until it appeared it would burst. As soon as the last one entered its doors the earth moved again, like a hungry giant opened and swallowed the church into a gaping hole of fire and smoke. I could hear the screams of those inside realizing their imminent doom.

Then there came another. He was dressed in the clothes of a Rabbi. Holding the same mask in front of him, he offered me refuge in the synagogue. Again, I could not respond. He ran into a building, which appeared to be a synagogue. It too met with the same fate as that of the church.

By now, everything was coming apart. The very fiber of the universe was coming apart, shattering into wisps of atoms, appearing like a cloud of dust. As the dust engulfed me, I felt the capability to move. I felt compelled to look down at my feet; I was standing on a log or bridge. On the right where my right foot was, the log was green and cool, and on the left, where my left foot was, the log was on fire. Down the middle, was a line that divided the green from the fire, neither overtook the other. Being pulled and thrust at the same time I was rocketed forward, landing in a beautiful meadow, covered in tiny sparkling flowers, all around me were gardens, rivers and dewdrops floating in the air, cooling my face, arms, and hands. The scent of the flowers and fresh grass was intoxicating.

In a clearing just ahead, I noticed a group of people standing together holding hands in a circle. I drew near to them as they beckoned me to come closer. There was a space open in the circle and they were waiting for me to take my place. I joined the circle, my hands clasped theirs and I turned my face to the place where I came from. There, through the trees, I could see in the distance the earth ablaze like a burning coal, setting over the horizon. I watched as it faded away, becoming filled with peace and joy, feeling relieved, being without burden for the first time in my life. When the final tip of the burning earth vanished, I awoke.

The Wedding

It was the day of the *fuqara* wedding. It was at least a two-hour drive, a lot of it flowing through the enchanting coastal forests and sometimes along the majestic beaches of northern California. We arrived at the Sufi center just before the sunset prayer. People were already lining up to perform their ablutions, and the call to prayer sounded, adding further sanctity to the celebratory atmosphere.

From the throng of people moving about, their *Muqaddim* emerged and welcomed me. *Muqaddim* is a Sufi designation given to one who represents the Shaykh. He introduced himself as Hajj Haroun. He, like Hajj Abdul Aziz, years before, was the leader of this particular group. He stayed with me almost the entire evening. I felt like he was chaperoning me, and afterwards I learned this was their practice with all visitors and newcomers.

I was deeply touched by their genuine courtesy with each other; they all treated one another with respect and nobility. Neither book nor creed could make a better argument for the veracity of their spiritual practice.

From the very first moment I arrived at the *Za`wiya*, I felt a kinship that went far beyond anything I had experienced before. It wasn't that most were of the same generation, or that we shared certain proclivities or social and economic similarities. It wasn't just the upheaval that swept into our lives from questioning norms, politics or diets and musical tastes.

It was a familiarity of the Soul.

Every one of the *fuqara* I encountered mirrored within me a likeness of heart and mind. It was a sense of what I would imagine it would be like to meet your biological father or brother for the first time, an unexplainable, almost sub-atomic, subconscious reality reconnecting in this world.

The double car garage of their house was transformed into a sacred space, for prayer and, tonight, for a wedding followed by a feast. Moroccan carpets were strewn across the floor; Arab calligraphy adorned its walls, with the names of God, His Prophets, and Messengers. There were prayer beads hanging from the walls, especially over a bookshelf that held several copies of the Qur'an and the *Diwans* of Shaykh Muhammad ibn al Habib.

Looking across the room, you could see faces from all over the world. It was a true statement to the universality of the path they had embraced.

As the *Adhan*, or call to prayer nearly finished, Haroun asked if I would join in the prayer, and I promptly agreed. He led me to an area where there was a water spigot. He explained the practice of *Wudhu*, a type of ablution that was a prerequisite to performing the prayer.

This was the first time I had performed *Wudhu*, following his patient instructions; I wiped the purifying water across my hands, face, arms, head, and feet. Wherever I placed my hands, I imagined blessing myself with holy water, sanctifying my body in preparation for the ultimate meeting. The water helped me put aside my mind, even the anxiety that was my constant companion melted with each intentional stroke of celestial water. Upon finishing the ablution, I felt renewed and ready for the presence of God in and through my life.

Right after the prayer, the bride and groom stepped up to the front of the room where the Imam stood leading the prayer. Cushions were placed one upon the other so that the bride and groom were visible to everyone present. The bride dressed in a traditional white Moroccan wedding dress, glittering with sequins, pearls, and lace. The groom was dressed in a tailored *Jalabiya*, a traditional Arab robe, leather socks, green turban and a large *Tasbih* upon his neck. *Muqaddim* Haroun sat in front of them and began with reciting the first chapter of the Qur'an, *al-Fatiha*. Beginning with the Qur'an evoked the sacredness present in every aspect of life.

After reading *al-Fatiha*, Haroun spoke about the meaning of marriage, underscoring the need to strike a balance in both their obligations to each other and their mutual obligation towards their creator.

The marriage vows in Islam are short and to the point. After the agreement of marriage was witnessed, the ladies present jubilantly ululated as is the Arab custom and the men stood up with loving enthusiasm saying *Allahu Akbar*. Both ladies and men lined up to greet the newlyweds with hugs of joy and mutual gratitude.

Transformational Turn in Life

The next morning, I was preparing to return home. I slept the night in their *Za`wiya*, sleeping on the floor upon a thin cotton mat. There was only one bathroom and there were already several people waiting in a queue to use it. I was invited to the head of the line as a thoughtful gesture towards being a guest in their center.

While waiting in the queue, I overheard one of the men talking to another, saying that he was going for a job interview and only had time to either take a shower or iron his shirt. He decided to have a shower. While in the shower, the other man, whom he had confided in, left his position in the bathroom line, and ironed the shirt. He placed it on a hanger near the bathroom door, to be easily discovered when its owner emerged from the bathroom. The man who ironed the shirt, asked me not to tell him who ironed the shirt. He exclaimed that Allah seeing him was enough reward. When the other man emerged and found his shirt, he looked around to see if he could thank that person. You could see his gratitude shining from his face.

Of all the experiences I had with this fine Sufi community, this was by far the most profound for me. It's one thing to sing, talk and chant, it's another to "live" by what you profess.

I departed that morning from the Monterey center in body only, my heart and soul still resonating with the whole experience. My mind was struggling to make sense of the split within me. On one hand I had never experienced what I recognized in the practices of Islam. To my mind and heart, it contained all I wanted in a path to Light. On the other hand, my habitual negative views regarding dogmatic "religions" as such were stifling me from coming to a resolution to move forward.

I first realized how profound my perceptions had changed when I stepped through the doorway of the commune. It was as though everything was tinted with a dulling, grayish shade of colorlessness. In the past when returning to the commune, I felt happy and excited to be back. This time, the glow that I used to experience was gone.

I heard voices coming from the kitchen, which was the common place for people gathering over coffee to discuss and share visions of the universe, personal experiences and sometimes long running debates on the veracity of different practices and religious beliefs. I was always keen on participating in these discussions, but this time it was painful, so much theory and intellectualizing with little reality. My recent experience with the *fuqara* mirrored a powerful contrast between discussing the menu and actually eating the meal. The chasm between those living a life of transformation and those only discussing transformation is as different as day and night.

Hopi Words of Wisdom

I retreated from the discussion to my shack in the backyard of the house. As I walked through the garden a campfire was burning near the pathway. Sitting near the fire was the Mohawk Indian warming a pot of tea leaves he had picked from our garden. He invited me to join him. After pouring the tea, we sat in silence; the only sounds were the crackling fire. We gazed at the night sky, full of endless majesty and wonder, as the heat of the fire was just right to cut through the coastal breeze of the night. The silence of the moment washed through my being, my body relaxed, the mind's tumult abated, and I felt my eyes focused clearly after being blurred for some time. We glanced at each other in recognition that we were both resonating with the same experience. There was no need to speak, to talk or to gesture in confirmation, we both just relished in the gift of this overflowing moment.

After some time passed, he turned to me and related a story called: *We are the Ones we've Been Waiting For.*

You have been telling people that this is the Eleventh Hour, now you must go back and tell the people that this is the Hour and there are things to be considered...

Who are you?

Where are you living?

What are you doing?

What are your relationships?

Are you in the right relation?

Where is your water?

Know your garden.

It is time to speak your truth.

Create your community.

Be good to each other.

And do not look outside yourself for that which leads you.

Then he clasped his hands together, smiled, and said:

"This could be a good time! There is a river flowing now very fast. It is so great and swift that there are those who will be afraid. They will try to hold on to the shore. They will feel they are being torn apart and will suffer greatly. Know the river has its destination. The elders say we must let go of the shore, push off into the middle of the river, keep our eyes open, and our heads above the water."

And I say, see who is in there with you and celebrate.

At this time in history, we are to take nothing personally, least of all ourselves, for the moment that we do, our spiritual growth and journey come to a halt.

The time of the lone wolf is over.

Gather yourselves! Banish the word 'struggle' from your attitude and your vocabulary.

All that we do now must be done in a sacred manner and in celebration.

We are the ones we've been waiting for.

— Hopi Elders' Prophecy

He paused after finishing the story and turned to me saying, "you know what you have to do, do not delay!"

Transformational Thoughts

I went to my room in the backyard with a fever for action. In every part of my being, I felt the bursting of a new day. Like the seed that thrusts through the layer of earth to reach the sunlight, my whole being was under the command of nature itself.

I hardly slept that night. Even though I was compelled and knowing that Islam was the right path for me, I felt I was being encased within a cocoon of darkness. My whole life began to pass in front of me. All the things I falsely thought, believed, and identified with, loomed large in my awareness. Each and everything that appeared closed in on me. It felt like I was being slowly suffocated by their presence. It was a "dark night of the soul," a crucible to endure. At the point where I thought I could no longer take the vision in, I heard a voice emerge accompanied by a sparking of light. It beckoned me, "Come, come as you are, but come." I followed that voice with my awareness until the darkness was overcome by the presence of that light and voice.

I had not realized that I had fallen asleep until I awoke with those very words, repeating on my tongue, "Come, come as you are, but come!"

As the sun rose, I packed a bag and informed Jerry and others that I was going down to Monterey to embrace Islam. I told them at this point I didn't care what they called themselves. I wanted what they had. Jerry accompanied me to Monterey, both of us going with the same intention.

Taking the *Shahada*

We arrived in Monterey late morning. Jerry wanted to stop for a coffee and breakfast before going to the *Za`wiya*. Although I would have preferred to go straight to the center, we stopped at a local diner. Jerry ordered two eggs over easy, bacon and a beer. I said, what's this all about? He said, "well this is the last time we will be able to eat pork and drink alcohol." I could not get behind this at all, reminding him that, in reality, once we have decided to follow the path of Islam we were essentially within its grounds, so to speak. He gave my comment little credence and went on to have his "last meal."

We arrived at the center and were welcomed into the house, where the living room was converted into a small meeting room. Hajj Haroun was sitting there with several of the *fuqara*. We happened to walk in at the very moment several people were taking their *shahada* (profession of faith). It was an auspicious moment to arrive. I informed Hajj Haroun why we had come. I said, "I want to be one of you, please accept me."

He instructed me to have a shower, while performing it with the intention to purify myself from the past. Afterwards, I came in front of these noble men of the *Darqawi* Sufi order; putting my hand in theirs, I recited the most profound words possible.

Ash-hadu an laa ilaaha ill Allah (I bear witness that there is no deity, no other, no other existent other than The One and only existent; One Reality with no partner to compare with Him), *Wa Ash-hadu anna Muhammadan Rasulul Allah* (and I bear witness that Reality, in Its Infinite expression of Mercy and Love, has echoed His attributes in the representation of the Prophet Muhammad).

Muhammad is the perfect mirror and access point to the eternal soul of humanity.

I remained in Monterey for several weeks. During that time, I learned the basic practices of Islam. Above and beyond the practices, there was the benefit of keeping company with the *fuqara*. Each member of this group was so unique in expressing their commitment to their path. Most were also well traveled, visiting living saints across the world, spending time with them and receiving knowledge, not only from books and words, but with direct transmission from these saints, heart to heart. The idea of transmission was most compelling. It was something I accepted very naturally. I had already experienced this through meetings with saints and spiritual personalities in the past. All this added to my commitment to further myself along this way in emulating the drive and appreciation of the people among the *fuqara*.

Shaykh Abdalqadir as-Sufi

Everyone at the center talked about their teacher, Shaykh Abdalqadir as-Sufi. There was much deference and reference to him almost in every conversation. All projects at the center were centered on his directions and leadership. When the news came that their Shaykh was coming to visit Monterey, there was a great sense of anticipation. I would note that this anticipation expressed itself out of joy but also some trepidation. I had read "The Way of Muhammad" and it was a transforming read for me. Many stories were shared about the miracles that surrounded the Shaykh and his vast knowledge and overall stature. I was very excited to meet him and, as a result, anticipated a major turning point in my life.

The day of the Shaykh's arrival was upon us. A separate house was rented nearby to accommodate him, specialty foods and teas were procured, and the center's kitchen was roaring in preparation to celebrate the arrival of the Shaykh with his favorite foods.

We were all waiting in the *Za`wiya* for the Shaykh's arrival, sitting shoulder-to-shoulder, singing the *Diwan* of Shaykh Muhammad ibn al Habib; all eyes were lowered, looking into their own hearts respectfully as the Shaykh entered the room. I remember getting all caught up in the excitement, the anxious anticipation; I really didn't know why I had succumbed to the collective emotion of the moment. I had no experience with him before, but it was impossible to avoid when everyone was resonating in the same way.

When the Shaykh entered the room, I could smell him before seeing him. He was wearing Oudh, a particularly pungent perfume made from Aloeswood infected by a fungus that transformed the sap into a unique perfume. These trees are found in Vietnam, Cambodia, and the Philippines. The fragrance was intoxicating and gripped me immediately upon detecting it. Although the Shaykh was in the room with us, we were advised not to look up at him at first, but to see him in your heart, and later you may have the opportunity to see him face to face.

The singing and chanting came to a halt as the Shaykh signaled it was time to end the ceremonial for his address. It was one of the most intoxicating speeches I had ever heard. The Shaykh also broached sensitive political issues. He underscored the need to be proactive on the world stage, insisting that spirituality find its balance and completion in worldly action.

Meeting the Shaykh

After the group session the Shaykh held individual meetings with all the new Muslims. There were about 8 or 9 of us. I was very nervous to meet him. I rehearsed what I was going to say to him, which started with a brief summary of my life. When I was called up to meet him, he greeted me warmly. I was just about to go into my story, when he abruptly and unexpectedly stopped me and said, "I don't need to hear your life's story, I can write it for you in less than five minutes!" He continued, "Everything you think you know, everything they taught you is a lie. If we can start with an agreement that you can accept this, then we can move on, if not, leave now."

Time froze. I had a second to answer upon which my whole life hung in the balance. My mind streamed with questions, doubts, and justifications to not agree; yet my heart, my recent experience with this community encouraged me to agree. In what seemed like an eternity, I answered, "I agree!" He smiled and asked me to kiss his hand, which I did. He said, "You made the right choice. I cannot promise you anything other than you will have a good time." At that, I moved back from the inner circle where he was sitting. Then it was my companion's turn, Jerry, who had been my teacher and leader of the commune for many years. Shaykh Abdalqadir asked him: "What do you want?" Jerry replied, "I want to be a Shaykh like you." Everyone in the circle raised their brows; there were even smirks and gestures of unbelief that Jerry would even voice such a desire. Shaykh Abdalqadir paused and said, "Right, you will be a Shaykh, under the following condition." Jerry answered, "I will do whatever it takes." Shaykh Abdalqadir spoke, squinting his eyes towards Jerry's face and saying, "For the next two years, you must sit by the men's washroom and make sure that everyone that enters has warm water to wash themselves after using the toilet and to make sure the facilities remain clean."

Jerry paused before answering, with just enough time for his face to turn red, lips quivering. He stood up with contempt and said, "You have got to be kidding. This condition is not only outrageous but asking me to commit to such a length of time does not take into consideration what I have to offer. I have to decline."

Shaykh Abdalqadir lowered his gaze and said that there was nothing more for him to offer and bid him farewell. When Jerry left the immediate circle, Shaykh Abdalqadir said to the rest of us, "That man does not realize what gift he declined." Later, one of the close companions of Shaykh Abdalqadir spoke to me in this regard, sharing his opinion regarding Jerry's rejection of the offer. He said, "If he only knew the burden and sacrifice that goes into becoming a Shaykh, he would have grabbed this opportunity with both hands. Cleaning toilets and providing warm washing water for two years! Anyone sitting in that circle, having been given the same offer would have jumped at that opportunity."

How can norms be broken for you whilst you have not

Broken the norms of the self (egoic-self).

— Ibn ata'Allah Iskandari

O seeker of truth, leave your desires behind if you want

Deeper divine secrets,

And then take onto the Path and maintain the

companionship....... Until all shadows vanish and the Original Love engulfs you.

— Shaykh Faytouri

While Shaykh Abdalqadir was with us in Monterey, many plans were discussed with him as to how to propagate Islam in America, as well as strengthen the existing group in knowledge and practice of the Sufi science of awakening. For the next several weeks, we awoke two hours before dawn to study Arabic, the Qur'an and, before the actual sunrise, perform the ritual *dhikr* of the *Darqawa*, which included the standing *Hadra* (Presence or Dance of the Sufis.)

The Morning Prayer was performed, and the recital of two Chapters of the Qur'an then followed: *al-Waqi`ah* and al-*Muzammil.*

Later in the afternoon, Shaykh Abdalqadir would address the community in the prayer hall or sometimes, when just sitting with the men in the living space of the house, now called the Mensa.

Propagation of Islam in America

On one of these occasions, the Shaykh addressed all the men, sharing his vision for us as a community. He spoke with a detailed analysis of the current state of the world and a plan to address its effect on our local circumstance. He briefly outlined a three-tier program that included a group to exclusively study Islam and the Sufi sciences, and a second group to travel the world akin to the lore of the "wandering Dervishes," and a third to train in the martial arts and military in preparation for open confrontation in the streets of America.

I was on board with the first two tiers of his program, but the third made no sense to me and viscerally made me sick. I felt a wave of anxiety run through me as my heart and mind could not line up with the idea of "open confrontation in the streets of America." I could not conceive of this as an actual future outcome. It seemed more a provocation than having its intellectual genesis rooted in reality. While caught in my thoughts, I hadn't paid attention to what he said next, nor what the atmosphere in the room was like. At that moment, he asked if there were any questions regarding what he was saying, or any comment. I reluctantly raised my hand, acknowledged, and responded with my view. I said that I believed that the application of the third tier as described was not only reactionary but without basis at this present time and in the future. The Shaykh immediately reacted energetically to my comment, not addressing it head on, but rather, making it a question of my loyalty. He gave me an ultimatum: either accept the components of the plan, as defined, or leave now.

I felt exactly like I did when I first met the Shaykh, when he emphatically said that everything I had been taught was a lie and to accept this premise or leave. I took the same tack as I did then. I had been with this group for several weeks now, listened to the Shaykh's magnificent talks and attended the most majestic invocations during the *dhikrs*. Although I did disagree with his postulating the need for the third tier, I decided to hold on a bit longer to see where all this would lead. Having a good opinion moving forward, I answered with an outward affirmative, but inwardly agreed only with conditions that I kept to myself.

That night, while sleeping on my mat in the prayer room, two close students of the Shaykh came to awaken me. It was 3am. They said you must come with us immediately to the Shaykh's house; he wants to discuss a very important matter with you. I rose to dress, but was discouraged to do so, as time was of the essence. I left in my pajamas with them and was brought to the Shaykh's house. I was asked to wait in an adjoining room separated by two French doors, draped with a thin curtain. I could see through the curtain, and there was the Shaykh sitting alongside a white board. I could make out a hand-drawn grid filled with details of dates, places, names and times. Once asked to come in, I was warmly greeted by the Shaykh and he said that he was so excited that he could not wait till the morning to share with me the new plan for the community, bringing me up to speed as to my role in making it happen.

The three tiers were all still in place, but the third was altered to only include personal education in the martial arts as a way of developing discipline and abilities to protect the community if needed. I asked, what happened to AK-47 training and street fighting with the "enemies of Islam"? He said that was yesterday! Allah is always on a new creation; forget about that, this is the new plan. He also threw in, "Why did you not get dressed before coming here."

Murabitun Movement – Setting Up the Rabat Center

The plan was to establish a "Rabat"[7] on the outskirts of Tucson, Arizona, and all of the community here and some from abroad would rendezvous there to participate in creating a new *Murabitun Movement.*

My role was to finalize the purchase of the house that would act as both Shaykh Abdalqadir's residence and the center fortress of the *Murabitun.*

Later, we called the house simply, the *Rabat.*

I was further instructed to travel and live in Tucson with a companion, Abdus Sabur. The Shaykh gave explicit instructions that neither one of us should ever be more than ten feet away from the other at any time. He also asked that we find an apartment that was no more than ten minutes away from the *Rabat.*

At that meeting I raised the issue of the Mohawk Indian that was living in the yard of our commune in the Bay Area. The Shaykh became very excited about the opportunity to meet the Hopi liaison. In the next few days my return to the commune was organized. I was to travel back with two seasoned students of Shaykh Abdalqadir to keep me company while

---

[7] The capital city of Morocco. It's used here as a metaphor.

transitioning from my previous life towards the new mission of establishing the *Rabat* in Tucson. They were also carrying an invitation addressed to the Mohawk, to be the Shaykh's guest in Monterey.

Sufi Boot Camp and the Significance of the *Hadra*

Shortly after embracing Islam, my entire past quickly retreated into the distant horizon, delivering me for the first time in my life with a sense of renewal and rebirth. My relationship, towards everything, had changed. A newly discovered, inner GPS awakened within me, guided by the unfolding wisdom teachings and transformative practices of Islam.

I recall Shaykh Abdalqadir's first words to me:

"Everything you have been taught to this point was a lie."

He required my acceptance of this statement as a prerequisite to staying on as a *faqir* (a wayfarer to a spiritual path) and, by extension, a student of his.

I struggled profoundly with the entire notion of complying with his conditions. I reasoned to myself that, surely, it all could not be a lie.

It was only later I began to understand what, in truth, he was really trying to say.

It wasn't particularly the content of my cultural upbringing or my education, both religious and secular, but rather the resultant construction of an ego-centered persona, driven and conditioned to be subservient to the lower tendencies of the self.

"Every living entity is sustained by its provider: soul or spirit.

Souls differ in their extent of consciousness, and thus, bodies and minds differ appropriately.

The human soul creates its own evolving self as a companion shadow. From the interplay of self and soul, personality emerges. Mind is an intermediate faculty between the soul and the body that exists through the senses, intelligence and memory.

The soul radiates qualities that are desirable, such as knowledge, life, ability, and numerous other attributes. The self, which carries aspects of its animal connection desires the soul's qualities and evolves through maturity of mind to spiritual wisdom, culminating in self-discovery, which is soul-realization."

— *Spectrum of Reality*, by Shaykh Fadhlalla Haeri

Shaykh Abdalqadir knew that the only way to break the hold of conditioned consciousness, was to turn away from it on whole, in hope that the real and Original Light of the soul would emerge, opening the potential to discover who and what I/you really are, i.e., Soul Realization.

This theme permeates all practices in Islam and is particularly emphasized by the instructions and practices in all the Sufi schools (*Tariqahs*).

It was reflected in the daily practices we performed as part of Shaykh Abdalqadir's community.

We prayed together, studied together and practiced conscious *Adab* (courtesies), which we all discovered was not an outer blueprint of behavior per se, but a practice of being present, aware with propriety, sincerity, humility and courage.

When gathered with others with the same intention, an X factor appears and multiplies the depth of its transmission for each one present, becoming the basis for the most transformative relationships one can have.

For the first five weeks after declaring myself as a Muslim, I remained at the *Za`wiya* in Monterey California. These five weeks were, for all intents and purposes, a *Sufi Boot Camp*. The new Sufi recruits were put to the rigor of *Fuqara Training*. It was obvious that although the "old" *fuqara* gave us special attention, making it their job to bring us up to speed with the practices of Darqawi Sufi Path, they did not exclude themselves from the same rigor and intensity of participating in the daily teachings, prayers, and general rules of conduct, i.e., the correct *Adab* – it was expected from everyone.

Each day would start at least one hour before the beginning of the dawn prayer. Every day, one of the *fuqara* was appointed to go around the *Za`wyia* and wake us from sleep. They made sure we were not only awake but moving towards dressing, and preparing for the first program of the day. If we remained in our beds, even for a few moments, we were often encouraged with a Zen like strike on the bottoms of our feet with a bamboo rod, accompanied with a verbal command to rise. Most of us new *fuqara* slept in a large carpeted converted garage. There must have been at least thirty men, each having their own bedrolls and personal items in a duffle bag behind their heads. It was amazing that within minutes of being awake, everyone rolled their beds up against the walls, securing their personal items. Once everyone's items were in place, colorful blankets were thrown on top of them, providing the perimeter of the entire room with makeshift seating. Prayer mats were unfolded and spread across the now opened floor.

The *fuqara* from the main house would file in as the space was being prepared; we all sat on the ground forming a circle, sometimes concentric circles, depending on how many people there were. Once all were present, sitting in place, a moment of silent gathered-ness descended upon the room, each heart in unifying resonance, and one with the other in the presence of stillness.

The Muqaddim, as he was known, was the leader of the community; he would give the nod to begin the liturgy of the morning. There were a variety of liturgies; anything from repeating the names and attributes of Allah, to extensive reading of the Qur'an.

On some mornings, we would begin with the singing of the *Diwan* of Shaykh Muhammad ibn al Habib, followed by a standing *dhikr*, called the *Hadra*.

It is most often performed in a circle, standing, holding each other's hands and moving in unison, while repeating traditional formulas in Arabic.

Its parts combine into a transformative experience that transcends beyond the body and mind, yet acknowledges and encompasses mind, body and spirit, in movement, sound and breath.

It is a metaphor, reflecting the journey, from the relative and conditioned consciousness, to knocking at the door of the Divine Absolute, i.e., God Consciousness.

There is always someone leading the *Hadra* who is in the middle of the circle, making sure that it remains stable and, when needed, making adjustments; it can be anything from a light tap to the chest, an embrace of the shoulders or sometimes removal from the circle, all in order to keep the flow and harmony of the circle intact. On the outside of the circle, experienced *Diwan* singers chant away in rhythm and movement with the sound and timing of each stage of the *Hadra*. The meanings of the *Diwan* swirl throughout the room like a mist of light, and the meanings flow into the expanding awareness and presence, aiding in inspiring the hearts yearning to union with the soul within.

> *Dare, O human being, to awaken! Harmonize your song; intensify your commitment. Consult your heart and your heart alone. Expose yourself to loving; seek the protection of Love. To arrive at true being, come past the curtain waving in front of the Divine Light, which is your own light.*

— Lex Hixon / Shaykh Nur al-Jerrahi

The first segment of the *Hadra* focuses on the Divine attribute of *The Living.*

The movements of the *Hadra* begin with the neck, dropping it down towards your chest while in an out breath, exclaiming *"Hayy"* (Life) followed by the head coming up, and knees slightly giving way, simultaneously exclaiming *"Llah"* (Allah) combined together, meaning "Living-Allah."

With body, mind, heart and breath synchronized, it is designed to shed and cause to fall away any attribution held within conditioned consciousness, of "otherness," while yearning for none other than The One and Only Source of Life itself.

In the second segment the movement changes and instead of moving only the head up and down, you begin to move your whole body up and down in place, your knees acting like springs, feet not leaving the ground, while in your heart acknowledging the Life Giver itself, your every breath exclaiming only, *Hayy, Hayy Hayy!*

Life, life, He is Life itself.

"Dance until you shatter yourself"

— Rumi

It continues until the leader of the Dance is inspired to bring it to an end, marked by reciting the prayer upon the Prophet Muhammad.

We would all quickly sit down, in circles, eyes focused downwards, abiding in the fullness of the Present. When everyone is in place, a portion of the Qur'an would be recited and the *Muqqadim*, or someone chosen by him, would begin a talk, which was commonly referred to as the *Dars* (Lesson).

The *Hadra* can go on for minutes, hours and sometimes all day and through the night.

I had been present in a *Hadra* that started after the evening prayer and went until well after dawn.

After the *Dars*, the *Adhan* was given, for the *Fajr* prayer.

We would pray at the beginning of *Fajr*, when the sun had just begun to tint the horizon with its golden light. Copies of the Quran were passed out and, as it was every morning just after the prayer, we would recite two *Suras*, the first was *Sura Muzammil* and the second *Sura ad Dukhan*. After these recitations, the copies of the Qur'an would be collected and we would break up into groups, separated by the level of proficiency in Arabic, studying the language of the Qur'an until the rising of the sun.

In these five weeks, I had gone through tremendous changes, I had lost about twenty pounds, exchanged my blue jeans for Yves Saint Laurent slacks and blazer, wore a conservative haircut, replacing the not-so-distant past longhair hippie ringlets that once draped down my back. I exchanged my beaten-up VW Karman Ghia with an Oldsmobile Delta 88, and sported one of the first Seiko digital watches. I also learned to make black tea, English style, which I learned later was a qualifying factor in facilitating longer and more repeated meetings with Shaykh Abdalqadir as-Sufi.

Return to the Commune

Upon returning to the commune, I was met with a great deal of consternation, for much of which I was personally responsible, as I came back a zealot, about entering Islam.

Although the folks of the commune heard that I had become a Muslim while I was away, several other members made their pilgrimage to Monterey to also embrace Islam as well.

Nevertheless, they did not hear from me until I returned. I gathered them all in our meeting room and without mincing words, exhorted them to embrace Islam. I was after all the appointed Emir of Murshid Hassan and most of the members of the commune had considered themselves under his guidance. Several came forward, but most declined. This was the beginning of the end of our commune. In the coming days, many began packing to leave, and others seemed to vanish without word or trace. I put my store up for sale and was able to sell it within a few days of the offer going out.

Since Randal Scott, Jerry and I were co-owners of the homes that made up the commune, we placed the property on the market, which was all sold within a week.

While I was tying up loose ends in the Bay Area, the Mohawk traveled down to Monterey to meet with Shaykh Abdalqadir. As his mission dictated, he put the 10 qualifying questions to the Shaykh. They were all satisfactorily answered, opening the way for the Shaykh and a small entourage to travel to Oraibi, to meet with the Hopi Council of Elders for the second phase, to qualify the veracity of the findings. After meeting with the council and satisfactorily answering all their questions, there was one more challenge to be met.

There is a sacred cave painting depicting the animal that the future Prophet would use as his mount. The painting was clearly identified as a camel.

Among the Hopi elders, only a few acknowledged and accepted the outcome of the findings. The majority gave limited, tepid acknowledgment, positing that there was a greater universal context to the results of the findings that can apply to many other religions and sacred ways. They held to a traditional understanding of the belief that the new Prophet would come from among the indigenous peoples, not people as far flung as Europe and especially the Arabian Peninsula.

There was one indigenous man that heard the news and returned to Monterey with the Shaykh and his entourage.

> *To God belongs the East and the West. Wherever you turn is the face of God.*
>
> — Qur'an 2:115

Down the Rabbit Hole

Within a few days of Shaykh Abdalqadir's return to Monterey, Abdus Sabur and I were off to Tucson, Arizona. After staying in a hotel for a few days we found an apartment. It only occurred to me after we signed the lease that I had not considered the 10-minute limit that the Shaykh asked us to abide by. I did not share my concern with Abdus Sabur; we were already having issues regarding the 10-foot restriction placed upon us. In general, I am a very laid-back person; yes, the Shaykh said never to be outside ten feet, but I took it in stride 10 feet more or less. It was not the same with Abdus Sabur. When we walked into a supermarket, or a Mall Shopping center, he would often play catch up with me, running towards me if we were even a foot over the prescribed distance. When I had to use the toilets, he would accompany me to the public restroom. I would normally find the humor and irony in this situation, but it soon became annoying to both of us.

This was an example of the kind of over the top, fanatical obedience to the Shaykh in my mind. As my time and exposure to the *fuqara* grew, I experienced more and more of the same behavior. When I broached the subject with a few of the more easy-going brothers, they ardently believed that the Shaykh's directions contain an insight that we were incapable of having or understanding. I was always encouraged to trust without hesitation, warning me that it was the only way to succeed on this path. As a neophyte on this path, for a time, I suspended and surrendered my common sense. For the most part I went along even when my gut was sounding the alarm and messaging caution. Being with the Shaykh and the *fuqara* was thrilling and exciting. We were always in revolution being encouraged by the evolution that clearly each one was individually experiencing. Anyone who knew Shaykh Abdalqadir, read his books, or heard his talks, would agree that he had great insight into the psyche of humanity, a grasp of all that was wrong in the world, a charismatic flare for drama, along with an evoking presence, transmitting his message, touching in a profound way not only the intellect of those listening, but also inspiring and awakening their hearts. He was an extraordinary being, but not perfect, as we imagined.

Shaykh Abdalqadir arrived in Tucson and immediately was installed in Rabat.

Down Came the Spider

I picked him up from the airport in a new Oldsmobile Delta 88. The interior was beige leather with an extended backseat for plenty of foot and headroom. The color of the car was dark green and topped with a black vinyl top. When the Shaykh first saw the car, he asked if it were mine, and I proudly said, yes. He commented that the color was *Darqawi* green. Upon sitting in the back seat, he asked if I would be his driver during his stay in Tucson. This is exactly what I had hoped for and what inspired me to buy this car. I was told that whoever drives the Shaykh around would have the coveted opportunity to spend time with him and converse with him often.

All went well for the first week or so, we regularly visited the Shaykh at the Rabat, I took him shopping and as foretold, and Shaykh Abdalqadir would talk to me frequently, sharing stories and teachings of the Sufi way.

One night, as I was dozing off to sleep, the phone rang. It was a call from Shaykh Abdalqadir. He asked that I come to the Rabat immediately, ending the call with, "I'll see you in ten minutes!"

I still had not timed the distance from our apartment to the Rabat; I had an idea that it was about ten minutes, but not quite sure. In any case, I dressed quickly, went down to the basement garage where my car was and sped off to the Rabat. Upon arriving there, I glanced at my watch, fifteen minutes had passed. I entered the driveway where, just beyond the pathway to the Rabat, I saw Shaykh Abdalqadir waiting at the front door, even though it was a dim light that cast over the front entrance, I could see him pointing to his wrist watch and shaking his head in the negative. I walked quickly to greet him. He turned away scolding me that I had missed an opportunity as he shut the door in my face.

The next day we did not hear from him. I was determined to make sure that if he calls again in the night, I would be ready to make it to the

Rabat in ten minutes. It was only a day later that he called again, this time nearly midnight. I was ready. I had the phone next to my bed, to pick up immediately. I went to bed in a jogging outfit, so as not to waste time getting dressed. I rushed down to my car that I had parked at the entrance of the garage, pointing outward for a quick getaway. With the pedal to the metal, I rushed off to the Rabat. As I rolled up the driveway, I glanced at my watch, this time; it was exactly ten minutes. The Shaykh was at the door, waved me in and disappeared into the Rabat. Reaching the door, I was invited in by a young student called Muhammad Qasim. He welcomed me in, asking me to sit on the sofa. After a few minutes, he brought me a warm glass of milk, accompanied with a message from the Shaykh, relating a tradition from the Prophet Muhammad saying that, he never drank milk in which there was not knowledge in it. After finishing the warm milk, I was excused and returned to our apartment in Tucson.

For the next few nights, I did not let my guard down. I was vigilant, prepared for a potential call from the Shaykh.

Some nights had passed, it seemed as though the lesson had been learned and that the Shaykh would probably not call. Then, at 3am the phone rang. It was Muhammad Qasim. He was extremely agitated; speaking quickly with urgency, he said that Shaykh Abdalqadir had been bitten by a spider and he was lying prostrate on the floor, he said come immediately to take him to the hospital. I was ready to move! Dressed as I was before, the car parked for the least time to get out of the garage. I was off like a bat out of hell for the Rabat. I can't really explain how, but I arrived in seven minutes this time. The door was open and Shaykh Abdalqadir was clearly in distress. Muhammad and I carried the Shaykh to the car, where he laid down on the back seat. We drove straight to the ER at the Tucson hospital. We carried the Shaykh into the ER waiting room, I was shouting, "We need a doctor now!" Within a few minutes a gurney was brought into the ER waiting room and they wheeled the Shaykh into triage. We waited anxiously for several minutes, before a doctor appeared. He explained that Mr. Dallas (Shaykh Abdalqadir's birth name) has an extreme allergy to spider venom and that he was being treated with the proper antidote. He then addressed me saying it's a good thing you got here in good time, if it were another few minutes, the outcome could have been much worse.

We waited until the anti-venom worked. Shaykh Abdalqadir quickly recovered.

We returned to the Rabat; it was nearly dawn. The Shaykh did not speak during our return to Rabat. When we arrived, he quickly retired to his room. He sent a message to me to remain until late morning when he would see me.

Later that morning I was summoned to his room. When I entered his bedroom, he was busy packing his suitcase. He explained that the spider bite was an omen for him to leave. He said this sort of event happened once before and, as it turned out, it too was an omen for him to leave. He showed me his personal copy of the *Diwan* of Shaykh Muhammad ibn al Habib. On the leather front cover was a black stain over an indentation, it looked as though a drop of acid landed there and ate away the leather. Shaykh Abdalqadir explained that while he was asleep last night, he awoke sensing that there was a dark presence in his room. He had the *Diwan* next to his bed and threw it up to the ceiling, where it hit with considerable force. He had killed the spider, but it was too late, it had already bit him. He had severe allergies from spider venom. He asked me to take him to the airport, as he was leaving immediately. At that point he thanked me for being there for him. He then removed his own green turban from his head and placed it upon mine. He also gave me a large leather bound *Maghribi* Qur'an, that is, it was written and bound in the Western part of North Africa and the Arab world. He said these are the two best things that he had to offer.

I asked when he might return. He answered that he would be in touch.

Shaykh Abdalqadir's Return to England

Shaykh Abdalqadir returned to England for several months, during that time we established a center and many *fuqara* came from all over the US and abroad to begin building what would become the foundation for the Worldwide *Murabitun* movement.

During this period, I worked wherever I could, mostly sales jobs. There were so many members of our community that could not work for one reason or another, so it fell on those who had jobs to support the community. Although I was not married and living simply, whatever funds I had were drained away until I had very little to show for my work. At one point, in order to make ends meet, I sold my *Darqawi* green Oldsmobile Delta 88 and bought a tiny used Datsun two seat, in which none of the windows rolled down. It was faded red and often needed to role downhill to jump-start the car. I was especially unhappy about this because this car was not suitable to drive Shaykh Abdalqadir around when he returned. I had really looked forward to doing so, but all hope was dashed with the Datsun.

Shaykh Abdalqadir Returns / Meeting Shaykh Fadhlalla

Grand Theft Auto

In the coming weeks I had better fortune in my sales job and thought that I would look for a suitable car to drive the Shaykh around.

I had been working at a local furniture shop. One evening, when I was returning home from my place of employment, I imagined with anticipation the return of the Shaykh and how if I had the right vehicle, I might have the opportunity of being his driver again.

While indulging in this fantasy I passed by a local Cadillac dealership and mused to myself, "Wouldn't it be great if I were to drive the Shaykh around in style and comfort in a brand-new Cadillac?" Following my fantasy, I pulled into the dealership and immediately noticed a dark green Cadillac Fleetwood with a luxurious leather interior.

A salesman approached me, who went into a sales pitch for the car. I went along pretending to be an interested buyer. He asked me if I wanted to take it for a test drive, and I agreed.

They made a copy of my driver's license and off I went for a "test" drive. (And what a test it became!).

While driving around the block, I imagined driving the Shaykh and spending quality time in his company.

At one point, I passed near the *Za`wiya* and was suddenly overwhelmed by a feeling that Shaykh Abdalqadir had arrived unannounced and was waiting at the center.

The sense of this possibility gripped me to such an extent, I was compelled to head right for the center. I arrived and pulled in the driveway and there, standing with all his suitcases, was the Shaykh.

I was stunned! My heart was pounding hard, I was astonished, delighted, surprised and mystified. I approached the Shaykh, greeting him and without thinking it through, I opened the trunk and doors of the Cadillac and invited the Shaykh to sit down.

He greeted me with an exuberant greeting, looking over the Cadillac, praising its color and comfort, and then asked me if this was mine?

I froze inside, wanting so much for this car to be mine, and without considering the repercussions, I answered in the affirmative. He answered "splendid" and requested me to drive him to his home, outside Tucson.

91

As we drove away, I became more and more anxious. What have I done? I asked myself. Surely, by now, the salesman at the Cadillac dealership is reporting the missing car. I was certain that they would call the police. During the drive to Rabat, my eyes darted repeatedly into the rear-view mirror, looking out for police. I was beside myself with fear. Not only have I endangered my own self but that of the well-being of the Shaykh.

The teaching and intimate conversation I had anticipated, in an atmosphere of tranquility, was not going to happen!

We arrived without incident at the Shaykh's house. I had one consistent thought and that was to get back to the dealership and return the car.

After unloading the trunk and depositing the Shaykh in his home I requested his permission to take his leave. To my utter dread, he requested that I come in and have some tea with him. I explained that I would not be able to do that, but he insisted and went immediately into directing me to the right kitchen cabinets where all the tea fixings were kept.

My mind was in a spin. I was sure that the police had been notified and there was a warrant or APB[8] out for my arrest and the return of the vehicle.

It was getting dark and I again approached the subject outlining the importance without giving the reasons for me to leave. He did not answer, rising from where he was sitting and making his way up the staircase to his room, he paused and said, "Please stay here tonight." He said that he wanted to go shopping early in the morning and, since it also was the first night, he was back from traveling would like to have me remain for the night.

I was stuck! I was up to my ears. On the one hand, I couldn't leave in fear of offending or falling out of grace with the Shaykh and, on the other hand, I was certain by now I was a fugitive from the law. Perplexed as to what to do, I opted to remain the night and sort things out the next day.

The next morning came bright and early and Shaykh Abdalqadir was ready to go out shopping. We spent the day between several Tucson malls and shopping centers, a restaurant, and a local health food shop. The day went on without incident. But for me it was a nightmare! I could hardly listen to all the sublime themes and subjects the Shaykh touched upon.

---

8 APB – All Points Bulletin – an electronic information broadcast system.

With all the noise going on in my mind and my emotions running wild, the best I could do was to mechanically nod and answer as though I got his point and praised God as a punctuation between what I did not hear or understand but appeared to listen attentively.

Back at the Shaykh's house, I now entertained the idea that I could make it back to the dealership with a clever story and avoid legal problems.

I again requested permission to leave, and he then reminded me that tonight there was a gathering of *dhikr* at the *Za`wiya* and that I should remain until it was time to go for the gathering.

My thoughts were now turning to being thrown into a jail cell, court proceedings and having to hire a lawyer. I was also thinking a viable defense, insanity, was the only reasonable plea.

The evening arrived and I was off to the *Za`wiya* in downtown Tucson.

When we arrived, we could hear the powerful rhythm of the standing *Hadra* and the melodious Andalusia themes applied to the singing of the *Diwan*.

The Shaykh swiftly alighted from the car and called to me to rush with him to the circle of the *Hadra*. We entered the room, and a place between the hands of the others opened, making way for us to join.

The Shaykh jumped into the middle of the circle taking the lead in the *Hadra*.

When the Shaykh entered the center of the circle, the intensity of the *dhikr* was raised. Everyone felt the quickening of their spirits as the Shaykh's presence infected the room.

I anchored myself with my eyes glued to the floor, focused on dissolving into the presence of the moment, the repetition of "*Hay La, hay la, hay la*" chased away my thoughts and anxieties, since borrowing the Cadillac.

I was in the front row of the circle. There had to be at least three concentric circles as the room was small and the number was great.

I remember wondering who all the people were that came tonight. I didn't yet look up as that was not the proper courtesy of this practice, but my curiosity took over and I raised my head to glance straight in front of me. To my utter astonishment, fear and perplexity, there, directly across from my position in the *Hadra*, moving in perfect sync with everyone else was the salesman from the Cadillac car dealership!

He stared back at me like a bull about to charge the Matador. He shook his head profusely; it almost looked like smoke billowed from his nostrils. He was, needless to say, very upset.

What was he doing here! In the *Hadra*, no less!

The *Hadra* lasted for another half-hour and, although the salesman hardly took his eyes off of me, there were moments where I could see and feel that the *dhikr* was getting to him.

I could sense, beyond his anger with me, his heart expanding.

Shaykh Abdalqadir ended the *dhikr*, everyone quickly sat down and as it is the habit of the *Darqawi*, the Shaykh spoke to the open hearts of the circle.

Everyone sat and listened attentively, soaking in the meaningful talk.

At the end, while the tea and biscuits were being served, I made my way towards the Cadillac salesman to finally face the music.

He was understandably angry. I approached him humbly. I was certainly not going to defend my actions. I was ready to do whatever he demanded, including going to the police with him and turning myself in, if he had already placed charges against me. As I approached him, I felt he strangely looked upon me like a disapproving father would look at a son, rather than a common thief. I apologized profusely imploring him to forgive me.

In a scolding tone, he proverbially raked me over the coals. He told me that I had put him personally through a great deal of trouble, worry and stress. I asked if he had reported my indiscretion to the police, he said no. I asked how he came to be here tonight.

He explained that when I did not return with the Cadillac, he was going to call the police, but he looked at the copy of my driver's license and knew the address of the house was nearby, so he went over to track me down. Knocking at the door of the center, it was opened by one of the *fuqara*. He was invited in and explained that he was looking for me. The *faqir* told him where I was and what I was doing. Then, he turned and told me that his salesman's name is Alan, but his real name was 'Ali and he was a Muslim. He explained that when he found out what this place was and that someone had told him about me, i.e., that I was a convert to Islam, he held back pressing charges and waited for this evening, expecting that I would show up and likely with the car.

He asked me for the keys after some more deserved scolding and made me promise I would never do such a thing again. I promised. He shared with me how touched he was with what he saw and experienced that night. He said he remembered going with his grandfather in Syria to homes and lodges where Sufis met on Thursday nights for the remembrance of God. It resonated with him and he was looking forward to returning under better circumstances.

Although, when I did ask him if I could have the car for another few weeks of *Fisabilillah* (for the sake of God) I think he contemplated hitting me at that point; of course, the answer was no!

Well, that was a great relief. I was very grateful that all did work out for the best!

Now, I was faced with another problem.

Taking the Shaykh Home in Another Car

I was supposed to take Shaykh Abdalqadir home after the *dhikr*. The Cadillac was now gone, and my car was a tiny two door Datsun, with missing windows and a smelly engine.

I borrowed the next best car in the community from my fiancé, more about that later.

She had an older and larger car and in somewhat better condition than my own.

As we left the *Za`wiya* with the Shaykh, I stood there with my fiancé's car door open and invited the Shaykh to sit down. He did, but I could sense that he was not pleased, and it was soon confirmed, because he did not speak to me the entire time we rode back to Rabat.

When we arrived, he immediately opened the car door himself and walked briskly to his front door, opened it and shut it leaving me in his driveway clearly, if only metaphorically, told off.

Several years later, when I was with Shaykh Fadhlalla at our center in Texas. Shaykh Abdalqadir visited us for a few days. On the last day of Shaykh Abdalqadir's visit, Shaykh Fadhlalla asked if I would take Shaykh Abdalqadir to the airport. I agreed. Up until this point, I had never spoken to Shaykh Abdalqadir about the Cadillac incident – it had been at least five years since the incident.

While the two Shaykhs were saying their farewells, I pulled my car up and opened the door, inviting Shaykh Abdalqadir to take a seat. It was not a Cadillac, but it was a late model, clean and presentable.

He approached the car; his body language and facial expression expressed some trepidation. Before taking his seat in the car, he turned to me and, with a playful, tongue-in-check stare, asked, "This is your car, isn't it?"

I answered in the affirmative, and he and I both had a good and long overdue laugh.

The Rabat Model / Meeting Sidi Fadhlalla

Shaykh Abdalqadir remained at the Rabat for several weeks. In this time, he established the Rabat model, initially containing the tripartite formula. There would be one group to travel the world, living on the God given Grace of others. The second group was to study martial arts and, in general, the Art of War. The third group that I was slotted into was to study the Qur'an and the Sufi sciences.

Shaykh Abdalqadir and Shaykh Fadhlalla Haeri

The venue for the third group was the Rabat. Shaykh Abdalqadir would meet with us daily for teaching sessions. On one of these sessions Shaykh Abdalqadir informed me that a very close associate was coming from the UK and joining our group. He personally asked me to look after him. I asked the other *fuqara* who he was. I was told, he was an Iraqi businessman, and his name was Sidi Fadhlalla.[9] Most of the *Fuqara* painted a picture of Shaykh Fadhlalla as a well-meaning mature, rich, businessman with little experience of "our" path.

---

[9] Since he later became a *shaykh* (a Sufi master), I'll refer to him as Shaykh Fadhlalla or, with his full name, Shaykh Fadhlalla Haeri, from now on.

Keeping in mind Shaykh Abdalqadir's request and after speaking to several people, I was left with what turned out to be a delusional impression that he was a neophyte, and it was up to me to bring him up to speed regarding our practices and, in general, the courtesies of our path.

When we reached the end of the teaching session, Shaykh Abdalqadir asked that I take Shaykh Fadhlalla Haeri to his hotel. Shaykh Fadhlalla did not show any reluctance when I opened the passenger door of my Datsun. He sat down without complaint or comment about the condition of my car. Even after the tattered roof inner lining fell across his head, he just brushed it aside.

Teaching The Teacher

As we headed down the dusty desert road towards the main highway, I started lecturing Shaykh Fadhlalla Haeri about being a *faqir* of the Shaykh. The duration of the dusty and sometimes bumpy road, to reach the highway, was about twenty minutes and I arrogantly filled this time with the most condescending and presumptive lecture, that would have very likely made someone else jump out of the car; but Shaykh Fadhlalla Haeri sat there, holding his right hand over his left at the wrist, his eyes looking down displaying all the signs of someone contained and steeped in heroic patience. While still going on, I started feeling constriction building in my chest and abdomen, feeling faint. I pulled the car over to the side of the road and, out of nowhere, burst into tears. Shaykh Fadhlalla Haeri compassionately reached over, putting his arm over my shoulders and with the other hand grasped mine and started to weep with me, our heads touching as two brothers may do in sharing a moment of grief or for that matter, even joy. The persona I was enacting broke apart. I looked over at Shaykh Fadhlalla with new eyes, embarrassed and feeling shame, Shaykh Fadhlalla smiled knowingly and with total acceptance. We both acknowledged the blessings of an opening of heart, my opening uniquely for me, his, uniquely for himself, shared at the same moment in time.

We were both suspended in time, out of time, until the moment came to drive on. This was the beginning of a lifelong relationship of mentoring, friendship and companionship that has been for me, the most beneficial, durable, and loving relationship I have had throughout my life.

Life in Tucson

Tucson Sufi Center

During our stay in Tucson, we established a Sufi Center in South Tucson, where several of our members lived. We also rented several small houses, built on one lot, called Las Casitas. We had daily gatherings of teachings and *dhikr* at the center as well as a robust *Da`wa* (Invitation to the Path) program that included visiting the quad at the University of Arizona on a daily basis, calling the *Adhan* and performing the midday prayer in front of all the students during their lunch break. Many students and interested individuals returned to the center with us, where they were informed about Islam and sometimes invited to embrace the *Deen* (religion). There were also many young people in Tucson interested in spirituality, and many of them came to visit us and several of this group embraced Islam. Over the better part of a year the center flourished, businesses were established, and a good part of our membership had become gainfully employed.

What's in a Name

During an afternoon tea with Shaykh Abdalqadir, he requested me to legally change my name. He believed it would facilitate a final seal from past identification with my background. I researched the legal path to do so and petitioned the court to be heard for a name change. While in court on the day of my hearing, I was informed that the presiding judge was very conservative and, in regard to name changing, he expects a good reason to approve it. When I was called before the judge, he read my petition out loud, clearly with disdain that I was changing my name from Abraham David Schatz to Mustafa Shawqi. With the courtroom full of people waiting to be heard, he asked me, "Why the hell do you want to change your good Christian name to (struggling to pronounce Mustafa Shawqi) Mustard Shaky?"

I answered it was for religious reasons. He snapped back, "Are you sure you are not changing your name to avoid any legal responsibility, like having made someone pregnant?" I answered, "No sir, like I said, for religious reasons only." He addressed the courtroom commenting that the world is going to hell in a handbasket when we see people taking on exotic foreign names over the ones given to them by their folks. He continued, that if it were up to him, he would deny the change, but the law was clear in this matter, and with a swing of the gavel my name was changed to Mustafa Shawqi. Having said this, for months after the name change, my electric bills, phone bills and other business communications came to me addressed to Mustard Shaky.

Many years later Shaykh Fadhlalla asked me about why I changed my name. He had a different take in this regard and suggested that I legally change my name back to my original name or at least to a western name. He believed it would help facilitate ease of transactions in the world. We were living in Seattle, Washington, at that time. I petitioned the court for the name change. I was in the courtroom waiting my turn to be heard. The judge's name was Abraham Bloomberg. It was my turn to be heard. The judge asked me why I wanted to change my name from Mustafa Shawqi to David Leonard Sterling (the new name we chose for the family)? I explained that it was for ease of transaction. I spoke to how with these Middle Eastern names we were often singled out for questioning at airports, ridiculed in the workplace and my children made fun of in school. Upon hearing this explanation, the judge placed his gavel down and asked that everyone in the courtroom pay attention. He said that it is incumbent upon him to grant the name change, but that it was a sad testament to the state of our country, when forced out of prejudice and ignorance, fine people have to hide their identity and conform to the current majority.

It's a damn shame, he said, Mustafa Shawqi is a beautiful name. He picked up the gavel and reluctantly granted my petition. What a difference between this judge and the one in Tucson.

Wife Hunting

I had been a Muslim for just over a year, when we settled in Tucson. Most of the members of our community were married with families, but there was a growing number of single men that recently joined our group, most coming from the Da'wa efforts that other male members were engaged in. In my previous life, I had always had the companionship of women, which now I sorely missed. There were single women in the community, but when I showed any interest and inquired about them, Shaykh Abdalqadir would find some reason to deem them a bad match. After many frustrating attempts, I complained to Shaykh Abdalqadir about my situation, seeking his positive advice. He seemed not to have too much patience for my line of inquiry, saying that if I wanted a woman to marry, there are plenty of them waiting out there in the world for someone like you. He instructed me to make two *rakaat* of *salaat* (two cycles of formal Muslim prayer), take some trinkets or whatever would be seen of value, look for the first woman that you fancy and marry her!

I took his advice, offered two *rakaat* and headed to an organic food and restaurant on 6th street in Tucson. I thought I would most likely find a discriminating female in such a place. I sat down at the juice bar area and waited for my bride to show up. After some time, I noticed an attractive young woman standing at the checkout line. I grabbed a bottle of carrot juice and got in line just behind her. I gathered my courage up to introduce myself to her, tapping her on the shoulder. I introduced myself and explained that I was a Muslim, found her very attractive and invited her to sit with me at the juice bar and get to know each other for a while to see if there is a compatibility. Upon hearing me out, I watched her face turn from white to red, both of us feeling very awkward. Her first reaction was no, she said she was not at all interested. I tried to reassure her that I was not a crazy person or a radical, but a Sufi, that adhered to certain etiquette that provided certain ways and means to interact with the opposite sex. I pressed her to consider giving me just a few minutes, after all, I underscored to her, we are in a public place, what is there to lose?

She still expressed her unwillingness to meet with me and asked that I mind my own business from here on out. I returned to the juice bar area and took a seat on the outside where there was a shaded open to the air area. Everyone leaving the food market had to pass by this area as they walked out. The young lady I spoke to started to walk by, and she paused, saying she would sit with me just for a few minutes. We talked for over an hour.

I shared with her what had unfolded in my life over the past year, becoming Muslim and joining the Sufi Community of Shaykh Abdalqadir. She was intrigued, resonating with me personally, but also, I found her a seeker as well, interested in exploring the path I was on. We made a plan to meet again for tea. I explained that it would have to be with another couple acting as chaperon, which was the etiquette for unmarried people to get to know each other. Within a few weeks we had met several times, getting to know each other, and I was growing closer to inviting her to embrace Islam and marry me.

After our last tea together, the woman I intended to marry informed me that her car would not start and asked if I would take her home. Being of chivalrous nature, I agreed, but with a great deal of trepidation. This meant that we would be alone together, and I was warned not to, out of caution that something untoward might happen. I ignored my gut feelings and agreed to take her home. When we arrived, it was already dark. Her house was dark, not even a porch light on. She expressed her anxiety about entering the dark house and asked if I would walk her to the door. I walked her to the door, stepped into the house making sure everything was all right as she turned on the lights.

She invited me to stay for a cup of tea before I left, again my gut told me not to, but "I" wanted to anyway. During our tea, I felt the strong attraction that any healthy man would feel under these circumstances. Before things got out of hand, I went for the door and explained that I could not stay. I explained that if we were to be alone, she would have to be my wife and until then this is a no go. She suddenly became very irate, shouting at me, asking me if I thought she wasn't good enough as she was? She then asked me to leave, saying that she would never become a Muslim and marry me, she wanted to be free to wear her hair out, and dress in a manner of her liking, not to be covered. I went for the door, reminding her that these were the conditions we discussed before getting to know each other, that I was committed to this path and if she wanted to be with me, she'd have to adhere to that as well. I closed the door and left.

After a week or so, she showed up at our center, asking the women to prepare her to say her *Shahada* and eventually marry me. From this point on, we communicated only by phone, making our plans to get married. I had been working two jobs to earn enough money to rent my own apartment. Up until her becoming my betrothed, I had been living with other single men at Las Casitas. I fully furnished the apartment and made arrangements for a wedding celebration to take place at our Sufi Center. I even bought a live lamb to be slaughtered for the occasion.

It was a few days before the marriage was to take place, when Shaykh Abdalqadir called me to catch up with my activities. I informed him that I was getting married in a few days. After hearing my news, he paused for an uncomfortable period of time. He then requested me to postpone the marriage until he returned to Tucson, which was to be within the next week. He also said that Shaykh Fadhlalla was also going to be in Tucson at that time and we all could attend the wedding. Although I really did not want to postpone the wedding, I felt compelled to, it was the way things worked when it came to Shaykh Abdalqadir, everything yielded and deferred to him.

Berkeley Biofeedback

Shaykh Abdalqadir arrived in Tucson, followed by Shaykh Fadhlalla Haeri, both within a week of each other. I was invited to serve them tea one afternoon. It was then that Shaykh Abdalqadir asked that I accompany him and Shaykh Fadhlalla Haeri to visit the Bay Area in California to research and review the development and cutting edge of Biofeedback taking place in Berkeley and San Francisco. Biofeedback had become a strong interest of Shaykh Abdalqadir, believing it might be a useful tool in developing deeper meditation and self-discipline. It was a great opportunity for me, and I agreed, although I was concerned that I would have to either marry quickly before leaving or immediately after returning. I preferred going through with it now and asked Shaykh Abdalqadir for his blessings. He dismissed the idea of marrying before we left, assuring me that she and I could wait until we returned. It was not easy to explain to her that we had to wait, she and I were very anxious to marry, and I had already bought the lamb and food, having made arrangements for a more immediate event.

We flew to the Bay Area, staying at the iconic Claremont Hotel in Berkeley. During our stay in Berkeley, I fell into depression and a fair amount of anxiety. In recent days I had spoken to my parents, and they were very distressed and felt betrayed that I had become Muslim, especially my mother, who begged me to come back home and abandon my commitment to Islam. My sister and brother and most of my friends felt that I had had a mental breakdown resulting in me becoming Muslim. All this added to the stress of having to postpone my wedding for an uncertain period of time. With all this impacting me, I was distracted and far from being present in the moment to benefit from the opportunity of the company of Shaykh Abdalqadir and Shaykh Fadhlalla Haeri. One evening Shaykh Fadhlalla Haeri called me to his room at the Claremont. He had prepared some tea. I dreaded visiting him that night, as I was feeling overwhelmed with anxiety and the idea that I would have to push through this meeting maintaining a false facade that all was well with me. There were two chairs and a lounge in the sitting room of his hotel room. He sat in one of the chairs and I sat in the lounge. Shaykh Fadhlalla Haeri seemed clearly concerned about me. His demeanor towards me was more personal, and his questions to me were empathetic regarding my health and state of mind. It was very unexpected, and I felt awkward and to some degree defensive that my agitated state of mind was showing. His concern and empathy were appreciated, but I felt he had nothing to offer me. At one point he came over to the lounge and sat beside me. He put his arm around me, clearly a gesture of concern. He asked me if there was anything he could do for me. Although at that point I deeply respected Shaykh Fadhlalla Haeri, I was veiled to the eminence of this man, no idea of the vastness of his knowledge and being. I reacted to him by dismissing that he had anything to give me, or the ability to fathom what I was going through. He offered me more than a friendship, but an open door to a mentorship that took me the next a year to realize and embrace.

After visiting several research laboratories focused on Biofeedback, we returned to Tucson, having been gone for the better part of two weeks.

No Wedding

Returning to Tucson, I was determined to restart the wedding plans. In the meantime, my fiancé was very anxious to marry; we spent hours nearly every day talking by phone, planning our life together.

One of Shaykh Abdalqadir's very close companions came to visit me at Las Casitas. He came with a message from the Shaykh. The message was that the Shaykh does not approve of this marriage, his advice is that the woman I choose to marry was not a good match for me and that I should immediately call the wedding off.

Needless to say, this message devastated me. I was suddenly thrust onto a crossroads. On one hand I was committed to follow the Shaykh, with the pretense that on the Sufi path, obedience to the Shaykh ideally was without question, and his inspired advice, even that it may appear contrary to logic or one's own sense of direction was immutable. The idea that I would go ahead and marry without his blessings would most likely mean expulsion from the community as well as going back on my commitment that I voluntarily made on his hand to obey.

That afternoon I mustered up the will and courage to call the woman I was going to marry and cancel the wedding. She pleaded with me to change my mind, she professed her love for me and disbelief that this was right and that somehow, I may have misunderstood the Shaykh's direction, but I made it clear to her, there was no mistake. Not wanting to endure any more pain from listening to her pleas, I hung the phone up saying I was sorry, but this must end here and now.

That very same night I was readying for bed in the apartment I had rented to live with my wife when there was a loud knock at my door. It was the woman I broke off with earlier that day. I asked what she was doing here, after all that was said between us. She implored me to leave the community with her now, to pack up and escape with her. She explained that her bags were already in her car and hoped that I would join her. It was extremely tempting, a part of me wanted very much to go with her, and another part wanted to hold to my commitment to the Shaykh and remain with the community. In a moment that could have gone either way, I closed the door while telling her again it was over, to go home and consider that this is all for the best.

There is an unexplainable alchemy that takes place when there is commitment and sincere seeking to live and be in harmony with the flow of truth as it unfolds in life's everyday occurrences. Regardless of the many twists and turns and the best of intentions gone awry, in the end there is an arc of ascension that one moves along towards higher consciousness and presence within the everlasting, timelessness of the now. All of us, including the Shaykh himself, evolve together. When I look back at this circumstance, having a potential marriage derailed, I can't but acknowledge that from my current perspective, all was for the best. This has to do with the unique destiny that each one of us is moment-to-moment manifesting. Everyone I have ever known that was involved with Shaykh Abdalqadir, whether they acknowledge it or not, benefited from his company. All together I am forever in his debt, having been surgically remolded, tumors and all removed, making it possible for a rebirth of my life path. Although today I could not follow him, what was mirrored in his company in the past remains a vital source and inspiration.

Breaking Norms

Throughout my stay in Tucson, Shaykh Fadhlalla Haeri played a key role in forging within me a broadening of my horizons, as it were. In one of our regular meetings, he informed me that he was leaving Tucson, with the intention of returning and establishing a more permanent presence. He asked me to research investment properties and meet with local businessmen and land developers to find the best opportunities for investment. I had no experience with this type of business, nor did I feel I had the acumen to engage and perform within this arena with any proficiency. I shared my reservations with Shaykh Fadhlalla Haeri and told him that he would be better off with someone with experience. He outright dismissed what I was saying and came back with a rebuke that included encouraging me to rise to the occasion. He said that I had all that it takes to embody the role he was requesting. Although he agreed that experience was important, at the same time he impressed upon me that he has in the past had many dealings with businessmen and property developers, underscoring that I had more than enough intelligence, and then some, to take on this role successfully. He counseled me to rent an office, furnish it tastefully and present myself to the local business community as a "representative" of a wealthy Arab sheikh, looking for property investments. His positivity was infectious and inspired me to take it on. He gave me a sense of potential I had not had before. I was energized by a powerful trust in the best of outcomes. I felt opened, in a new way towards the reality that God's grace and generosity can unfold in ways and means not immediately available to the mind and its calculations, but to provisions abounding from where we do not know, trusting, until they manifest, one way or another. In any case, it was clear it is not about the outcome, but the depth and quality of journeying through life with the best opinion of God and His cornucopia of effulgent grace.

I set out, charged with clarity of heart and mind to establish the office. We rented a modest, but upmarket space in a local business center, hired a local secretary and opened for business. I furnished the office with floor seating, Persian carpets (borrowed from a local Iranian carpet dealer) and natural sheepskin rugs strung about the entire office. It was exotic to say the least to have an office appear this way. When meeting with local businessmen, I asked them to remove their shoes and, instead of coffee, we served green mint tea. It was interesting to see suited businessmen come to our office, not expecting to have to remove their shoes, sit on the ground and drink Moroccan style tea for a business meeting. Most felt awkward and put off guard, and were generally feeling uncomfortable in this atmosphere, but others were impressed. In any case, we did present ourselves as representatives of a rich Arab sheikh. What else would you expect?

Our meetings went on for several weeks until we finally narrowed it down to a few promising properties. We passed on all the potential investments to Shaykh Fadhlalla. Over the years, it escapes me whether or not he purchased property in Tucson or not, but for me, it was an exercise that left an indelible mark on the landscape of my life. It was through this exercise, I believe, I began to call on the resource of that experience, knowing that it would apply to many, future circumstances, adding to the overall quality and depth of my life, both in the business and personal engagements.

Another challenge to requiring me to rise to the occasion was Shaykh Abdalqadir asking me to head a new publishing company that would exclusively publish his books and other relevant works in line with the community doctrines. We coined the name Iqra Press Inc. for the publishing company.

Although I had no experience in publishing, Shaykh Fadhlalla Haeri again played a pivotal role and encouraged me to see myself as a publisher and be confident that I could handle whatever challenge may come along if I approached it with humility and honesty, recognizing it is all in God's hands. He stressed the importance to acknowledge that any affairs that we engage in are predicated on God's will and permission. He taught me to take permission before acting and announcing it with *"bismillah"* (in God's name and His will), so that all will be for the best. He also mentioned that there were many experienced people to call on and take counsel with when it came to practical matters, but not to forget or diminish in any way the power and absolute reality that is behind all relative realities.

Within less than a year, we published several books and works by Shaykh Abdalqadir, such as, *Jihad a Ground Plan, One Hundred Steps, Future Islam a Manifesto, Indications from Signs, One Hundred Steps* and many more.

.

To Atlanta, Then to England with Shaykh Abdalqadir

Making *Hijrah* (Migration) to Atlanta

In what was to herald the last days of our sojourn in Tucson, a group of African American Muslims from Atlanta, Georgia, visited us at the center. They had read several of Shaykh Abdalqadir's books and traveled to Tucson to join our community and invite Shaykh Abdalqadir to visit Atlanta. After that meeting, it wasn't long before Shaykh Abdalqadir gathered all the people in the community together at the center and announced, in his words, that it was time to "gather up the tents of our caravanserai" and move to Atlanta to join our community with the new Atlanta group. At that meeting, Shaykh Abdalqadir instructed several members of the community to leave that day, by sunset. I was in that first group. Within a matter of a few weeks, what had become a thriving community in Tucson, had all but disappeared. There were some few new people that needed time to pull up their tent stakes, but eventually, all made *Hijrah* to Atlanta.

Instruction to Move to England

We arrived in Atlanta and were welcomed generously by the community there. After some time, we rented a large house and established our Sufi Center. I remained in Atlanta for several months until I received instructions directly from Shaykh Abdalqadir to come to England. He invited me to live at Wood Dalling Hall, a 16th century country estate, outside of Norwich and to take the position as head administrator of The Darqawi Institute that was centered at the hall.

I had been working selling waterbeds at a local shop, saving just enough money to purchase a one-way ticket to London.

A day or two before departing, I had called Shaykh Abdalqadir to confirm my arrival. While on the phone with him the conversation turned towards the subject of the young American Indian man called Tiku Nur, who we had met as a result of Shaykh Abdalqadir's visit with the Hopi community in Oraibi, Arizona. Tiku Nur was living with us in Tucson. He had recently embraced Islam and migrated with us to the community in Georgia.

Shaykh Abdalqadir suggested that it would be a great benefit to not only him, but also others if he could come to England as well. He requested that I helped in this matter.

That afternoon, I traded my round-trip tickets into two one-way standby tickets to England and, within a few days, Tiku Nur and I were off to England.

Our flights were booked from Atlanta, through Dulles Airport, in Washington DC.

The Secret Agent and a Meeting with Destiny

Upon our arrival at the airport, we were told that due to several crashes of the DC 10 in the last few months, the FAA had grounded the entire fleet until the cause was determined. This impacted our situation directly in that the DC 10 was the most used aircraft for overseas flights, limiting seating on the new Boeing 747, which now was the only aircraft going overseas.

Upon arrival in Washington, we immediately approached the check-in counter and inquired about the possibilities of getting on a flight with our standby tickets. The counter agent told us that it would not be possible for us to get on that flight or any flight in the foreseeable future, until this DC 10 situation was resolved.

Neither of us had the means to upgrade our tickets.

Both Tiku and I faced having nowhere outwardly to turn for help. So we both decided to be patient and vigilant with trust and hope that a way for us would be opened somehow.

It was now three days and we were living in the airport, sleeping in shifts in the waiting area and taking sponge baths in the restrooms while we looked out for each other's privacy and the ever-present security guards, who were by now becoming suspicious towards us as they started seeing us more regularly.

We had no money for food either. At the food court, there was a Mexican restaurant in which one of the workers was aware of our plight, and he took pity on us, providing a generous serving of leftover food at closing.

Each night of these first three days, as the overseas flights readied to take off, I would join the line of boarding passengers in hopes that we would be allowed to board with our standby tickets. We approached the same flight agent inquiring about the possibilities that we could get on with our standby tickets. His answer, while shaking his head in the negative, was, "Unless you upgrade your tickets, there is no way!"

It was now the morning of the fourth day, and I was taking what now became a regular walk through the terminal, and I found myself at the Concord arrival lounge. It drew my attention as the ground crew made a big fuss about the Concord arriving, a red carpet was being rolled out to welcome the elite passengers from overseas. There was a lot of activity, lights flashing, and attendants were moving about. I lingered, intrigued by the whole spectacle, finding it ironically entertaining.

As the double doors of the Concorde lounge opened, to my surprise and delight, the very first person to come off the plane was Shaykh Fadhlalla Haeri. I was flabbergasted, my mind raced with thoughts of possibilities and expectation that his arrival would be our ticket out of this situation. I knew him as a generous man and I was certain that once he heard our story, he would help us, and we would be on our way.

We both rushed to embrace each other, and excitedly he inquired as to our situation. I explained our circumstance, clearly underscoring the need to upgrade our tickets to complete our flights to London, from where he had just departed.

As he reached into his pocket, I expected that his hand would emerge with cash solving our predicament; instead, his hand emerged clasping what appeared to be a plastic or possibly small wooden set of prayer beads. He handed the beads to me saying, "*Husbun ullah wa ni`mal wakeel*, say it over and over again, and all will be well".

With that, he swiftly walked away.

I was initially stunned and disappointed. I thought that he should have at least rolled off a few hundred dollars from his billfold along with the spiritual advice. I clenched the prayer beads with a strong conviction that all will be well.

From that moment on, I was absorbed in the meaning of the formula Shaykh Fadhlalla gave me. "Trust in Allah for He is the best Guardian of our affairs."

The sun was setting, and it was that time again to make our way to the counter for the evening flight to London. All other overseas flights were beginning to board.

Like the three nights before, I began my approach to the Pan Am ticket counter. I could see the glance of the ticket agent waft over me like an icy chilling breeze.

With my prayer beads in hand, I approached the agent and asked for the fourth time if there was a possibility to get seats on the flight. The agent looking weary shook his head and said no. I began to turn and walk away, when he called me back and asked what I had in my hand? I explained that it was a rosary. He followed up, asking me what was I saying on my rosary?

At this point, I knew something had shifted. There was a sense of Presence in this moment. I turned to him and said, *"Husbun ullah wa ni`mal wakeel"*.

He asked if I understood the meaning. I said: "Trust in Allah, for He is the best Guardian of our affairs."

Tears welled up in his eyes. He called me back to the counter. He asked me if I was a Muslim. I said yes and explained that we were on our way to see our teacher in England, to further our knowledge on the path to Light. He waved me to come close and whispered in my ear, that he was a "secret" Muslim working for Pan Am. He was afraid to be open with his Islam as there was a great deal of ignorance regarding Muslims and Islam among his colleagues. Although his nametag read Alan, his name was Ali.

He asked for our standby tickets and, before our eyes, with a stroke of a pen and a few sticky tags attached to our tickets, made our tickets valid for the upper first-class deck of the Pan Am Boeing 747 flight to London.

We were stunned. He hurriedly ushered us onto the plane, up the stairs onto the upper deck. Just before the plane lifted off, our Muslim friend `Ali came on to the plane, inquiring if we were comfortable. We expressed our gratitude to him profusely. I also explained how I came to be reciting the formula on my prayer beads. This touched him even more, as he held his pointer finger, pointing to the sky, saying Allah is the best of planners! I also expressed my concern for his job, after changing our tickets the way he did. I asked him what would happen to him.

He smiled from ear to ear and said, *"Husbun ullah wa ni`mal wakeel"*.

"Trust in Allah, for He is the best Guardian of our affairs."

The Norwich Community

For the past year I had heard so much about the Sufi Community in Norwich, it was already a legend in my mind. Some of the brothers from Norwich retrieved us from the airport and, without pause, we were off to Norwich. It was already late in the evening when we arrived in the northern town. Tiku and I were split up and hosted in different homes of the *Fuqara*. I was generously welcomed in the home of Abu `Ali with his family of two wives and several children. Although they had little space and means, I was lovingly accommodated before being passed around to several of the *fuqara's* homes throughout Norwich. After a few weeks, Hajj Abdul Aziz Redpath came to take me to my new post and residence at Wood Dalling Hall. As we traveled towards our destination, Hajj Abdul Aziz advised me not to have too much expectation regarding not only my new position, but the state and condition of Wood Dalling Hall. He informed me that activities at the Hall were few and that renovations were taking place at the hall. After about an hour's drive, we arrived at the gate house where there was a young man and his family waiting to let us through. His name was Abdul Razzaq from Ireland. The road to the hall was muddy, from the constant downpour. I could see the Tudor period hall emerging through the blur of mist and rain. It was an ominous site, something out of a Hollywood period piece. We arrived at the back kitchen entrance; Abdul Razzaq entered first fiddling with the electrical panel as there was no power coming to the building. He finally got a few fuses in place, and we entered the building. I realized now why Hajj Abdul Aziz had been talking to me about Wood Dalling Hall and now felt some trepidation. Looking up from the ground floor of the hall, I could see right through to the roof. Every floor, with the exception of the staircase leading up to the attic room, was without floorboards. The inside of the hall had been stripped of floor boards, walls and ceilings, leaving only a skeleton of its former self.

I was escorted to the attic room where I was to be accommodated. It was like the attic in a typical horror movie that you wished the protagonist of the film would not enter with their failing flashlight while following strange noises that they heard.

In the corner of the room was a small wood burning stove and to its right was a stack of sheepskins, which would serve as my bed. Hajj Abdul Aziz, told me that this is where Shaykh Abdalqadir used to stay when he visited the hall, indicating to me that it is a *Barakah* (Blessing) for me to be taking this room, albeit it was the only livable room in the entire mansion. Hajj Abdul Aziz gave me a bag of groceries bidding me farewell.

I remained at Wood Dalling Hall for several months, enduring an exceptionally cold winter with little contact with others.

When Shaykh Abdalqadir heard of the state of Wood Dalling, he sent for me to come to Norwich. Having nowhere to stay, I moved into the Norwich Mosque, with several other single men, living in a small annex at the back of the mosque between the prayer hall and the ablution area. We earned the right to remain in the mosque by keeping it, its ablution area, kitchen and the bathrooms clean and helping with its general upkeep. I was not allowed to work, relying on the good graces of the community for food and clothes. I remained in the mosque for approximately three months.

There were several excursions to visit other communities in England; one exceptional visit was to Manchester to attend an *Urs*[10] led by Sufi Abdullah, a tall, gracious, generous man, who always had charity passing both from his hands and heart.

The *Urs* and Sufi Abdullah

The *Urs* was in a huge public facility in which there was a soccer field attached to it. Upon entering the grounds, I was struck by the sheer spectacle of thousands of people – men, women and children – surrounding the center of the soccer field where several large metal pots of food were being prepared. These were no ordinary pots; some stood three to four feet tall, accessed by step ladders and foot stools, where both men and women took turns, stirring the pots, not with ordinary spoons, but with some more like wooden boat oars. As they stirred the pots, they recited "*La ilaha illa Allah*, there is no god, but the One God." With each stroke they enfolded with love and gratitude the acknowledgment of The Source of all things. There seemed to be an endless parade of people, bringing meat, vegetables, and spices, and pouring them into the pots in preparation for the feast that was to come.

On the other side of the field was a huge circle of people sitting on the ground, reciting litanies, and repeating the names and attributes of God. I found a space in the circle and sat down, entering the inner feast of hearts swaying to a heavenly rhythm in Divine invocation.

I had my hands lifted in prayer, nearly covering my face, when I noticed straight across the circle a young man with an outstanding long

---

10 Urs (from Arabic `Urs) or `Urus (literal meaning 'wedding'), is the death anniversary of a Sufi saint, usually held at the saint's shrine.

black beard holding his hands like myself. He was staring directly at me. I noticed that he was looking at me, making a prayer; his eyes darted from looking into his hand and then over to me, his face and presence illuminated with light. I knew he was including me in his supplications, and I made the intention to speak to him after the circle of invocation was over. When all was said and done, I moved across the now dispersing circle to find this brother, but he was nowhere to be found. I asked around, describing him to others but no one was able to help me locate him. By my description of his dress and turban, the consensus was that he was one of the community Shaykhs, a young teacher named, Noor e Muhammad.

As we shall see, these events were destined to play an important role in my future.

We returned to the mosque in Norwich after the *Urs*.

It had been nearly a year since I had arrived in Norwich and it was coming up to my third month living in the *masjid* (mosque).

Unable to work because of immigration restrictions, I grew tired of relying on the good graces of others to support me. My clothes had become old and tattered, and food and other personal care items started to become less available as time passed.

The Master Plan

I decided to leave Norwich.

It was not only these issues, but I felt strongly that this community was no longer for me.

I loved the people individually, but as a community, there were issues that I could not reconcile, and no longer could I go along with what was contrary to my understanding of the *Deen* of Islam and, in general, contrary to my common sense applied to the circumstance. The proverbial straw that broke the camel's back was Shaykh Abdalqadir instructed the community to come up with a new community model that all could live by. The model was to include the wisdom and experience of Islam we had collectively and to underscore equity for all, especially the women of the community.

A task force was assembled to include one man and one woman, and they both hand-picked several people to be part of their respective committees. After some time, a plan was constructed and a meeting was called in the *masjid* for it to be presented to the rest of the community for a vote of consensus, yea or nay.

Of course, Shaykh Abdalqadir had reviewed the plan beforehand and, although I did not hear it directly from him, he had given his seal of approval.

The plan was presented in the mosque with most of the Norwich community present. Shaykh Zam Zami (a ranking member of the community) was to chair the meeting that evening.

The overall gist of the plan was to calculate an inventory of all property held, individually and collectively. This included homes, flats, cars, electronics, and monetary sources. The said properties would then be split in two, half going to the women in the community and the remaining to the men. Women would move into half the houses, have use of half the resources of the community and vice versa. Families would be split also in two, divided into homes and shared through a scheduled visitation roster. To be clear, married couples would be split up, i.e., all men living together and women in their own houses and flats. Upon hearing the plan, most community members agreed with the underlying principles and applications.

I was shocked to see the tacit capitulation to this Orwellian nightmare. The plan included the dissolution of the family unit, as well as an extreme reengineering of the social structure and economics of the community, which reflected more of a Marxist/Stalinist scenario than a prophetic model of enlightened living.

One brave member of the community, Abdul Moumin, stood up and strongly objected to the plan, pointing out its waywardness and disconnection to the prophetic model. He questioned the plan leaders, how would he and his wife or other married couples see each other casually or intimately? The head of the women's group quickly retorted that he or she would have to make an appointment with their spouse for both casual and conjugal visits. Upon hearing this answer, Abdul Moumin, called out to his wife in the meeting to leave with him immediately. As they left the prayer hall, he shouted out to the rest of the community that if they adopted such a plan, it would mean ruin for them all.

Shaykh Zam Zami called for an immediate vote, consensus was reached, and the plan was passed and adopted by the community.

After the vote, Shaykh Zam Zami also stood up and announced that, although he chaired the meeting and the vote, he announced his own personal rejection of the plan, and said further, that it was madness and scolded the community for mindlessly accepting something so far from the teachings of Islam and utterly void of basic common sense.

He said he would have nothing to do with this plan and would leave the community if the plan was actually implemented. He stood up, storming out of the prayer hall, calling out to me to follow him to his house. I went with him. That was the beginning of the end for me in this community and as well for Shaykh Zam Zami.

I had already been praying for a way out, but after the adoption of the new community plan, I was set on leaving as soon as possible.

Prayers Answered

The following *Jum'ah* (Friday's Congregational Prayer) proceeded as usual, the mosque was filled to the brim with members of the community as well as student Muslims and other expats working and living in Norwich.

Over the past year, I had come to recognize many of the local Muslims, some by names, most others by their faces. There was one Egyptian man, Faisal, who always hugged me before leaving the mosque and today was no exception, but this time as he was hugging me, he reached into my front pocket. My knee jerk reaction was to grab his hand. I instantly felt that he had put something in my pocket. With a great deal of ambiguity, he quickly explained himself, asking me not to see what he had placed there until he left the mosque. When he left, I reached in my pocket and there was a roll of 50-pound notes, a total of 750 pounds. This was what I had been praying for, a way out of Norwich and a return to the US.

That afternoon, I went shopping on the high street for new clothes and accessories. I packed what little I had of my possessions at the mosque and, without telling anyone, I went to the Norwich train station. At the train station I called Shaykh Abdalqadir from a Telephone Box. After greeting him, I explained I was at the train station, committed to leaving Norwich. I made it clear to him that I could not be convinced otherwise and as my last act, I requested Shaykh Abdalqadir to suggest the best place for me to go. He answered, go to Shaykh Fadhlalla. We exchanged greetings of farewell and I was off to London on the next train, to Heathrow and on to San Antonio, Texas where Shaykh Fadhlalla was establishing a center.

The Prophet's Mosque in Medina

The Destiny Bus to Medina

Jumping ahead a bit, after some years living in San Antonio, I had made a plan to visit Mecca and Medina with my good friend and brother, Hajj Ahmed Mikel.

We arrived in Jeddah in the middle of the night, then took a taxi to the bus station where there were special buses to take us directly to Medina, where the Prophet Muhammad is buried.

While on the bus to Medina, there was a man sitting directly behind us who impressed me with a familiar presence. I turned around to look at him several times but could not connect where we had met or if we even had met at all. After some time, he obviously felt the same as he began to lean over the back of our bus bench trying to get a better look at me. It was awkward and strange but, as time passed, I felt stronger that we had a connection going on here.

Then, out of the blue, he shouted out loud *"Allahu Akbar"* and proceeded to climb over our back seat, landing in our laps, being that the aisle was crammed with standing riders.

He gave me a big hug, started weeping and repeating *Allahu Akbar* over and over again.

I exclaimed, "What's going on? Who are you?" He looked at me, with loving eyes and said, "I am Noor e Muhammad, and do you not remember me, from Birmingham, England, from the circle of *dhikr*, that afternoon celebrating the *Urs* of Sufi Abdullah's Shaykh?"

As soon as he said that his face and presence clicked into focus. I recognized him as the man who was sitting across from me in that prayer circle, I said yes! We embraced each other, both of us awestruck and crying tears of joy. How could this be! How?

"I tried to find you after the prayer and I couldn't," I said. He replied that he had also been looking for me, that we must have crossed each other in the hall.

Then he said, rhetorically, "Do you know what I was praying on that day?"

"Let me tell you!"

"When I saw you sitting across the circle, I was so touched that you, unlike myself, who was born into Islam, you came to Islam as a sincere seeker with clear and with strong conviction. I felt blessed to be in the same circle with you.

"My prayer that day, so many years ago, was that one day, I would meet you at the Prophet's Mosque in Medina, that we would sit in his presence together and here we are on a bus in the middle of the night, on our way together to the Prophet's Mosque."

The conversation turned towards where we would be staying in Medina. I explained that we had not prepared any accommodation; we had just arrived that night from overseas and proceeded to the bus station, fortunately getting seats on the last bus to Medina for this night. He said, "Don't worry, my good friend is going to meet us at the bus station. He's a generous man and I am sure he will open his home for you as well."

When we got to the bus station in Medina, his friend was waiting there. There was a Mercedes in the parking lot and, as we approached it, Noor e Muhammad's friend got out of the car and as soon as I saw him, I was again struck with awe and astonishment, I recognized him. It was Faisal, the very man in the Mosque at Norwich, years back, who had hugged me after the *Jum`ah* prayer and placed the 750 British pounds in my pocket. We rushed to embrace each other, we were all stunned and dyed in the color of gratitude, speechless, in tears and acknowledgement that God was in charge. Faisal later shared with me that the funds he passed on to me were from his father, to gift as a gesture of love for the Prophet Muhammad.

Hajj Ahmed's Shoes

During our stay in Medina, Hajj Ahmed and I would visit the Prophet's Mosque regularly. At the time of our visit, the mosque was being expanded, remodeled and refurbished. There were many collapsed columns and loose rubble spread about, most taped off for safety. The normal shoe racks were also disorganized, as they were scattered and moved from their usual areas and hard to find, so we had to make do and leave our shoes wherever there was space. On our first visit, we moved as close to the Prophet's tomb as we could. The tomb was surrounded by a metal filigree enclosure, probably made of silver and brass. If you got close enough you could peer inside where the actual tomb was, rising from the ground: an elongated mound covered with a green cloth embroidered with Qur'an and supplications. Next to the Prophet, was a smaller mound where the Lady of Light, Fatimah Zahra, the Prophet's daughter, was resting. At each corner on the outside of the tomb stood religious enforcers. These were quasi guards, holding thin whip-like sticks that were used to whip people who approached the tombs too close with varying intensity, accompanied with verbal admonishment, encouraging visitors to behave towards the Prophet's tomb as prescribed by their Wahhabi dictates. They had their job cut out for them. Muslims from all over the world, representing hundreds of different cultures and languages, expressed their love for the Prophet and Lady Fatimah in a myriad of ways. Some became very emotional and outwardly expressed their love and yearning, addressing the Prophet Muhammad directly for his help and acceptance. You would commonly hear the heart's call with the words in Arabic, "Yah Allah!" (O Allah!) followed by "Yah Muhammad!" (O Muhammad!). Upon hearing people say "Yah Muhammad!" the guard would immediately address and admonish those seeking intervention from the Prophet Muhammad. They shouted out, "No! do not say, O Muhammad, only say O Allah." They would tell everyone that it was *haram*, forbidden, to "pray" to the Prophet, only to Allah. But it discouraged the people only a little. Many bore the whipping and verbal abuse. It appeared that the sting of the whip only encouraged them to express their love and passion for the Prophet and his blessed daughter.

Hajj Ahmed and I were sitting close to the containment wall that was the foundation of the enclosure. We both simultaneously became aware of a sweet and increasingly intensely intoxicating perfume wafting through the Prophet's Tomb towards where we were sitting. Our eyes met, sparkling with the mutual acknowledgment and wonderment of the perfume that was beckoning us to draw closer. We were both aware that the guard standing only two feet away had already whipped back many visitors that wanted to draw near to the enclosure; nevertheless, we inched forward, making headway, if only in small bits. We came closer and closer to the tomb of the Prophet and were met with not only the intense odor pouring from the grave, but also with the intoxicating perfume of the garden beyond. We were as close to the mounds of Light that was physically possible. Although the guard clearly saw us, his face became glazed over, as though he did not see us; he did not once admonish us or threaten us with the whip from his punishing hand. We sat in silent ecstasy for an incalculable time; we only rose, as the call for the sunset prayer rang out from minaret towers surrounding the mosque. After prayer we headed out from the mosque to where we had left our shoes. My shoes were there, exactly where I had left them; Hajj Ahmed's shoes were gone. After such an encounter, nothing, not even losing a pair of shoes, was going to diminish our state. Hajj Ahmed accepted his loss and, in bare feet he made his way with me back to where we were staying. On the way, we stopped at the Souk, or marketplace, and Hajj Ahmed purchased a new pair of shoes. The next day we entered the Prophet's Mosque, but this time we agreed to be more strategic in placing our shoes. We found a cleared area, where the new marble for the mosque was being stored. There were spaces between the stones. It is there where we placed our shoes, his and mine right next to each other. That day was another amazing visit to the Prophet's tomb. We met many wonderful people and enjoyed long periods of meditation and Qur'an recitation. After the sunset prayer, we went to find our shoes, mine were there, Hajj Ahmed's shoes were gone. Both of us thought that the shoes gone missing again were a sign and felt a strong pull to be open and aware of what the sign was pointing to. The next day was our last in Medina. Hajj Ahmed had already purchased two pairs of shoes from the market and in our farewell visit to the Prophet's grave, we were going to pay strong attention to where we left our shoes, with the strategy that they would be so cleverly hidden that no one could possibly find them except us upon return. Nearing the outside perimeter of the mosque, we noticed a large concrete pillar that was opened at the top.

The pillar was surrounded by warning signs that this was a construction zone and to stay out. We slid under the boundary tape and found the pillar had a hollow interior. We both placed our shoes inside the pillar, one on top of the other. We covered the opening of the pillar with bricks and rubble. We were certain that this time our shoes would be safe. It was approaching our time to depart and was just after the late afternoon prayer. We greeted the Prophet, made our prayers, and left the mosque to retrieve our shoes. We approached the pillar with a great deal of confidence that all was well and that we would certainly find our shoes. The bricks and rubble were still piled upon the opening hollow of the pillar. I was the first to reach in and pull my shoes out, but when Hajj Ahmed reached in to remove his shoes, they were nowhere to be found.

This was the third time Hajj Ahmed's shoes were missing. We were both astonished and perplexed. There was no reasonable answer to apply to this unsettling event. This time we went to the hypermarket and Hajj Ahmed bought a pair of flip flops just in case they too would turn up missing in the coming days.

Upon our return to San Antonio in the US, we visited Shaykh Fadhlalla and recanted the story to him. He remarked that it was and still remains a custom among the Prophet's followers to take the shoes of a guest when they visited your home so they would not leave. He said it was an invitation from the Prophet to stay for a while.

San Antonio, Texas, with Shaykh Fadhlalla Haeri

San Antonio

A few days after arriving in San Antonio, Texas, Shaykh Fadhlalla Haeri arrived as a newly minted Shaykh, having been given *Idhn*[11] from Shaykh Abdalqadir.

Although I was not committed, as a *Mureed*, to either Shaykh Abdalqadir or Shaykh Fadhlalla Haeri, I came to San Antonio on the counsel of Shaykh Abdalqadir to be with Shaykh Fadhlalla Haeri.

Shaykh Fadhlalla Haeri was inspired to build a *madrasah* (school) that would become a resource, mainly for American Muslims and expats that were rediscovering their *Deen*. A large piece of land was purchased approximately one hour outside of San Antonio, near the town of Blanco, Texas. The property would become known as *Bayt ud Deen* (Door to the Religion).

Shaykh Fadhlalla Haeri initially had the help of several of Shaykh Abdalqadir's students. At this point there was no clear delineation between Shaykh Fadhlalla's work and that of Shaykh Abdalqadir's. Over time, Shaykh Fadhlalla Haeri's projects clearly took on their own unique direction eventually and naturally taking on their own life apart from that of Shaykh Abdalqadir's. As *Bayt ud Deen* was being built, there was a blending of Shaykh Abdalqadir's community members and that of Shaykh Fadhlalla Haeri. After the *madrasah* was built and Shaykh Fadhlalla Haeri came into his own so to speak, rifts in the fabric of the blended community began to appear, culminating eventually in Shaykh Abdalqadir and Shaykh Fadhlalla Haeri going their own ways.

---

[11] Permission to transmit spiritual knowledge to others as a Sufi teacher.

Bayt ud Deen

Shaykh Fadhlalla Haeri continued the regular practice of *Laylat ul Fuqara* every Thursday evening after sunset. Students would gather for reciting songs from the *Diwan* of Shaykh Muhammad ibn al Habib, followed by repeating the names and attributes of Allah, in the fashion of the Moroccan Sufis of the Darqawi way. These gatherings would take place either at Shaykh Fadhlalla Haeri's home compound, where a special hall was constructed for this purpose and other teaching situations, or at what we called "the small mosque" at *Bayt ud Deen*, until the main mosque was completed as part of the overall *madrasah* project.

It had been the better part of a year since I arrived in San Antonio. I had taken part in the in-town living project, which was called "New Light Village." It was a housing complex located in a not so savory part of town. Over a dozen families connected to Shaykh Fadhlalla Haeri moved in en masse, taking over most of the rental property. The managers and owners of New Light Village granted us unlimited use of their on-sight meeting hall, which we converted to our mosque and teaching center. I had recently married, and my wife Nafisa and I had an apartment in the Village.

Shaykh Fadhlalla Haeri's focus was centered on building the *madrasah* and, unless you were in some way directly involved, time with Shaykh Fadhlalla Haeri was scarce. New Light Village for me was also challenging. The appointed *Amir*, or leader, of our group was in my view abusive and clearly relished being in power. Many of the programs he initiated had ulterior, self-serving elements in it. It was clear to me that he had his own agenda hiding under the cloak of his altruism.

In some way it reminded me of the people who authored the "master plan" in my last days in Norwich. Granted, it wasn't about self-aggrandizement or financial gain as I deduced was going on in New Light Village, but there was still an underlying self-serving agenda.

I lost interest in what was going on in San Antonio and, by extension, Shaykh Fadhlalla Haeri. It just seemed to me, as it did in Norwich at that time, a path I could not go down.

The next *Laylat ul Fuqara* was taking place at the small mosque in *Bayt ud Deen*. Shaykh Fadhlalla Haeri was going to be there as well as Sidi Hosam Rauf, an old and honored friend of Shaykh Fadhlalla Haeri. I intended to inform Shaykh Fadhlalla Haeri that night of my intentions to leave this community and revisit Norwich, connecting again with Shaykh Abdalqadir.

After the *dhikr* was over, there was always time for socializing with each other. Shaykh Fadhlalla Haeri would always call several people up to his table and engage with different people. I moved close and was generously invited to sit nearby. When the time was right, I took the opportunity to inform Shaykh Fadhlalla Haeri about my intentions. He noticed I was trying to get his attention, so turning to me, he asked what was on my mind. I told him that I was planning to leave the community here and join with Shaykh Abdalqadir again. In a most unexpected and surprising manner, he responded, saying "Well, you're a Shaykh, why tell me?" If I were naked as the day I was born, it would not go far enough to communicate what I was feeling; embarrassment does not describe how I felt. He then asked, "Why are you going?" Now trembling, feeling dreadfully uncomfortable, I answered, to see Shaykh Abdalqadir. He answered back, "I am Shaykh Abdalqadir! Now what do you want?" His words, like sharpened arrows, were a direct hit, collapsing the walls of my misguided conception, leaving me naked to the truth that had been in plain sight in front of me through this whole time. In what was like a mini death experience, I witnessed my life for the past year in a raw unveiling of my blind arrogance.

At that moment, I realized for the first time how I had been asleep, without awareness, in obstructed consciousness, and in absence of presence of heart. For the first time, I saw Shaykh Fadhlalla Haeri in the real sense and I was shattered; I curled over onto his lap in tears, repeating *Astaghfirullah* (I seek forgiveness), over and over again.

He lowered his head to whisper in my ears, "Congratulations!"

Sowing up the Pieces and Off to Hajj

Shaykh Fadhlalla Haeri then reminded me of the time when he invited me to his hotel room at the Claremont in Berkeley two years back. He continued and revealed that evening before I came to visit him, he had met with Shaykh Abdalqadir in which, among other issues, they talked about me. Shaykh Abdalqadir said that he had no more to impart to me and asked Shaykh Fadhlalla Haeri to take me on as his student, but after meeting with me, he realized I was far from ready to not only hear this, but to recognize and accept him as my mentor, until now. As I raised myself up, keeping my head lowered in the realized humility of my ignorance, I thanked the Shaykh and asked to remain and serve in any way he deemed fit. On that evening Shaykh Fadhlalla gifted me with the opportunity to make the Hajj, the pilgrimage to Mecca and a visit to the Prophet in Medina. Sidi Hosam was planning on going, but was unable to make it that year, so he gifted me with the means to make the Hajj in his stead.

In the meantime, Shaykh Fadhlalla put forward a plan for a group of us to visit Arabia and the Emirates with the idea to raise funds for both the *Bayt ud Deen* project and New Light Village. I was part of this team, and it was 1981.

We combined the pilgrimage of Hajj with an extended visit afterwards to Riyadh and later to the Gulf states.

At the Military Housing Complex in Riyadh

In Riyadh we were generously provided accommodation at the military housing complex. We had befriended a Saudi air force captain, training at Lackland Air force Base outside of San Antonio Texas. He offered his family residence to us during our visit to Saudi Arabia. There was a large mosque at the center of the housing complex that I frequented during our stay. One morning at the *Fajr* (before sunrise) prayer, I arrived early to read the Qur'an and take advantage of the expansive, quiet space of the mosque before others arrived for prayer. As *Fajr* approached, an automatic, prerecorded call to prayer rang out echoing across the buildings of the housing complex. It was at least a half hour since the call was sent out and no one showed, except one man who had already been in the mosque, unseen behind one of the many pillars. He appeared, reciting *Iqama* (Call to *Salaat*) for the prayer and waved me on to join him.

After praying together, he asked me to remain. He introduced himself as the chief Imam for the Air Force. He inquired why I was in Saudi Arabia and how I came to this mosque. We talked for a while; he genuinely expressed his happiness in meeting me and offered to help connect us with people that could financially assist us with our projects. He invited us for dinner the next night. That day we explored Riyadh, meeting with people organically and sharing many cups of coffee, tea, and sweets. We were very impressed with the level of openness and generosity of the everyday people we met. There was one thing that stuck out in blatant incongruity; there were areas between opulent neighborhoods and also commercial areas that were packed with shanty towns where people were literally living in informal settlements, their homes constructed with a mix of wooden pallets and empty discarded refrigerator boxes. There were some made with broken assorted offcuts of bricks, clearly left over from other completed building sites. The people we met in this place were mainly poor African and South Asian workers and servants of Saudi families. In one of these settlements, a man from Sudan approached us; he clearly was excited to see us, having heard from others that we were new converts to Islam. He invited us to his home for lunch, which was one of many shelters constructed as I described above.

Meal with Muhammad Amin of Sudan

We entered through a burlap curtain that was the front entrance to his home. There were pieces of cloth sewn together on the ground into a makeshift carpet, surrounded by pillows made from stuffed discarded rice sacks. In one corner was a two-burner gas stove sitting on a plastic folding table, an electric water kettle, billowing steam, filling the already poorly ventilated desert heated space with even more heat. Electricity was available by tapping into existing lines that fed the nearby Saudi homes and businesses. Our friend, Muhammad Amin, busied himself preparing tea and lunch, excitedly sharing in broken English about his family back in Sudan, his wife, children, and elderly parents. He treated us like family, heart-full, overflowing with exuberance, joy and gratitude that transformed this poor hovel, into a spacious palace garden of light and beauty.

When we mentioned the disparity between how he lived and the Saudis around him, he quickly answered, reminding us that Allah is the provider and things could be worse, expressing gratitude with what he had.

He served us boiled eggs, swimming in olive oil and salted *Za`tar* (Middle Eastern spice mixture). Hot bread arrived just in time to dip into the food he generously prepared. With the pronouncement of *Bismillah!* We huddled close together, shared the food, eating from one plate.

Going to Visit Amir Sultan at His Palace

We remained with Muhammad until late afternoon, returning to the hotel to get ready for our dinner meeting with the Imam of the Saudi Air Force. After we performed the sunset prayer, a message came to our room that a car was waiting for us in front of the hotel to take us to our dinner engagement. The Imam's driver was waiting for us in a shiny new Mercedes with blacked-out windows, looking very much like an official government vehicle. The driver was a Yemeni who spoke some English. He was wearing a traditional Yemeni style *Keffiyeh* (A traditional Arabian headdress) and robe; we couldn't help but notice he also had a dagger tucked into his waist belt. We drove for quite a while, leaving the center of Riyadh towards the military containment area. We asked where we were going, and our driver answered to the Palace of Amir Sultan. At the time, we did not know anything about him, later learning he was the defense minister who would become the crown prince to King Abdullah in 2005. The Sultan's powerbase lay in his control of the regular armed forces, and his status as one of seven full brothers born to the kingdom's founder, King Abdul-Aziz Ibn Saud, by his favorite wife.

Among the Clueless

We entered the compound of the Sultan on a paved road that stretched in front of us for at least half a mile. We could see his palace emerging at the end of the road. As we grew closer there were several armed checkpoints where we had to stop and be reviewed by the guards. Before entering the circle driveway that led to the entry of the palace, there was a plaque with the name Al-Yamamah Palace. The doors to the palace towered over us, rising at least fourteen feet, gilded in gold, and adorned with Islamic geometric patterns carved into each door panel. There were several security guards armed to the teeth, but smiling as they opened the doors, welcoming us into the palace. The interior foyer ceilings were at least five meters high at the center of which was an enormous crystal chandelier, so wide and tall it had its own entry panel to change bulbs and make repairs and large enough to accommodate two men working from the inside. There was Italian marble everywhere and strewn throughout were Persian carpets, many made of silk and each large enough to be the footprint of a modest house. We were escorted to the reception area, another large room where the walls were covered with pictures of the royal Saudi family going back to King Abdul Aziz. Many of the photos depicted Saudi kings and princes meeting with world leaders and businessmen, others official portraits of the royal family.

At the very end of the expanse was a dining table with sixteen chairs, each had a traditional European place setting in front of each chair. Through an entryway opposite from where we came in, the Imam appeared, welcoming us in, and inviting us to sit down in an alcove lounge area, next to the dining table. He informed us that the Crown Prince Sultan would be with us in a moment as well as other military officials, joining us for dinner.

It all began to dawn on us that we were about to meet the designated heir apparent of the Saudi kingdom.

The Imam asked us in detail about our projects. He explained that the prince was very keen on helping Muslim communities, especially projects that included new converts to Islam. In the past he had supplied educational materials, copies of the Qur'an and scholarships to Islamic educational institutions in Saudi and abroad.

I noticed that there was a sudden rise in activities with the kitchen and serving staff, and within moments the Amir was arriving with an entourage of military officials, generals and other family members. We were warmly greeted by the prince and by most of the military, although I saw several looks of suspicion directed at us as well as some cynical stares. We all took our places at the table; dinner was quickly served, and without much ceremony, everyone dug in. The prince did most of the talking, everyone else paid deference to him at the slightest indication that he might speak. There was definite tension at the table. I could only guess that would be the case when you were sitting with a man who had not only your career in his hand, but your life as well.

Although there were only about eight of us having dinner, the amount of food that was being served was enough for three times as many people. There were three kinds of meat, several rice and barley dishes, as well as a variety of salads and breads and, of course, overflowing glasses of Pepsi. At the end of the meal, we retreated to the alcove lounge where we had been sitting earlier. The prince had to leave for a few minutes; we were left with the generals. There was not a lot of small talk and some walked around the room in pairs having their own discussions. I too got up and moved around the room, reviewing the photos and paintings. I came near the kitchen door, where there was a round glass window portal through which you could look inside the kitchen. I peered in and noticed that the servants were discarding all the leftovers into the trash – the meats, salads, breads, everything. I thought that this couldn't be right. In my naivety I thought if the prince knew that the food was being trashed, he certainly would do something about it. When he returned, I waited for the right moment to bring this to his attention, being careful not to cause any embarrassment to the prince. When I told him, he responded with an exuberant, *Mashallah! Hadha min Fadhli Rabbi* (That is, God has willed. This is by the overflowing generosity of God), he went on to say that God was so generous to us, that he had given us more than we needed, and we have to throw it away. I was astonished at his response. I thought, could not this food be distributed to the poor, or taken home by the servants that work at the palace? I was thinking about earlier that day, having lunch with Muhammad, who worked for the Saudi Government, and I was sure he would gladly and gratefully accept the leftovers.

As the evening grew to a close, I felt more and more uneasy about accepting any help from the prince. I went back and forth in my mind about it, considering whether it was morally imperative that I reject his help because of the twisted way he understood God's blessings and provision. On the other hand, I thought of accepting his help; it could be providing him with a positive contribution to his *Akhira* (The Hereafter).

A Million-Dollar Offer from the Prince

We were readying to leave when the prince asked to see me privately in his office that was adjacent to the dining hall. He led me to a room where he sat down at a very large hand carved wooden desk, inlaid with ivory, turquoise and abalone, flags of the nation and other different branches of the military. He immediately began writing something on an official letterhead, finishing with his signature and seal, he handed me the letter. Simultaneously, while reading the letter, he said that on behalf of the Kingdom of Saudi Arabia, he bequeathed us with a contribution of one million dollars. I was speechless not only due to the immense gravity of this generous contribution, but also because I was still struggling with accepting the money at all, due to my concerns about the source of these funds. In that moment I capitulated to his generous act and thanked him profusely. He asked that we see his personal secretary in the morning to finalize the transfer of funds. On that we were escorted out of the palace to the car waiting to return us to our hotel.

The next morning, we visited the offices of the prince's secretary, a very bookish Pakistani accountant, who assured us that the funds would be transferred to our account with the following condition. The stipulation was that he would visit our community first before the funds were distributed. At the time, this condition didn't raise any red flag or issue; I chalked it up to their methods to verify contributions were legitimate. It made sense, so I did not give it much thought. He also asked us for our air tickets and hotel bills. He said that from now on we are guests of the Kingdom and our flight costs will be refunded to us and all our expenses including the hotel bill will be paid for by the prince himself.

For the next few days we ate, shopped, and moved about Riyadh, with a document in hand, stating that we were official guests of the kingdom and any expense or services rendered to us would be compensated directly by the prince's office.

Return to *Bayt ud Deen* / Off to Pakistan

Million-Dollar Contribution Retracted

We returned to San Antonio with the good news and waited for Amir Sultan's secretary to arrive and hopefully sign off on the funds transfer.

Within days of our return, the Saudi consulate notified us that the Saudi envoy arrived in Houston and that he would be visiting us in San Antonio within a few days. We prepared a guest accommodation for him and arranged for him to meet several of the families involved in both the *Bayt ud Deen* and New Light Village projects. He arrived as planned and we took him first to the house of our Imam at New Light Village. Everything went downhill from there. He came looking to disqualify us, and from the get-go he found fault and reasons to be critical of everyone and everything we introduced to him. He was rude and condescending to our Imam and questioned his training and understanding of the duties of a "religious" leader and, at one point, he even doubted his ability to recite the Qur'an and asked him to read *Suratul Fatiha* to prove his knowledge. The final straw was when he visited our mosque, he heard the community reciting a litany of *dhikr*, inquiring to us why we were doing this *"Bid`a"* (i.e., it has no basic in the Qur'an and *Sunnah*) in the mosque. We politely explained that we were a Sufi Muslim Community and that *dhikr* was an everyday part of our practice, individually and in congregation. The Saudi envoy vehemently shared his disapproval of our community. He stated without question that the funds would not be transferred and even went further by extolling us to reform ourselves and return to the real and true path of Islam. Before leaving he offered to send teachers to us from Saudi Arabia if we were willing to change our ways.

I was still very naïve and ignorant regarding the diverse perspectives within the community of the world's Muslims. Although I was somewhat disappointed, I was not deterred in my belief that help would come one way or another in ways most likely unknown and expected. One thing was without doubt: informed by my past experiences, I knew that we all receive our provision in precise measure and often from where we do not know, so that we may be in gratitude and awe to the overflowing generosity towards The Source of all things.

Support for *Bayt ud Deen*

The *madrasah* at *Bayt ud Deen* was well on its way to being erected, and support came from many different directions and, although it was not revealed publicly, we all knew that the lion's share of support for the *Bayt ud Deen* project was directly from its founder Shaykh Fadhlalla Haeri.

While the finishing touches were being made on the *madrasah*, there was a plan developing to send a group of Western, mostly American, Muslims to Pakistan as part of a project conceived between Shaykh Fadhlalla and a new member of our community, a Pakistani student named Dr. Khalid Iqbal.

The Pakistan Connection

Dr. Khalid came from a small village in Pakistan called Ahmedpur Sharqia (Ahmedpur East). Although he came from a relatively well-to-do family of land and business owners, there was a desperate need in his village for medical care and business skills training, especially for disenfranchised women, young and old.

Shaykh Fadhlalla saw this as an opportunity for American Muslims to serve by helping to establish a free clinic, a women's training center and a Sufi center. The center would be a place of sharing with the community at large their inspirations and experience of Islam, not just as shared religion, but as a transformative ethos of practices and teachings that not only led them to the *Deen*, but became a constant source of inspiration to live fully in the recognition of the Ever-Present One.

In 1981 my wife and I set out, with others from our community, to live and serve in the villages of Pakistan.

Before leaving for Pakistan I met with Shaykh Fadhlalla, as he wanted to greet me before we traveled. In that meeting he instructed me to keep a journal/diary containing my up-and-coming travel experiences in Pakistan.

The following stories are taken from that journal.

Note that they are not exactly in chronological order, although I have tried to organize them here as such.

To Pakistan and Beyond

I recall the very first morning in Ahmedpur. Since we arrived in the darkness of night in Karachi, we did not see much to get a feel for where we were as we were taken immediately from the airport to the train station for an overnight journey to Ahmedpur, its location being well into the interior of the country.

Vibrating from the constant movement over the past 24 hours, I awoke to the sound of the call to prayer. Each Muezzin's voice, rising from the dozens of mosques, chimed in creating a beautiful cascading symphony of heart. Each *Adhan* flowed over the other, echoing in perfect harmony, announcing the beginning of a new day, new opportunities of awakening for all to acknowledge and respond dutifully upon their waiting prayer mats.

Shaykh Fadhlalla saw this mission as two-fold. Firstly, it provided an arena for Westerners to live among people that were not over exposed and spoiled by the commercialism and excessive living in the West. These were people who lived simple God-fearing lives and the trappings of the Western world. With less emphasis on the outer, simple inner qualities were more cherished. Consequently, real relationships were developed easier. Our stay among these people affected us greatly. We were often pushed to the limits. We experienced how dependent and spoiled we were by the way of life we had in the West.

For the first few weeks, it was easy. But when the novelty wore off, it was like we had become afflicted with withdrawal symptoms and had checked into a country-sized rehab clinic, after being addicted to some powerful drug. It was accepting and coming to terms with our inner and outer condition that made our stay in Pakistan one of the most transformative times in our lives. We came away with a profound appreciation for what Allah had given us. We learned a great deal about our personal limitations and the extent of our sincerity for the path we were on.

Secondly, our stay among born Muslims was an inspiration and benefit to born Muslims around us as well. Wherever we met Muslims in Pakistan most responded with love and welcoming. We were often taken into people's homes and treated like their own children, brothers, or sisters. This was the most beautiful part of our stay. Our presence amongst them brought about a reassessment of their own practice of Islam. It is all too often that born Muslims take for granted the great gift of Islam they had been given. This is the great blessing that Islam has for its sincere followers. As new converts enter the fold, the whole is benefited with the freshness and added vitality. This is the way it was at the historical beginning of Islam, and the legacy of that model remains as vital today as it was then. In contrast to this, in a Western society we are veiled from witnessing many human situations and inner states of being, which inhibit the development of the heart.

First Morning

As the sun generously rose and the curtain of night was lifted from the stage of the first day of our journey, I was suddenly struck with both excitement and apprehension, about the prospect of venturing out of my room and into the streets of our new life. I could hear the clatter of hoofs, and bells, voices, and smells, all blending together beckoning me to see first-hand how it all fit together. Building my resolve, I walked out the door and met with the new world around me.

In front of our house was a poorly tarred road, on which a parade of horse drawn carriages, motor bikes, bicycles and motorized kamikaze rickshaws, racing up and down. They were like oversized bumblebees, buzzing along in a competition of who could produce the most noise, smell, and visual pollution. I would have given them all the first prize!

Across the road was a *"Chai Khana"* ("Tea House"), where they sold hot tea, sweets, and Pepsi Cola. The bottles of which were all scripted in Urdu. I managed to order a Pepsi and slowly sipped it in pace with my new surroundings. I was bemused and enchanted with it all. Although I had never experienced anything like this before, it all felt familiar to me. It slowly drew out of me a sense of ease, belonging, and recognition of the universality of humanity. As I stood up from my chair, I arose with a new sense in myself. I was no longer in my own eyes a foreigner, but a brother who comes home to discover and be discovered by others as a kindred spirit.

It is amazing how as human beings we are not so different from each other. The basic elements are there in each one of us. It is only expressed and developed differently depending upon our upbringing and overall outer circumstance.

Dr. Khalid's House

We had met Dr. Khalid Iqbal in College Station, Texas, in the USA, where he was working as a research assistant on the "Star Wars" defense project. We had our center of activity in Texas near San Antonio. As part of our projects, we would often go out to different colleges and universities, looking to share our path with others. From time to time someone would embrace Islam, or a born Muslim would meet us and soon after reassessing their lives, change themselves in a more spiritual direction. This was the case with Dr. Khalid Iqbal. He made a 180-degree turn in his life; he left his work at the university and returned to serve his community that he had left behind in Pakistan. It was with his invitation and support that we were able to carry out our projects in Pakistan.

Dr. Khalid's house became our home for some time before we had our own center. We were immediately made to feel at home and were brought into the family in every way.

Once we got to our center, others from America and Europe joined us. We now had regular teaching and our circle of *dhikr* was growing.

Shaykh Sayed Ikram Hussain

First Meeting with Shaykh Ikram Hussain

Pakistan is a synthesis of feudal landowners and tribal chiefs, who held a lot of power and control over their people. When the British colonized the Indian Subcontinent, they were able to rule through the strategy of "divide and conquer," in spite of their small numbers.

Summer nights in Dera Nawab Sahib were not much different than the days. They were hot and uncomfortable. It was so hot this particular summer that our bed pillow covers felt as though they had just been steam-ironed. I used to wet the sheets of my bed and wrap myself up in them. But it was a short-lived comfort. The sheets would dry within a few minutes.

On one of these summer nights, we came to hear about a Sufi Shaykh visiting our village by the name of Shaykh Sayed Ikram Hussain. We were invited by one of the Shaykh's local *Mureeds*, Hakeem Iftikhar, for a meeting.

We came to the house where the Shaykh was having a *Majlis* (Gathering).

139

It was in a large open room with plenty of cushions along the walls. After removing our shoes and greeting everyone upon entering, the Shaykh stood up and kindly invited us in welcoming us with love and warm embrace.

After all the introductions were made, the Shaykh requested everyone besides our group to leave the room; he also requested the curtains be drawn and the doors locked.

Once there was only our group left, the Shaykh began to question us about what we were doing in Pakistan. He inquired about the name of our Shaykh and asked us individually about ourselves and our stay in Pakistan. During the course of our meeting, Shaykh Ikram leaned over and reclined on some pillows under his arms, with his legs stretched out. We thought nothing of this, but soon, there were rumbling and sounds of agitated people outside the door.

Suddenly, there was a breaking sound, and the door came swinging open, forced by several of the people outside. They were visibly very agitated and upset; one had a machete in his hand. There was a flurry of shouting and gesturing, but clearly their concern was about the well-being of the Shaykh. Shaykh Ikram laughed a bit and assured them he was fine and then instructed them to leave immediately until they were asked to return.

We found out through our interpreter that the Shaykh's *mureeds* were so upset due to the fact that they saw Shaykh Ikram reclining. Under normal circumstances, in public, the Shaykh would never recline. They extrapolated from seeing his unusual behavior that we might have poisoned or cast an evil spell on the Shaykh.

After he learned the reasons for their concern, Shaykh Ikram confirmed their reaction and informed us that he never reclined in public and would do so only with his family and close relatives.

Once the agitation of the people outside subsided, Shaykh Ikram went around the room questioning us about what we had learned and how we had benefited from the Sufi path.

Each one of us had a turn in answering the Shaykh's questions. The answers varied from person to person. Listening attentively, the Shaykh appeared not to be impressed with any of our answers until it came to the last person to respond, who was `Ali Abdul Aziz, the youngest among us – he was 18 at the time. `Ali answered that he knew nothing, was new to the path, but expressed eagerness to learn. Upon hearing Ali's response, Shaykh Ikram declared that `Ali Abdul Aziz was the only Sufi in tonight's circle.

Shaykh Ikram asked us about our practices, especially inquiring whether there was one central practice. I responded by sharing the practice of reciting the *Ismul A`zam*, which means "The greatest name of God – Allah", in a technique passed down to us from Shaykh Fayturi of Algeria. It is performed by pronouncing the name of Allah in an elongated fashion, much like the Hindu recitation of the universal sound of "Om."

He asked me to demonstrate the technique, which I started to do, but then he stopped me, saying that I was not performing it correctly. He then began to demonstrate the correct way it was meant to be done. He also showed us how to improve the overall effect of the practice by adding certain techniques that he demonstrated for us. Needless to say, his knowledge and authority took us all aback. None of us expected that in this remote Pakistani village, a local Shaykh would not only know of this practice, but also instruct us in the best and most efficient and accurate way to perform it.

Our meeting with Shaykh Ikram was the beginning of a relationship that spanned over decades, expanding the horizons of our work in Pakistan and beyond.

Development of Close Relationship with Shaykh Ikram

My wife and I became very close to Shaykh Ikram. While living in Karachi for nearly a year, Shaykh Ikram would visit our home nearly every month, during his regular visits with his *Mureeds* in Karachi. He especially took a liking to my wife, Nafisa, who he renamed Rifat, often discussing healing methods with her as well as encouraging women in general to be more proactive in sharing the Sufi path with other women. He always addressed her as his daughter.

Nearly always upon his departure from Karachi, he would take me aside and ask me the following: "Hajj Mustafa Shawqi Sahib, will you not remain in Pakistan for the rest of your life?"

He often included in these questions remarks to me like, if I stayed, he would make sure that a grand shrine would be built at the site of my grave and that people would come from all over and sing the *Diwan* as well as make supplications for me and in my name. Shaykh Ikram had a great sense of humor, but I always felt uncomfortable, taking it too seriously, even though I knew he was kidding – at least about the Shrine part of the offer.

In answering the question of remaining in Pakistan, although I could not rule the possibility out, I could not make the commitment to spend the rest of my life there. He would often press me to give him a definite answer, but until the very last time he asked, I could not say one way or the other.

After a year of proposing to me that I remained in Pakistan, I finally responded to his question with an enthusiastic yes! Upon hearing my answer, Shaykh Ikram shook his head and finger at me in the negative and said, "We don't need you, go back to America!"

He continued; "Your light here is like a candle in the bright sun, it will make little difference, return your light to America where that light will shine brighter."

We all laughed, and I made my plans to return to the States.

After several weeks of arranging our departure, Shaykh Ikram returned to Karachi to see us off to the States. At that last meeting, he hugged me whispering incantations of prayers in both my ears, he then placed his right pointer finger in the middle of my chest and wrote the name of Allah in my heart. After tracing the name three times, he kissed my chest, while rising as he looked directly into my eyes. I was instantly transported into a sense of timelessness, his eyes portals to my own heart, a taste of which I can return to even now.

The Search for Opium

While living in the capital city of Karachi, my wife had come down with a serious ailment that was life threatening. Shaykh Ikram visited us in Karachi regularly and, being accomplished in the art of healing, he prescribed a combination of Barbarous, lemon and six grams of opium to be made into a paste, rolled into balls the size of chickpeas, and taken over a period of several days. He assured us that this would cure the situation immediately. I was stunned that he suggested opium, as it was not only illegal in Pakistan, but that if a foreigner like myself were to be caught with it, I would be locked away in jail with little help from anywhere to get out. I expressed my concerns to the Shaykh about the opium and he responded with a little giggle and assured me that I would be fine. With that he suggested a few places for me to begin my search and left our home saying he would return in a few days to check on his patient.

That afternoon I ventured out into the marketplaces and bazaars that foreigners rarely see. Kharadar was a bazaar close to the waterfront area near the Karachi port. There were things there for sale that were not for regular consumption. Things like condoms, old girly magazines, love potions and all kinds of occult crafts and spells. There were also many herb shops and local healers who had their offices there. I began asking for opium at the herbal shops but was met with anger and warning that I would be arrested or beaten. Some shop owners chased me with sticks and others pushed me out of their shops. I had been searching for several hours and had not had any clue or direction where to turn next. I wandered further into the bazaar and came to a clearing where there were many flower and sweet shops. In the middle of the bazaar, was a man moving through the open area of the market, walking on his hands. His legs were knurled and crossed over each other. Every inch of his body was covered with sacks of skin like so many Christmas ornaments hanging on a tree. There were hundreds, from very small sacks to ones the size of a golf ball. He could hardly see as they dangled from his forehead over his eyes. He was begging for food and money. I was taken deeply by this site. I reached in my pocket and took all the money I had with me. The money I brought to buy the opium and gave it to him. When I placed it in his hand, he prayed for me. We greeted each other and soon parted. I was now without money and my patience for this search had run out.

I started to make my way out of the bazaar. As I followed the route I had come, I suddenly became disoriented as to what direction to go. There were so many twists and turns, alleyways and streets all looking the same. As I stood there deciding which way to go, I suddenly felt a tugging on my sleeve. I looked down expecting to see a child begging or something like that. What I saw was a man sitting on a clean white sheet, wearing the most impeccable clean and white clothes. At first, I treated him like a beggar. I said *"maaf karow,"* which means, "forgive me" in Urdu. He responded in English "No, please, forgive me. May I have a word with you please?" He beckoned me to sit down on the sheet with him, which I did. He then asked me what I was doing in this place. I explained to him more or less what I was doing there. I left out the part about the opium, as I was still suspicious of the intention of this man. He then told me what he was doing there and why he tugged on my sleeve to join him. He said that the night before he had a dream that his now dead Shaykh had come to him, instructing him to come to this bazaar and sit on a white sheet, and wait for an unusual man to appear. He said I was the unusual man. He then asked what he could do for me. At this moment, I knew that there were other forces at play. That all that had happened was part of a plot yet to unfold and become known. I humbly told him about my wife and the prescription of the Shaykh for her ailment. As I spoke, I would see his eyes swell with tears. He reached for my hand and consoled me that Allah and his *awliya* (Friends of Allah) were looking after us. He produced from behind him a black leather bag, the kind a doctor would have. He reached in and pulled out several small bags of herbs and mixtures, along with a small brass scale. In one of the bags, was a black tarry looking substance. It was opium. He removed it from the bag and weighed the opium; it was exactly six grams as Shaykh Ikram prescribed. The man gave me the bag and said that this was the reason he had been instructed to come here today. He lifted his hands in prayer and we both stood together. I was now considering how I was going to pay him, after I had already given away all my money. Before I could inquire, he grabbed my hand and said that the opium was a gift to me and my wife and that having fulfilled the instructions of his Shaykh was enough payment for him. With that he asked to be excused. I suddenly heard my name being called from somewhere out in the bazaar. I turned and looked to the direction the voice was coming. I saw nothing. By the time I turned back to face this man, he was gone. Not a trace of him, his sheet, or marks on the ground. He had just vanished. I didn't even get his name.

I returned to my house and mixed the mixture as prescribed by Shaykh Ikram. I gave the homemade pills to my wife, and, within a few hours, the symptoms subsided and, after a few days, she was well again. The exception being that the opium had made her a bit intoxicated. She complained how she felt like she was floating. I thought this was due to the effects of the opium. After a few days, Shaykh Ikram came to visit as promised. He tended to my wife. He came and asked to see the pills I had made. I will never forget the look and smile on his face when I showed him the pills. He just smiled and said "too big." He took a knife and cut each one into four. We all had a good laugh that day.

The Belly of Satan

One day Dr. Khalid had come to Karachi to visit us and to see his relatives. He had a cousin, called Rasheed, who owned a new restaurant at Clifton. Rasheed requested Dr. Khalid to take him to visit Shaykh Ikram at his home in Hyderabad, which was about a five-hour drive from Karachi. I was asked to accompany them. I had never been to Shaykh Ikram's house. I considered it an honor that we were allowed to visit him. Shaykh Ikram refused to allow any of his students to come to his home. He lived in a very humble home, made of mud brick. He liked it that way. He knew that if his students came, they would want to move him out to a better and bigger place.

We arrived at Shaykh Ikram's in the early afternoon and he generously welcomed us into the courtyard of his house. We were soon served tea and some simple sweets. As the tea was being served, the Shaykh asked Rasheed to hold out his hand with his palm up. Rasheed complied with the Shaykh's request. The Shaykh then reached behind him and brought out a stack of small denominations of rupee notes. He then started placing the money one note at a time in Rasheed's hand, counting each note. He went on and on until Rasheed's hand was overflowing with rupees. Rasheed became more and more agitated as the Shaykh continued. Finally, Rasheed, politely requested the Shaykh to stop. Shaykh Ikram answered back saying: "But isn't this what you came here for?" You could see the shock in Rasheed's face as the Shaykh revealed the real intention for the visit. Rasheed, feeling exposed and cornered, replied in the affirmative. He had come not for a spiritual reason, but to ask the Shaykh to pray for his new business and that it would be a success. The Shaykh said that he was not against this request, only that he wanted Rasheed to be open and honest about his intentions. The Shaykh agreed to pray for him under the following conditions. That Rasheed kept to his prayers and that he did not rush after money. That he must take care and not run after the *dunya* (this world). He warned Rasheed that running after money would lead to disaster. Rasheed accepted the Shaykh's consul and promised to heed his warning and injunctions.

Several months passed after this visit, when one afternoon I received a phone call from a mutual friend of Rasheed's. It was news that Rasheed's daughter had been shot and killed. I rushed over to Rasheed's house and found his entire family wailing in the parlor. Rasheed appeared from the upper level of the house. He rushed over to me, in tears. I inquired what happened. I was told that Rasheed was upstairs cleaning a rifle he used for target practice. There was a phone call from his business that something had happened to the receipts from the night before. There was money missing and Rasheed had to go down to his business immediately and take care of the matter. Rasheed rushed out the door in a panic, leaving the rifle on his bed, loaded. His small son and daughter entered the room and seeing the rifle started to play cowboys and Indians. His little son aimed the rifle at his sister and pulled the trigger, killing her instantly.

When Shaykh Ikram was told of these events, he was so upset that he refused to visit Karachi for three months. He called it the belly of Satan.

Life is full of lessons. Some come to us like a fragrant breeze, others like being hit by a train. There is no doubt that if one is sincere to God and to themselves, then the lessons of life will come in a way like the breeze. But when one is thick and without fear of consequences, then the lessons knock louder at the door.

The *Urs* at Mustafabad

There is a Sufi tradition of commemorating the passing on of an enlightened Shaykh or *Wali u`llah* (Friend of God). In the Indian sub-continent, this tradition is referred to as an *Urs*. These celebrations often go on for days and act as a focal point for adherents of the Shaykh to gather from all over the world, meeting each other and communing in their dedication to the path. There is usually lots of Qawwali singing and plenty of food and tea going around the clock. During the gathering, a living Shaykh sits at the head while the singing and celebrations are going on. As the singing and momentum of the gathering grows, many of the attendants enter into states of varying degrees of spiritual intoxication during which they experience moments of connection with the zone that is timeless, spaceless and boundless. They often get up and dance around, some collapse in exhaustion and others in spiritual ecstasy.

We were invited to one of these gathering by Shaykh Ikram, who was the head and living spiritual inheritor of the Shaykh whose *Urs* we were attending.

It is traditional at these gatherings for those attending that when they approach the Shaykh, also known as the *Pir*, an offering is made, most of the time in sums of cash money.

I was sitting near to Shaykh Ikram during most of the *Urs* and observed that when money was offered Shaykh Ikram held his right hand open, never clasping the money with his fingers, but carefully sliding the money off his hands directly behind him. There was another devotee sitting directly behind Shaykh Ikram, who gathered the cash and pushed it through an opening of the tent. I was curious to see where all the cash was going, so I briefly left the main area and walked behind the tent. Extending from the back opening, was a line of people, mostly poor, destitute women, children, and men, crippled or blind, waiting to receive their portion of the offerings that were being distributed. I learned later that this was done under the strict order of Shaykh Ikram, where every coin collected would be fully distributed to the needy and that nothing should be left at the end of the *Urs*.

As we approached the environs where the gathering was taking place, I could feel the radiation of light coming from all directions. This feeling grew stronger as we approached closer and closer. Upon arrival we were immediately whisked away to a room that had been prepared for us near the main field where the gathering was taking place. The room was filled with the sweet smell of incense and rose water had been sprayed on the walls and floor. There were several beds waiting for us to rest on. Each was clothed in satin covers, and they were covered in thousands of multi-colored rose petals. Several young men who brought us rose and almond flavored milk, followed by tea and sweets, attended us too. It was so sweet. We were humbled by the way we were treated.

Shaykh Ikram's Healing Rain

After some time, we were invited to the *Majlis* where Shaykh Ikram was holding audience for those who wanted to seek his advice and blessings. When I saw Shaykh Ikram this time, I noticed a radical difference in his state. He appeared to my perception larger, and his face glowing with light. He gestured that I sit near him. There was much conversation between the *paan*[12] chewing and cigarettes. The attention was dispersed throughout the room, with little focus on anyone in particular. I felt more like an observer and remained mostly silent throughout. Then Shaykh Ikram turned to me and asked that Dr. Xaigham translate from Urdu to English. The Shaykh started to direct his conversation directly to me. His topic was sincerity and its virtues. He went from speaking about it in general terms to speaking directly to me and addressing my own personal sincerity for the path. I felt very uncomfortable at first having the diagnosis of my illness laid bare to everyone present, but soon I accepted. I closed my eyes and with a clear resolve opened my heart and mind to the words of the Shaykh. I imagined his words to be like healing rain, washing away the dust and dirt that had accumulated there over time.

---

[12] A betel leaf with various ingredients in the leaf.

I sat with inner stillness hanging on to each meaning and savoring the passing moments. The Shaykh seemed to go on for some time, when I started to hear other people in the room crying and others reciting praise to Allah under their breath. I was not aware of what was affecting them so profoundly. I considered that it might be what the Shaykh was saying to me, which they had applied to themselves. I continued to listen to the Shaykh's words, when I became acutely aware that I had been listening to the Shaykh's instructions to me, as though he were talking in English, directly into my heart. I listened to the voice of the translator, but there was none. It was the Shaykh speaking directly to me, and I understood every word. I could hardly contain myself. I opened my eyes and saw the faces of those around me all in recognition of what I had finally come to realize. I looked for the translator; he had gone some time ago. I was so overwhelmed that I leaped across to where the Shaykh was sitting and collapsed in his lap in tears. He began to stroke my head and laughed and recited the *ayah* of Qur`an, which says: "Allah is closer to you than your jugular vein." (*Surah* 50, *Ayah* 16)

From that moment on my state had changed; I was given a taste and glimpse of an inner quality mirrored in the overflowing presence and kindness of Shaykh Ikram.

The entire evening that followed, the singing, the dancing, all the hugs and tears, were all dyed with the flavor of this experience. In the early morning hours, the festivities drew to a close and we all retired to the beds in our room. Shaykh Ikram insisted that he sleep in the same room with us. He requested that we all remember our dreams that night.

I reflected on what he said with my experience of this day, that we are already living in a dream. We believe the parameters of our sensual experience to be the bounds of perception. How foolish this assumption is. Our senses are but limited organs of experience exposing only a small degree of what is possible for the human heart to perceive. There are greater inner senses whose scope spans wide into the more subtle worlds. We are blind and asleep until there is an awakening to the inner light. That light's source is from the infinite reality, boundless and forever giving, if we are fortunate to catch a glimpse of it, and combine it with our want to its source, we have certainly fulfilled our potential, and true joy will be ours.

Shaykh Ikram Visits South Africa

My last meeting with Shaykh Sayyid Ikram was while he visited South Africa.

The year was 2002 and the Shaykh was well advanced in years and had become frail.

It was evident that he was at the edge of his time in this world. During his days with us, he generously offered his time and energy, making *du`as* (supplications), prayers, sharing stories and wisdom teachings to all who were in his presence.

I was honored by him always as he made sure whenever there was a gathering, I would sit near or next to him. He often affectionately called me his *Pehlwan Khalifah,* which literally means [His] "Wrestler Representative". If there were biscuits or sweets, he would hand feed me one after another until my mouth was full to the brim. It was sometimes embarrassing, but each time he put something in my mouth it was his love and light that went straight to my heart and illuminated my being.

Shaykh Ikram in South Africa (2002)

Khalifah Certificate

In 2003, I received a letter from Shaykh Ikram. It contained a handwritten calligraphy of a certificate, made out to me, and signed by him officially entering my name as one of his *Khalifah* (successor/representative) in his spiritual lineage.

I keep it in my office, near to my desk alongside a picture of him.

They remind me of the reality of a sign in the Qur'an that says:

> *"And do not speak of those who are slain in Allah's way as dead; nay, (they are) alive, but you do not perceive."* (2:154)

Shaykh Ikram lived each day in the "way of Allah," I bear witness that his life goes on.

He passed away in 2007.

Khalifah Certificate (In Arabic and Persian)

بسم الله الرحمن الرحيم

خلافت نامہ

اَلْحَمْدُ لِلّٰهِ الَّذِيْ نَوَّرَ قُلُوْبَ الْعَارِفِيْنَ بِاَنْوَارِ الْمُشَاهَدَاتِ وَزَيَّنَ صُدُوْرَ

الصَّادِقِيْنَ بِخِلْيَةِ الصِّفَاتِ وَالْكَمَالَاتِ وَجَعَلَ ذَاكِرَهُ وَسِيْلَةً لِوُصُوْلِ الْحَاجَاتِ

وَصُحْبَتَهُمْ ذَرِيْعَةً لِّحُصُوْلِ السَّعَادَاتِ وَالصَّلٰوةُ الزَّاكِيَاتِ عَلٰى سَيِّدِ الْكَائِنَاتِ

وَاٰلِہٖ اَصْحَابِہٖ اَجْمَعِيْنَ الِجُيُوْعِ الْحَسَنَاتِ كَمَا قَالَ النَّبِيُّ عَلَيْهِ التَّحِيَّاتِ وَاتِبَاعَاتِ الشَّيْخِ فِيْ قَوْمِهٖ كَالنَّبِيِّ

فِيْ اُمَّتِهٖ لَہٗ حَمْدٌ وَنَعْتٌ مِيْگُوْيَمْ يَلْتَجِيْ بِہ شَفَاعَةِ شَفِيْعِ الْمُذْنِبِيْنَ صَلَوَاتُ اللهِ وَسَلَامُہٗ عَلَيْہِ وَعَلٰى عَلَيْهِ

اَجْمَعِيْنَ شاہ اكرم حسين كرچون حاجى مصطفىٰ شوقى

امتجلی اللہ توآرا بسوے اللہ و متفرق بشوق لقاء اللہ یافتم بجانب ارشد كامل حضرت شاہ بنجاد

حسين خليفہ حضرت شاہ على قبلی خلافت سلسلہ عالیہ باودام هر کرا رجوع بسلسلہ من باشد و دست بیعت و

ہم نسبت را بہم رسانم و فقہ اللہ تعالٰی بالاحکام الشرعیۃ وثبتہ اللہ تعالٰی بطریق الاوراد

چنانچہ پوشانیدم خرقہ و بستم دستار خود را و عبد کرم اپنج در مشائخ باشد کہ اگر در محشر مرا ذنی و اجازتی

از جناب کبریا و حضرت رسالت مآب صلی اللہ علیہ وسلم و پیشگاہ حضرت علی مرتضٰی ائمہ معصومین

علیہم الصلٰوۃ والسلام بشفاعت او بادشد شفاعت او نمایم واگر ادا قرب منزلت نزد حق تعالٰی از من زیادہ

ترباشد شفاعت از من در یغ مدارد اَللّٰهُمَّ نَوِّرْ قَلْبَهٗ بِنُوْرِ مَعْرِفَتِكَ وَاشْغِلْهُ بِاَشْغَالِ

جَلَالِكَ وَجَمَالِكَ وَثَبِّتْهُ عَلَى الصِّرَاطِ الْمُسْتَقِيْمِ اٰمِيْنَ اٰمِيْنَ

بِرَحْمَتِكَ يَااَرْحَمَ الرَّاحِمِيْنَ تحریری فی التاریخ ۹ ربیع الثانی ۱۳۲۳ هجری.

151

Shaykh Abdul Mabood al Jilani

For every rule, there is an exception. These exceptions are often referred to as miracles or just lumped together under the category of "unexplained phenomena." Exceptions exist in space, on earth and, in the case of Shaykh Abdul Mabood Jilani, his exceptional life and condition were a prime example of the rule.

He was most likely born in 1823 and traveled the world for over 160 years. He was a fighter for truth, a healer of hearts and an example of the highest, in his obedience and trust in God. Whenever I sat with him, his lessons were not spoken, but transmitted by his beingness. Teachings poured from his hand when he lifted it, from his eyes when he glanced in your direction and from his heart, which even being encased in a fragile, ancient shell, beamed out the light of God's sacred Presence.

He always had time for me and welcomed me as part of his family. He left me **five gifts** that became enduring features in the rose garden of my life:

The first was that nothing, no matter how small, is outside the Magnificence of God.

Secondly, that unless one takes the time and develops patience, through reflecting on Allah's Presence and Design, much of life's secrets will be missed.

Thirdly, no matter what we do to preserve life or to make things happen, it is ultimately in Allah's plan whether a thing will be or not.

Fourthly, people will see what they want to, regardless of the facts.

Finally, there is an appointed time and place for all things. Our plans are but fantasy-filled wishes, unless they are first and foremost, submitted to and aligned with what Allah wants. "We plot and Allah plots, surely Allah's plot will come to pass." (Qur'an 8:30)

First Meeting

The Shaykh had much to give in the way of lessons in life, yet most people flocked to him in hope of gaining extension of their lives through his blessings. He knew this and still was willing to allow thousands to see him weekly for his blessings.

In the winter of 1982, I was living in the capital city of Pakistan, Islamabad. We had rented a large house in a well-to-do area where there were many international embassies and consulates. It was a welcome change of pace after being in Punjab for nearly 8 months. The weather in Islamabad was much more bearable. On one afternoon, I was visiting what locally came to be known as the "*Jum`ah*" market. It was held every Friday before and after the congregational prayers of *Jum`ah*. That morning, as I was strolling along the rows of crafts, foods, and Afghan carpets, a man came out of the crowd rushing towards me as though he had some urgent message to deliver. As he came forward, he waved and waved his hands, like someone flagging down cars after an accident. Once upon us, he grabbed my hand and asked me if I was an American Sufi. I answered: "I am at least one of the American Sufis in Islamabad." He said, "You must follow me immediately; my Shaykh is waiting to meet you."

We were escorted to a waiting car and taken to a house in one of the better areas of Islamabad. There was a long line of people waiting outside, mostly women and children. We were taken to the front of the line and led into a small bedroom where there were several people sitting on the floor around a single bed. Everyone in the room had a reverent demeanor. There was little talking and, when someone spoke, it was whispered. On the bed, there was what appeared to be a lump right in the center covered by a blanket. I was instructed by our host to sit quietly and soon the Shaykh would awaken and we would have a meeting with him.

Looking at the blanket, I could hardly imagine a full-sized man under it. Whatever was under that blanket could not be bigger than a small child.

After some time, tea and lots of whispering, the blanket began to move. I could hear breathing and a slight moan. Then, a small hand emerged from the cover. It remained out and visible for some seconds before the rest of the Shaykh's body emerged. I had never seen or have yet to see again a hand quite like this one. It was almost skeletal, the skin was transparent, and you could see the bone and veins. Soon, the rest of this being emerged with him repeating the name of God, Allah… he was out, adjusting his hat, and glasses, smiling and looking around the room, examining every one of us thoroughly. When his eyes focused on me, he asked me to come closer. He grabbed my face in his hands and asked me if I was Iranian. I answered that I was an American. After introducing himself as Shaykh Mabood Al-Jilani, he smiled wide and asked me my name and the name of my Shaykh. I began to tell him, but before I finished naming the entire name, he stopped me and said, "Yes! Yes! Your Shaykh is the son of Shaykh Ahmed Haeri from Karbala."

I was shocked and overwhelmed with emotion. Tears ran down my cheeks. How did he know this? What an extraordinary meeting! The Shaykh saw my surprise and delight and went on to tell me how he had met my Shaykh's father at the Delhi Mosque in 1890 or something. I was further surprised at the dates. If he had met Shaykh Ahmed Haeri at that time, as the date now was 1983, then this Shaykh had to be at least in his nineties. I asked the Shaykh how old he was. With a big smile on his face, he said, 159 years old! I sat with the Shaykh for several hours, drinking more tea and having light conversation. I was soon asked to come back another time and visit the Shaykh in a more intimate way. I asked his leave and, with a kiss on my forehead, we left his presence. That night I called Shaykh Fadhlalla, and told him about this extraordinary meeting, and the news that this Shaykh knew his father. Shaykh Fadhlalla asked his mother and she affirmed that Shaykh Ahmed had told her about a visit to India as a young man.

More Meetings

The next day I was very anxious to visit the ancient Shaykh again. I was again escorted to the front of the line of people all waiting to see and receive the blessing of the Shaykh. There were many women with their children wanting the Shaykh's blessing on them for long life and health. As I sat there watching one after another, the Shaykh tirelessly placed his hand on the head of each child and mother and read a prayer over them.

He took no money or asked anything for himself.

On one of the first few occasions that I visited the Shaykh, an old man had come to the door of the bedroom and was having a hard time opening the door. The Shaykh, noticing the struggle gestured to us to help him and said with cheek, "Let that old man in." The old man sat down next to me. I leaned over, asked how long he had been coming here, and how long he had known the Shaykh. He said, "All my life; the Shaykh is my father." I asked him how old he was. He said ninety-nine years old. There was a young man who was serving the tea every time I was there. I asked him about his relationship with the Shaykh, another amazing answer. He said he too was the son of the Shaykh. His age was 28.

I found out later that Shaykh Abdul Mabood had 500 children, grandchildren, and great, great grandchildren. He had been married several times in his long life to women from all over the world. Amongst his children, his youngest was 28 and his oldest, nearly 100.

That night, I again communicated with Shaykh Fadhlalla the amazing things about Shaykh Abdul Mabood. This time Shaykh Fadhlalla instructed me that each time I visit Shaykh Abdul Mabood, I should bring with me five gifts for him. This seemingly very simple instruction was to be a difficult task. I was asked to visit him every day. What gift do you bring to a 160-year-old man?

The Five Gifts

As I was standing in the Bazaar in Islamabad, frozen, and perplexed by my task of what five gifts I could buy the Shaykh, it suddenly dawned on me that really it didn't matter. They could be anything. I just had to walk, with heart empty, mind clear and "see" what Allah would guide me to. As soon as this was clear within me, I was able to quickly buy five different items; they ranged from a plastic perfume container to a metal bracelet – with names of five close members of the Prophet's household. All the gifts fit into a small bag. Once I was done with shopping, I was off to the Shaykh's house to deliver his gifts.

Upon entering, I was taken immediately to his side. By now, I had grown very fond of him and he of me. He greeted me with a kiss on my cheeks and asked if I had anything for him. I brought out the bag and gave him the first gift my hand touched. It was a bracelet with the Prophet's family's names on it. When he saw it, he lifted it closely to his face and began to examine it with great interest. He turned it sideways, upside down, looked at the back, all the time reciting the Divine name, Allah, Allah! He looked like a child completely absorbed with a new toy, but even more so. He must have spent at least ten minutes turning it in every possible direction. He put it down and I brought another out. He repeated and gave the same one-pointed attention to the second gift I had brought. This went on through the other gifts. He looked at each one, although it may have been cheap plastic or metal, he held it and cherished it as though it were precious metals and rare gemstones.

It was a lesson for me. He took in life completely. He saw the divine in everything. He saw the traces of the Master of the universe in the smallest and seemingly insignificant things.

After reviewing all the gifts, he said he had something for me. He reached down under his bed and brought out some food that was left on his dinner plate. He said that he was saving this for me. He picked up a spoon, scooped up some rice and little bits of meat and spoon-fed me. There were exactly five bites.

Each night I returned to the Shaykh's house with five new gifts, and each time there were five bites of food waiting for me. On several occasions, I would ask the Shaykh about his life and experiences. Whenever I would inquire in this way, he would often play down the significance of his life and refuse to talk. But sometimes a flood of stories would come from him. On one of these nights, he told us the following tale.

The Caravan to Mecca

Around the turn of the 20th century, Shaykh Abdul Mabood was on his way to the pilgrimage in Mecca, on a camel caravan from Syria. He was accompanying his teacher, Shaykh Ahmed Mekki. The journey took three months, and along the way there were many difficulties, not the least desert robbers.

On one afternoon, they came across another caravan heading east to China. They shared a camp that evening and exchanged stories of their lands and experiences. The leader of the caravan warned the pilgrims to be very careful in the next few days, as there were reports of the presence of an infamous thief in the area. His infamy was based on the fact that he was a ruthless man, not caring whom he robbed or killed and not even sparing the caravans of pilgrims.

The next day, while having traveled for many miles, the Shaykh's caravan stopped to perform the afternoon prayer of `Asr. As they were doing their ablutions, shouts were heard from all quarters of the caravan. Soon, there were shots heard and the caravan was under siege by the band of thieves under the leadership of the infamous marauder, whom they had been warned about the night before.

The thieves were relentless in their appetite for blood. Many Hajjis were killed, and the caravan was ransacked. Shaykh Abdul Mabood could see the chief thief in the distance. Like a proud king or landowner, he remained away from the camp until most of the damage was done. Then he entered the camp to survey the booty his men had collected. As he moved through the crowds of the vanquished Hajjis, all heads bowed in fear of catching his eye and disfavor, risking death or a beating.

As he came closer, Shaykh Abdul Mabood lifted his head and challenged the chief thief. He admonished him for laying siege to a caravan of helpless Hajjis on their way to the holy pilgrimage. Most were astonished at the courage and bold stance the Shaykh had taken. Fear ran through them though; fear that this would be the invitation of their deaths. The thief addressed the Shaykh, saying, "Do you know who I am? Do you know that I have killed men for less than what you have done today!" The Shaykh answered, "I only fear Allah, my life is in His hands and in His hands only. If it be that I should die today having challenged evil, then let it be so."

The thief dismounted his camel and approached the Shaykh. He addressed the Shaykh saying, "I fear no man or God, but I am the one feared by all!" The Shaykh answered, "Then, I pity your illusion, and I will pray for you to repent." The thief was so impressed with the Shaykh's courage, that he had all his men gather around Shaykh Abdul Mabood to introduce him as an equal to himself. He extolled the Shaykh's courage in standing up and speaking to himself. In respect to Shaykh Abdul Mabood, he let him live and brought to him a gift of three camels, laden with gold and silver. Shaykh Abdul Mabood asked his Shaykh if he could accept the three camels of gold and silver from the infamous thief. His Shaykh was clear and direct in his response. He could not accept these gifts, as they were surely stolen from others. It would be *haram*.

As Shaykh Abdul Mabood returned to where the thief was to refuse the gifts, the Shaykh surprised everyone when he, in fact, accepted the gifts. The thief was gratified and, with his men, disappeared into the desert. Shaykh Abdul Mabood had now become an outcast. His Shaykh refused to see him, and he was sent with his camels to the end of the caravan, forbidden to eat, or fraternize with the rest of the caravan's Hajjis. He even was stoned and spat on several occasions.

After many days, the Shaykh's caravan came across the royal caravan from the Khalifah of Turkey. There was blood everywhere. The infamous thief had laid siege to them several days before. He had stolen all the gift supplies that the Khalifah had sent to Mecca and Medina to help for the Hajj. There were also three camels of gold and silver taken. This was a special gift from the Khalifah, intended to feed and clothe the poor Hajjis on pilgrimage. From the back of the caravan, Shaykh Abdul Mabood came forward with the three camels of gold and silver and placed their reins in the hands of their rightful guardians. A roar and cheer went up throughout the two caravans. Shaykh Abdul Mabood was now a hero. As the roar and shouts praising his insight and courage died down, his own Shaykh emerged from the crowd. As he approached Shaykh Abdul Mabood, he bowed slightly, taking Shaykh Abdul Mabood's hand and kissing it, saying from this day forward he was a Shaykh of the *Tariqah*.

This was the story of how Shaykh Abdul Mabood received his *idhn* to be a teaching Shaykh in his own right.

Over One Hundred Years of Pilgrimage

Shaykh Abdul Mabood's wife invited me one night for dinner. It was the first time I had the opportunity to visit and chat with his wife and the rest of his family in a less formal way. That evening I noticed that there was a plaque on the wall, written in Arabic, and sealed with a wax impression that appeared to be the seal of the royal family of Saud. I asked about it and this is what I was told:

> *After he had performed his pilgrimage to Mecca and Medina, Shaykh Abdul Mabood remained in the Hijaz teaching. King Abdul Aziz bin Saud had just recently taken control of the country and was under tremendous pressure from the Wahhabi scholars in Riyadh to control the emerging influence of the Sufis in the Hijaz as well as the Shias and their interests in the shrines of the members of the Prophet's family. Succumbing to their threats, King Abdul Aziz launched a campaign against these two groups by destroying the Sufi shrines of the awliya and those of the Shi`as.*

> *Shaykh Abdul Mabood, after having petitioned the King on many occasions to stop these activities, met with treachery. The king had put a warrant for the Shaykh's arrest. The Shaykh banded together with others wanting to preserve these holy places and waged battles against any army that attempted to hurt or destroy these shrines. The conflict raged on for many months. The warrant for the Shaykh's arrest had become a bounty hunt as the king placed a large sum of gold on Shaykh Abdul Mabood's*

head. After some time, the Shaykh was arrested and brought to stand trial in the court of King Abdul Aziz. The trial lasted for a few minutes, the charges were read and the sentence handed out.

The Shaykh was brought in front of King Abdul Aziz. Shaykh Abdul Mabood's head had already been wrapped in cloth and the axe and chopping block were already in the courtyard of the palace. The king leaned over to the Shaykh and asked if there were any last words. The Shaykh began to recite several poems about the qualities of the Prophet's family and how they should be remembered and cherished for all times. The king was moved to tears. For not only were the words of the Shaykh overwhelmingly beautiful, but the king recognized those poems as having been written by his grandfather and recited to him by his grandmother almost every night.

The king ordered the cloth to be removed from the Shaykh's head and for him to be set free. The king approached Shaykh Abdul Mabood and humbly requested his forgiveness. From that day the king ordered that the shrines and holy places of the Sufis and the Shias be left in peace. As a personal show of gratitude to the Shaykh, the King decreed that from that day forward, Shaykh Abdul Mabood would be the guest of the kingdom on the pilgrimage to Hajj. The kingdom of Saudi Arabia would cover all of his travel expenses and costs to stay in Mecca and Medina. The Shaykh was given an official plaque with this decree. It was this plaque I asked about on the wall.

Prior to receiving this gift, the Shaykh had already performed the Hajj for many years. When I had met him in 1983, he had already completed over 100 pilgrimages to Hajj. As far as we know, he holds the record for attending the pilgrimage.

His wife went on to tell me that Shaykh Abdul Mabood remains in bed most of the year. A few weeks before Hajj, he starts to move around more and a few days before he sets off to Hajj, he walks around, full of energy. She said that his hair turns from white to gray and even turns black as the Hajj approaches. In her time as wife of the Shaykh, he had lost and grown another set of teeth. As a junior wife, she remembered coming into a household of two other senior wives and that the Shaykh had several sets of teeth come in and fall over his lifetime.

Getting the Shaykh's Life Story

I would often contact Shaykh Fadhlalla Haeri about my daily experiences with Shaykh Abdul Mabood, relating the stories and circumstances that have marked his epic life and what impact he has on all those who visit him. Shaykh Fadhlalla asked that I request the Shaykh to dictate his life's story. He asked me to emphasize how it would be inspiring to many as well as deserving to be documented and heard.

On my next visit to the Shaykh, I brought up the idea and asked him to share with me the events, experiences and stories of his life. Upon hearing my request, he shook his head in the negative and, with a cheeky smile, told me that I was too late; there are already two who have taken down his life's history in detail and are keeping it well preserved for when the time is right to enter it into the record.

I was shocked and surprised that it was already done, boy was I naive! I asked where I could reach these most accomplished journalists? He turned, facing me with that glint in his eyes and face and pointed to his right and left shoulders, saying they are here now and have always been with him throughout his life. It clearly dawned on me now, what he was saying, of course! It was the two recording angles that sit upon all our shoulders, recording all of our lives to be included in the record of our life's book to be opened on a day to come, to stand in testimony of who and what we are as we enter the doors of the next experience.

Shaykh Mabood, speaking gently and softly to me, said that these were the only journalists of his life.

Even though the Shaykh declined to share his life's story, I could not let go of the idea of chronicling at least some of his vast and long life and sharing it with others. There is so much there I thought that would benefit others, so I came up with a plan to secretly record him while I was encouraging him to tell his life's story and asking relevant questions.

So, on one of my visits, I hid a tape recorder in my inner coat pocket and strung a microphone down my sleeve to my wrist. I didn't feel altogether right about doing this, but I felt compelled and determined. I came to his home and was welcomed in by his family as usual. I was led into his room and sat down at the edge of his bed as was now the habit of most days while visiting him. Shaykh Mabood normally would greet me and reach under his bed where he would bring out his dinner plate with the five morsels waiting for me, but this time he did not move. He sat still with his head supported by his hands and remained quiet and motionless. I knew something was wrong and that somehow, he knew I had been devious and that he may even had known that I had the recording device under my clothes. After several awkward and uncomfortable minutes, he turned to me and said that if I wanted to hear some of his life's story, I should turn it off. Needless to say, I was embarrassed and felt ashamed to have tried such deception. I immediately opened my coat and removed the recording device and the microphone. He looked at it and then looked at me with the most loving eyes and smiled and said, "OK! I will tell you some stories." His son came into the room to bring tea and remained to translate as the Shaykh generously shared some of the stories and adventures over the last 150 odd years of his life. As the evening went on, he got tired, and we asked permission to leave. I rose up from the bed and put my coat back on and went to kiss his hand as I had become accustomed to just before leaving; but this time, he pulled me back, indicating that I sit down again. He reached under his bed and brought up the plate with his left-over dinner and fed me the five morsels that I had missed earlier. Then we parted.

Diwan Marathon

On another visit to Shaykh Mabood, this time early one morning, I brought him my copy of the complete *Diwan* of Shaykh Muhammad ibn al Habib. Once I placed it in his hands, he inquired what it was. I explained what it was in general and what it meant to me. I sang a sample of it, choosing a short *Qasida* (ode in which God is praised) which he clearly delighted in. His eyesight was very poor and often he would have to bring whatever he read right up against his face, literally an inch or two from his glasses that were at least a quarter of an inch thick as it were. He opened the *Diwan* to the first page and lifted it to his face. This was about 10AM and he did not finish reading the Diwan, reading it entirety by the way, until just before Maghrib. There was a group of people visiting along with myself. No one dared seek permission to leave so as not to disturb the Shaykh's reading. As the Shaykh turned the pages of the Diwan, he would exclaim "*Subhan Allah* (Glory be to God)" loudly, or "*Allahu Akbar*," only lowering the book from his face to rest his arms and at one point to excuse whomever wanted to leave. At the end of this marathon session with the Diwan, he finally reached the last page, put the *Diwan* down and turned to me and said, "This is Good, really good!"

The Wing Commander

As mentioned above, I was asked by Shaykh Fadhlalla to research Shaykh Abdul Maboob's life for the possibility of writing his biography and what happened when I brought up the idea with him. Here, I will add another attempt of mine.

I asked one of his close students if there was any one person who had known the Shaykh and his life details the best. I was told about a wing commander, who was currently serving in the air force and stationed in Peshawar.

Peshawar in 1983 was a teeming town, full of traders, fighters, refugees and western government agents. The streets were filled with fighters from all over the Muslim world. There were Uzbeks, Tadjiks and even a spattering of Africans and Americans. Guns were everywhere and the air was filled with the excitement of men returning from battle. Traders of all kinds of contraband were tugging at the arms of everyone. You could buy anything in Peshawar, from opium to anti-tank missiles. There was no enforcement of law, only the law of the tribes and the strength of the fittest.

I made my way to the air force base outside the city. It was an unassuming air base with little bungalows and not an aircraft in sight. It looked more like a Boy Scout camp than a military base. I was escorted to the officers' lounge and was asked to wait until the officer I was looking for was located. After some time, I was escorted again to a small office on the outside of the camp. A private, who was the secretary of the wing commander I had come to visit, greeted me. He asked me the nature of my visit, and when I explained it to him, he was surprisingly not surprised, though it was an irregular reason for visiting an air force base. But this was Pakistan, and I had come to appreciate the common saying that "anything is possible in Pakistan."

While waiting to see the wing commander, I was served tea. Everything was very typical and nothing out of the ordinary. After some time, I was led into the inner office where the wing commander was waiting. We greeted each other and he immediately came down to business and asked me why I had come. When I mentioned Shaykh Abdul Mabood and the purpose of my visit, the wing commander changed his stance completely. He froze and did not move for some time. His eyes became red, and I could see that he was trembling. I asked if he was all right, and he nodded in the affirmative. He said that he was unable to tell me anything. I pushed a bit and told him that he had come highly recommended by several of the Shaykh's students. I said that I had come all the way up here to see him in this regard and I did not want to leave empty handed. The wing commander froze again for a few moments and said that he would ask his guide and oracle if he had the permission to speak to me. He excused himself for a few minutes while he inquired and said that I should remain here and wait for him. I agreed and waited.

I waited and waited, minutes turned into hours, and by now most of the day had passed. I kept inquiring (to the secretary) about the wing commander and was reassured that the wing commander would keep his word. I had now been there for about 3 hours when I heard a strange sound coming from behind the door to the next room. With the sound I felt the wood floor beneath me give way a bit and then return with a vibrating sound. At first, I thought nothing of it; maybe it was an aircraft landing or some machinery. The sound and the vibrations became more intense. They were definitely coming from the hall or rooms nearby. The private secretary stood up suddenly; I could see panic in his face. He left the room. Before leaving, he told me not to be concerned, and that the wing commander was on his way to see me. I was perplexed, what did the noise and the wing commander coming to see me have in common?

The sound from the other room became louder and louder, the floor was bending deeper and was increasing in vibrations. Then the sound was in the next room, and when I stood up, in a knee jerk reaction, the door flew open, and from it, the wing commander leaped out. He threw himself into the air and landed with a crushing and clanging sound that was nearly deafening.

He was covered head to toe with steel rings and chains. His head had a metal cap on it, with a spike coming up from the middle. This was attached to his head with small chains that came up from a neck brace, which was locked on him by a huge padlock. Each arm had eight or nine iron rings wrapped around it from the upper shoulder to his wrists. Around his body, there was like a suit of armor, but dull and thick, like ship plating. His legs were like his arms covered in irons; each ring had a chain attached to it, which connected in two directions, upwards towards his waist and downwards to his feet. On his feet, he wore iron clogs with nails between his toes. In one hand, was a spear and, in the other, a begging bowl shaped like a gourd also made from cast iron.

He leaped and wailed, walking around me. Half the time he danced like a mad man, the other half leaping uncontrollably into the air and crashing down, on the floor, unable to hold the weight of what he was wearing.

I stood in shock. My mind was still. I could only witness. It went on in a frenzy for about thirty minutes. The floor beneath heaving and bending, the pictures and plaques on the walls fell from their mountings. His voice grew louder and his speech more obscure.

The sounds of the chains grew louder and louder, clanging and clinging, almost deafening to the ears. In his hand a spear, moving up and down as though in preparation for an attack. He went on and on in a trance-like state. I could see the exhaustion on his face, but that paled compared to the look in his eyes, and his occasional glance at me swept me out into his world. I had to hide my eyes, as I feared getting lost in his glance. With all the drama of a final act of theater, the wing commander collapsed on the floor near where I was sitting. His body trembled and tears were flowing from his eyes. He looked at me and then, with a surprisingly lucid voice said: "I am unable and unworthy to even speak about a being whose blessed feet have touched the holy places over a hundred times." With that he closed his eyes and passed out.

He awoke after a few moments; his eyes had returned to the present, and he apologized if he had startled me with his appearance and carrying on. He explained that he had become a member of a sect of Sufis that wore irons and weights to symbolize the prison of the body to the soul. Thus, chains were an example of the attachments we have to this world. He danced and chanted to tune himself to the souls of enlightened beings, to directly receive their advice and teachings. As we spoke, I felt that he was being sincere in the desire to help me, but that it was beyond his ability at this time. He looked up into my eyes and asked me to forgive him all the trouble he might have caused. At that very touching moment, a bird landed on the windowsill next to where we were positioned and began to sing the loveliest song. The golden light of the afternoon sun graced our faces as we both enjoyed the message of our little friend. No words were spoken after this moment. The wing commander got up, with some difficulty, I must say. I stood up and we both left the room at the same time.

Shaykh Abdul Mabood Jilani died on 30th November 1985 (16th Rabi-ul-Awwal 1406 AH). He was 162 years old, give or take.

Before he died, he gave me a formula that when recited in difficult and overwhelming situations, would bring about resolve in your favor. It was revealed to him on a battlefield while fighting the British somewhere in history. Being outnumbered and outflanked, he turned to Allah, requesting His help. He heard the voice of an angel speak to him with the following phrase:

Hasbi Rabbi Murabbi (My reliance is on my Lord sustainer who sustained).

Repeat 100 times, followed by a salutation to the Prophet Muhammad. He told me to share it with others. I offer it up here for anyone in the path of Allah to use when turning to your Creator in an overpowering circumstance.

The Autonomous Tribal Areas

After meeting with the wing commander, I returned to Peshawar where I remained for several days exploring the city. I had met a local, Safdar Khan, who acted as my guide and introduced me to many wonderful people. He had met Shaykh Fadhlalla in Karachi at one point and, when he heard that I was coming to Peshawar, he generously offered to make introductions for me. Just past Peshawar, near the border with Afghanistan, are the tribal areas that are pretty much autonomous. These areas are self-governing, loosely administered by the central government. Foreigners are encouraged not to enter this area, adding a disclaimer that the government was not responsible for any mishap that might occur while visiting those areas.

Safdar Khan insisted I visit those areas, where there were many tribal locals eager to meet me. We set off through the Khyber Pass and entered Afghanistan. Along the way, we came to a military checkpoint where traffic was held up while papers were checked, mostly truck drivers' licenses were reviewed for legitimacy. Also, there was a lot of drugs and weapons trade on this road. The checkpoints acted as a deterrent for these activities. While waiting in line for our turn to pass through, a group of armed Pashtuns was approaching us from the side of our vehicle. They came upon us abruptly. I sensed some hostility focused on us and, as I was assessing the moment, one of them lifted the barrel of his gun and held it to my cheek. I froze, and my host vehemently objected. Then both broke out laughing; the barrel came off my face, and while my assailant was still giggling, he reached in and hugged me, asking me to forgive him, explaining it was only a joke. You can imagine that I was remiss in appreciating the humor of the gesture. We all got out of the car, and greetings were exchanged along with much embarrassment from the one who pointed his weapon at me.

I learned later that these were friends, and some were relatives of Safdar Khan. They were expecting our arrival and were waiting at the checkpoint. They were there to escort us to their village. The man who had put his gun to my face was a known assassin and smuggler. It was some consolation that he was a distant relative of my host; it was his unique expression of welcoming me, deranged as it was.

My host gave me insight as to why; this area was rife with assassins and smugglers. Assassins could carry out their deeds in Pakistan proper and retreat, over the border, where they could easily disappear in the no-man's land of the tribal areas. Smuggling was rife in this area due to its proximity and shared borders with China, Afghanistan, Indian administered Kashmir & Tajikistan. Chinese goods were heavily taxed and tariffed when shipped directly into Pakistan through normal channels. It became commonplace that a well-connected Pakistani could order items from China, have them smuggled into the tribal areas, and delivered by smugglers for a reasonable fee. While I was in the territories, I witnessed air conditioners as well as refrigerators being hauled by camels as we waited at official checkpoints. The Pakistani authorities turned a blind eye to this activity, many being on the payroll of the smugglers.

The tribal areas were also a reserve of traditional Pashtun culture and traditions. During my stay among the local villagers, I came to appreciate their way of life. Many of those I interviewed defended their customs and vehemently expressed they would not want to have it any other way. During our departure from the tribal areas, we personally got to experience their traditional application of tribal law when our car was damaged on the trunk road on our way back to Punjab. The story follows.

The Car Accident and the Local *Jirga*

We arrived at the village compound of the local tribal people, staying with them for about three days. At that time, we were informed about the skirmishes in some areas, which I thought were on the Afghan border but still in Pakistan because the borderline wasn't clear to me, but I later realized that the area where the skirmishes took place was across the border and within Afghanistan. Many Russians were captured and killed. There were always armed guards wherever we went while visiting other small villages and shrines. I began to appreciate the semi-autonomous life of the people who lived in these tribal areas. Especially after we were on our way back to Peshawar on the main trunk road out of the tribal areas, when our car was side-swiped by a commercial truck, basically ripping the front and side panels off our car, which made it impossible to drive back. We all got out of the car, a crowd of local bystanders and road vendors who had witnessed the crash gathered around us. After some time, they split into two distinct groups, one advocating for us as the victim and the other, seemingly taking the truck driver's side, defending him in front of our new litigation committee. A local official, representing the tribal elders arrived, calming down the ever-increasing emotions that were developing in the crowd. We were asked to bring our case to the local *Jirga* (or *Jirgah* is a council of tribal leaders), where a group of the local elders were already in session hearing other cases and passing judgments; our case was expedited to be heard immediately.

The *Jirga* was taking place in a large open room with only a few chairs and small serving tables scattered around the room. Deep red Afghan and Baluch tribal carpets lined the floors. Large raised Divan seating lined the perimeter of the room, where everyone sat close to the floor. The walls were covered with tapestries, carpets, and many samples of local craftsmanship: copper plaques, brass items and lots of handmade weaponry manufactured locally, especially samples of the AK-47, a local favorite.

We were asked to come forward, the truck driver and our group moved to the front of the room. They heard us both out, each relating our version of events that led to the crash. The elders called for witnesses, and there were several that came from the site of the accident. After the hearing, the elders counseled openly with each other on the matter, surprisingly arriving with a swift judgment. They determined that it was the fault of the truck driver, that he was seen swerving his truck to avoid a collision after veering over to oncoming traffic. What followed was the most unique outcome I had ever seen and exemplified the character and veracity of the tribal counsel's fair and generous practice of justice. The head elder pointed to a trunk that was sitting at the side of the room to be brought over to the front where we were all sitting. The trunk was clearly ancient, banded with hand-beaten iron over lacquered hardwood. There were iron chains strapped around for an added layer of security. The chest was so heavy it took two men struggling to carry it over, touching the ground with a loud thump. The chains were removed, and the trunk opened. I was close enough to peer into the trunk. It was filled with stacks of banded currencies. They were predominantly Pakistani Rupees, but there were also numerous stacks of US dollars, British pounds, and others I did not recognize. There were also small to medium leather bags that clanged as they moved, hinting precious metals. The elder's hands emerged out of the trunk with several stacks of Rupees. He called us forward to accept the cash as restitution for the damage inflicted on our vehicle as well as enough funds to stay locally until our vehicle was repaired. He then turned to the driver, having found him at fault, admonished and ordered him to pay back the Elders' Counsel for the cash they had provided us as well as a hefty fine for reckless driving. I was so impressed with how they handled this situation. In a Western court, there would be court dates and court dates postponed, lawyers involved, often costing more than the damage reimbursement – all in all much more complex and convoluted.

After the elders finished speaking to the driver, he turned to us and apologized on behalf of the people and to the Elders Court for the incident.

I was perplexed and wondered how they were able to extend the restitution to us on behalf of the driver. We discovered that all truck drivers had to have local permission to drive through their territories. The permits were costly and the business that utilized the main truck roads that were essential for trade and transport of goods and services, after all it was the only road connecting the tribal areas of Pakistan proper with Afghanistan. The employers vouched for their drivers and were contracted to make good any fines or levies that may be charged against them.

After only an astonishing 24 hours, our car was repaired good as new and we returned to Peshawar.

Invitation for Jihad

Meeting with Tajik Mujahedeen

It wasn't but a few days after returning from the tribal areas that I had a chance meeting with a group of Tajik Mujahedeen taking a break in Peshawar. I was having lunch at a local restaurant when we started up a conversation. They were intrigued that I was a new Muslim and kept me engaged in conversation with them for several hours. Their *Amir* invited me to travel to their base camp, just inside Afghanistan, about five miles from the frontline of engagement with the Russian military. I was very hesitant to accept their invitation, but the *Amir* pressed me, saying that his men would be inspired by my presence and that he would personally guarantee my safety. He underscored the point that it was not too far from the NWFP[13] border and a safe distance from the actual fighting. I guess being young with a highly developed sense of adventure, I agreed to go with them to their base camp.

We were to leave the next morning at dawn.

The Tajiks came to my hotel as promised, arriving in a caravan of Mitsubishi SUVs. I was invited into the lead car and sat with the *Amir* until we reached the NWFP/Afghanistan border, where there was the first Pakistani checkpoint. I had just been there a few days ago and it was all too familiar. I felt a bit of trepidation, more than the last time I came through, especially since I had a rifle pointed at my head. The Tajik *Amir* asked that I lie down in the back storage area and cover myself with a blanket. He said that the authorities might be touchy about them being with a foreigner, especially traveling onward towards Afghanistan. I hid in the back until we cleared the checkpoint. We traveled through Jamrud, which is a small village settlement near to the Khyber Pass.

Jamrud is infamous for local manufactures of the AK-47 and a Bazaar full of illegally imported items from the Border States. We stopped there for an hour or so. I got a chance to walk around and visit some of the manufacturing stalls that lined a designated part of the village where weapons were being manufactured. It was amazing to see their ingenuity in making the replicas of the famous Russian rifle. They cast steel right into molds in the ground, molds that they made themselves with the most rudimentary equipment. They also produced bullets. There were many other items, several I could not off hand identify, but there was a lot of

---

[13] North West Frontier Province, of Pakistan, now called, Khyber Pakhtunkhwa, borders Afghanistan. The tribal areas are within this province, but they have historically been pretty much autonomous.

activity, each stall was busy churning out their special brand of weaponry. I also saw delivery trucks marked clearly with Made in the USA on their crates. These were the same crates I had seen in the movies that carry guns and ammunition.

We arrived at the base camp in the late afternoon. I knew before we arrived that we were close, as I could hear the thunder and blasts of ordnance in the distance.

On approach to the Tajik camp, we passed a broken-down mud structure that was guarded by several armed men. The *Amir* pointed it out to me, saying it was where they kept Russian prisoners. He said that he would take me back here sometime later to see them.

The base camp was set up in an old abandoned schoolhouse. There were lots of activities around the compound, armed militia, Tajik, Baluch, and I was told also some Hazara as well, manning the camp. They invited me into the main meeting hall, introducing me to the *Amir*'s commanders and some more of his men. The room was crowded with several dozen fighters. They had prepared a special welcoming lunch for us.

I sat down near the front with the *Amir*. He had gone for a meeting, leaving me uncomfortably behind with the other Mujahedeen. Although I was met with warm greetings by most, several of the fighters looked at me with suspicion and concern. They had been infiltrated before by spies and agents and took a cautious approach with me. Some glared at me like they were about to question me.

Eating a Meal with My Right Hand

The food was ready to be served. Young men brought table cloths made of hand-woven tribal designs. They stretched them out in front of where we were all sitting. After the table cloths were in place, large platters overflowing with rice, meat, raisons, pine nuts and herbs were evenly placed along the table spread. There was another round of platters full of freshly baked Tandoori flat breads and salads as well. No one began to eat, just yet. They were all waiting for the *Amir* to return. Before he came in the room, another platter was brought in that elicited some smirks and comments that passed around the room. It was a tray especially for me that contained a Western style place setting with serviettes, proper forks, and a knife as well as a separate glass for water. The *Amir* arrived and with the invocation of *Bismillah*, everyone reached in with their hands and began eating. I was uncomfortably singled out with this tray setting. Some of the fighters glanced at me in a way that made me feel awkward, as an outsider. I wasn't going to have any of this, so I moved the tray away from me and said, *Bismillah*, and reached in with my right hand, rolling a large ball of rice and meat and depositing it enthusiastically in my mouth. The men around me noticed, and smiles and laughter broke out. The fighter right next to me shook his head in an affirmative manner, slapping me on the back and declaring, *Masha'Allah!* You Muslim, *Alhamdulillah!* (Thank God!) From that moment on, the stares of suspicion and concern evaporated. I was transformed and accepted as "one of the brothers."

That night, I was escorted to an open area where the men had built a bonfire and were sitting around in conversation and drinking the local sweet green tea. I was asked so many questions about my conversion to Islam and how Islam was spreading in the West. Most of the men had never met one or even thought that there could be American Muslims. There was an overflowing of joy and happiness that flowed between us that evening and, from then on, I was treated as one of them, with some deference to my being their guest.

The next morning, I met with the *Amir* in the main meeting hall. He informed me that he would be gone until the afternoon, but he was leaving me in the good hands of his youngest son Ahmed.

A Young Tajik Man's Family History

Ahmed and I got on well from the get-go. You could observe in his manner and etched in his face, that a young man, not yet in his twenties, had seen and done things that no young person should endure. He shared with me a little of his family history, especially what led up to them forming a Tajik militia to fight off the Russians. They lost everything; their village and way of life were erased when the Soviets invaded. He also recalled to me that this was not the first time that they as a people experienced this level of upheaval. During the British attempt to occupy Afghanistan, they experienced similar oppression and destruction. He was proud of his heritage as an ethnic Tajik as well as an Afghan. Ahmed shared with me that, by the time an Afghani boy reached the age of six, he was already familiar with weapons, able to shoot, and clean and maintain a rifle in good order.

Cache of Weapons

Later that afternoon, Ahmed took me to a weapons storage bunker to show me their cache of weapons and ordnance. In the corner of the bunker was a small, locked room that Ahmed opened on the direction of his father to show me what special types of weapons they had collected over time. One was especially pointed out to me, an antique British Enfield Rifle, fully restored and ready to use. He picked it up and handed it to me as a gift from his father. It came with a bandoleer worn across one's chest full of matching caliber bullets for the Enfield. I was taken aback by being offered this gift. I was initially intrigued, it being an antique and all, but it came with a conditional message from Ahmed's father that I should be armed while I was at the camp, to be ready for any unexpected events. It was a harsh and true reality that this camp was not a country club, but it was a forward positioned camp to stage raids on the front lines and in Kabul, which was but a few hours away.

Tragic Loss of the Eldest Son

That night, we gathered again in the main meeting room. The *Amir* turned to me during a session of sharing stories of their exploits in engaging the Russians. I could see that his eyes were tearing up as he began to tell me a story of how he lost his eldest son in a recent raid in Kabul. They had intelligence that a KGB cell had set up in the basement of a house in Kabul. He, his son and a small contingent of his men breached the basement of the house, while his son laid explosive charges to destroy the facility. The room was already full of electronic and satellite communication devices. Once the charges were laid, they would detonate from a safe distance. His son was the last one left in the building when KGB agents became aware of the plot and rushed into the basement and seized his son. The *Amir* was watching through binoculars as his son was arrested and the agents were about to dismantle the charges. In a split moment decision, he ordered the detonation, blowing up the building with his son. He painfully explained that it was the only choice to make. He knew that the Russians would torture his son to death and the decision to blow up the building was the best for his son and their cause. I reached over and touched his arm, he wept openly, and the men around lowered their heads and collectively mourned their loss.

After a minute or two, he looked up, smiled and declared that his son was a *Shaheed* (a martyr) and that he was now honored both in this world and the next. Upon his declaration, everyone in the room shouted *Allahu Akbar* repeatedly, gaining courage and fortitude from each word, acknowledging the sacrifice his son made and the decision he had to take when he ordered the blast sealing his son's fate. He then looked at me and said that he would take me as his son and encouraged me to consider joining them actively in their Jihad against the Russians. Although I was deeply touched, I declined his offer. I told him that I was not a fighter and that in any case I would be a detriment to anyone fighting with me. I told him that I would be too afraid and most likely be paralyzed with fear if I even attempted such an endeavor. He smiled at me, saying, "Don't you think we are all afraid?" He went on to say that when you are in the moment, facing death fighting for justice against tyranny and oppression, Allah takes away your fear and replaces it with abandonment for the promise of high station in the hereafter.

I insisted that I was not suited for this and asked him to be excused from his consideration. He smiled, accepting my response and said that Jihad is on many levels, not everyone fights with a gun, but some with words that support God's aims here and all over the world. He thanked me for coming and he shared that my presence among his men encouraged them and was inspiring for them. He shared a vision that their cause is more than local, but universal.

The next morning, we departed. The men lined the road and bid me farewell.

The *Qalandars* of Islamabad & The *Pir* of Dewal Sharif

For the better part of a year, we were living in Islamabad, the capital city of Pakistan. Some of our friends rented a home in the prestigious section of the city, near Margalla Road, which hugged the foothills of the Himalayas and was the main route to Murree – a famous vacation-stop in Pakistan and a transit point for people visiting Pakistani Kashmir. Our center was in a section called F7.

My wife Nafisa had left for the States, and I remained alone for the next six months.

I recently met Mushahid Hussain, who was the editor-in-chief of the Pakistani English newspaper called, "The Muslim." He offered me a position as an English editor, which I accepted and worked daily in their offices in Islamabad. It was during this period I met Shaykh Mahboob and the Qalandar Sufis that attended the Shrine of Bari Imam.

The Shrine of Bari Imam in Islamabad

The shrine was just outside Islamabad commemorating the great Sufi saint, Shah Abdul Latif Kazmi, also known as Bari Imam, or Bari Sarkar (1617 – 1705).

Bari Imam was a 17th-century Sufi ascetic from Punjab, who was one of the most prominent Sufis of the Qadiriyya order of his time.

He is venerated as the patron saint of Islamabad[14] in Pakistan.

He was born in the district of Chakwal to a family descended from the Prophet Muhammad, through the linage of Imam Musa al-Kadhim.

---

[14] The shrine of Bari Imam was located outside the historical city of Rawalpindi in a place called Noorpur Shahan. A new city of Islamabad was built outside of Rawalpindi in the 1960's as the new capital of Pakistan, whose original capital was Karachi. Islamabad then grew to include Noorpur Shahan.

What we know of the life of Bari Imam is known essentially through oral tradition as well as numerous poems and songs written and catalogued in various publications that contain teachings from Sufi saints of both India and Pakistan. Bari Imam remains one of the most popular and venerated saints of Punjab.

Shaykh Fadhlalla had visited the shrine and asked me to visit Bari Imam every Thursday night. I was to sit by his tomb and sing from the *Diwan* of Shaykh Muhammad ibn al Habib. For the better part of six months, I visited the shrine as instructed.

Refusing to Become *Mureed* of *Pir* of Dewal Sharif

On one of these visits, I was walking through the courtyard surrounding the shrine on my way to the building that housed Bari Imam. I noticed a large group of people sitting in the courtyard near the entrance of the mausoleum. As I passed by, one of the people stood up and approached me and requested that I come and meet their *Pir* who was present with them. I was always up to meeting and connecting with local Sufis, so I accepted his invitation and joined the circle around their *Pir*. I was introduced to their Shaykh, the *Pir* of Dewal Sharif. From the moment I sat down, I felt uneasy – my stomach tightened and generally felt on guard. The *Pir* requested me to sit in front of him. Urging me close, sitting knee to knee, he grabbed my face and through an English-speaking interpreter, said to me that, from the moment he saw me, he recognized me as his *mureed*. I answered him politely, saying that although it was an honor to be invited to his circle, I already had a Shaykh and thanked him again for his offer, but I must refuse. Upon my decline of the *Pir's* offer, many of his *mureeds* shouted at me; they chastised me for refusing the offer. The *Pir* himself pushed further, saying that he was my real teacher, and that any other *Pir* was less than his status and argued for me to reconsider. At that point, I was taken over by my instincts and went into flight or fight mode, choosing flight, I stood up and, without further ado, I quickly walked away. As I walked away, I heard those around the *Pir*, hurling insults at me, some I believe were cursing me for my refusal to surrender to their *Pir*.

A *Malang Qalandar* Protecting Me from the *Pir* of "Devil" Sharif

I returned to my mission, walking towards the tomb of Bari Imam, to sing and make *Du`a*, under the canopy of the *Wali's Barakah*. Before entering the tomb, there is a series of columns that line the entryway to the mausoleum. Sensing a presence, I then noticed there was a *Malang*

Qalandar (permanent inhabitant of the shrine) hidden behind the upcoming column. As I passed him, he grabbed my arm and pulled me behind the pillar. He spoke perfect English, asking me with sarcasm what the *Pir* of "Devil" Sharif said to me. I shared what happened and he laughed; shaking his head profusely, he said we must make him pay for his abuse of me. I explained to him that I was not interested in pay-back in any way against the *Pir* and that all I wanted to do was carry on to the shrine. The *Qalandar* said that he had been observing me for several months and that if it were not for his presence at the shrine, I would never have been able to fulfill my instructions from my *Pir*. He said that he was protecting me this whole time and that it was now urgently needed to come with him and confront the Evil *Pir* once and for all, making it clear that I was under the umbrella of the *Qalandars* and to leave me be. Hand in hand, we moved towards the circle where the *Pir* of Dewal Sharif was sitting. As we grew closer, the *Qalandar* asked me to observe the condition of the *Pir* and his students when we approached. What followed next was nothing short of a miracle. The *Pir* and his *mureeds* started to moan, several rolled over onto the ground holding their stomachs as though they were in great pain. As we moved even closer, the *Qalandar* began to laugh. He repeated over and over "*a`udhu billahi mina Shaytan ir Rajim* (I seek refuge in Allah from the outcast *Shaytan*)." The *Pir* stood up with all his *mureeds* and fled the Imam's compound. The *Qalandar* said that evil cannot remain when a *Qalandar* is truly present. He claimed that if he had come any closer to the group, some of them might even have died.

From that day forward, whenever I returned to Bari Imam, the *Qalandars* of the shrine greeted me with great warmth and assured me that all was, and will be, good during my visit. I often would sit with them for a while before entering the tomb. They would share stories of their lineage and how many of the *Malang Qalandars* present at this shrine have special gifts and *Karamat* (Supernatural wonders), mostly unknown or publicized to anyone, but they knew among each other.

At a *Qalandar's* Home

After some months of regular visits, one of the *Qalandars* invited me to his home in Islamabad for dinner. I was surprised that he even had a home. If you saw him at the shrine, wearing ragged clothes, his hair matted and his body covered in beads and chains, you would think that he lived in the jungle or something similar. We walked to his home near the shrine; it was a traditional mud constructed house with palm leaves for a roof. There was, however, a kitchen and sitting area appointed with several nice Sindhi mats and carpets. There was a woman cooking food. I didn't inquire if she was his wife or servant, but when the food was ready, she brought it outside to the back of the house where there was a small walled courtyard. We ate and had tea and exchanged many stories; mostly he did all the storytelling. I asked him if he had a special *Karamat?* He rolled up his lungi and showed me his legs that were riddled with cobra and scorpion bites. He claimed that no poison could kill him, let alone affect him in a bad way. He even claimed that being bit made him feel strong, strength in the form of total reliance on God being his healer and protector.

That was the last time I visited the shrine of Bari Imam as I soon returned to Karachi on my way back to the States.

More Extraordinary Encounters in Pakistan

Lonely in Pakistan / Meeting a Generous Host

During the last few weeks in Pakistan, I had moved from Islamabad to Rawalpindi, staying in a house that belonged to relatives of Dr. Khalid Iqbal. It was a modest home in a sub-middle-class neighborhood, in a very busy and noisy part of Rawalpindi. I was offered a small room in the upstairs of the house. The owners of the house were no longer living there and the only place that had a bed and cupboard was a storage room converted to a sleeping room originally intended for a housemaid or cook.

The bed in the room took up two thirds of the space and with the cupboard it was difficult to negotiate the space for anything but sleeping. Outside the room was a stair landing that I used to pray; it was the only space big enough to lay out a prayer mat.

It was a very lonely time for me. The house in Islamabad was closed down and everyone I knew from there was either gone or traveling. It would be a few weeks before I could leave the country. Out of loneliness I increased my correspondence with my wife Nafisa as well as the rest of my friends and family back in the States. I had compiled a stack of unsent mail and one evening I decided to make my way to the GPO (General Post Office) in downtown Rawalpindi. It was open twenty-four hours a day, so at about midnight I set out and arrived at the GPO on a local rickshaw. The GPO was indeed open, and surprisingly there was a line waiting at the only open window to buy stamps and mail items. I entered the back of the line and noticed a finely dressed man come behind me. What first drew my attention to him was that he wore a Chishti Cap or hat, and his shoulders were draped in a beautiful white scarf that reminded me of a scarf I had purchased in Mecca when I went for Umrah (Minor Hajj) last. There was also the scent of Oudh that wafted over me, my most favorite perfume oil.

After a few moments, our eyes met again, but this time, there was a palpable sense that we had met before, but I could not place the where and when. As I contemplated exploring with him, i.e., where we might have met, he tapped my shoulder; I turned and he opened his arms, coming in for a big hug. He was so excited, I was also, but I had not yet connected where we knew each other. By this time, I really didn't care. I was so lonely; it was enough to meet someone so enthusiastic. He then unfolded the story of how we met. Several years ago, while visiting Saudi

Arabia, in which we met with Crown Prince Sultan at his royal palace, we also made an Umrah before heading out to Riyadh for that meeting. During our stay in Mecca, we regularly patronized a small restaurant directly across from the Harem Sharif (The Great Mosque of Mecca, which surrounds the *Ka`ba*). It was owned and operated by a Yemini family. They specialized in roasted chickens freshly baked in a traditional mud oven. Regardless of the many evenings and daily visits to this establishment, we never had to pay for our food. When we asked for the bill, the waiter would always say it had been covered. One evening, we were determined to find out who had been paying for us in hopes to thank him. The waiter pointed him out just as the food arrived at our table. We decided to eat first and then approach our generous host to express our gratitude. But after finishing the meal, he had already gone, but not before I had clearly seen his face, sealing it in my memory, musing that someday we would meet again, and I could thank him properly for his generosity. Today, that day had finally come.

The same man was standing right behind me in the lineup in the middle of the night. We met years later in a country far from the Arabian Peninsula. We were both in tears, so happy to meet after so many years. We were awestruck and recalled together the Qur'anic saying in chapter 8, verse 63, "Only Allah can bring the hearts together." We rejoiced in each other's company and in the awesome majesty of God's decree. From that moment until I left Rawalpindi my loneliness ceased.

Urs of a Chishti Shaykh

I explained my circumstances to him. He said it could not have been a better time for us to meet as he was there for a weeks-long celebration of the *Urs* of his Chishti Shaykh that was being held in various locations through the Islamabad and Rawalpindi area. That very night we left together, arriving at a hall in Rawalpindi that was vibrating with the sound of Qawwali singers, people dancing in ecstasy, pots and pans clanging as a stream of endless food was being served to all including a line of poor being fed into the early morning hours. I entered the main hall, found my place near to the front where the *Qawwals* were singing, and was immediately swept away in an overwhelming presence of remembrance of the One and Only, and my loneliness was only a faint past memory. We celebrated for days. During the daylight hours we visited his Sufi friends, sharing intimate stories and experiences on the Sufi Path. In the evenings we gathered for *dhikr* in circles that united every heart together into one vibrating entity, overflowing with the Light of Remembrance of the Ever-

Present Oneness.

There could not have been a better send off for me than these last few days in Pakistan. I left, reluctantly. I had come to consider Pakistan my home, a place I imagined remaining in forever, living and dying in this blessed land. It was, however, not my destiny, and although I traveled extensively in the world after my stay in Pakistan, even living in various countries, Pakistan always remained in my heart as the only place I had ever considered my home.

Meeting the Agha Khan

During my last week in Markaz, F7 in Islamabad, I had left the house during a warm Ramadan afternoon. I walked around our neighborhood to cool off from the blistering heat of the day. F7 straddled Margalla Road on the north side and Srinagar Highway to the south. A few blocks away were the Karimabad Jamaat Center, where the local Ismailia Community met for their prayers and celebrations. I had no particular route in mind later that afternoon. I found myself walking towards the Ismaili Center. There was a large group of men walking towards me. I could make out the stragglers at the end of their line coming out of the Center. They were all huddling around a central point in the crowd, but from a distance I could not make out what the entire hubbub was about. As I grew closer to the crowd, I noticed they were surrounding an individual who was, by the body language of everyone around him, revered immensely. At the time I had no idea who it was, until I caught up with them on the roadside, where they had stopped for a moment to listen to the man at the center of the gaggle of devotees. As I passed, I greeted everyone with Salaams, and their honored guests also answered back wishing peace upon me as well. He reached out to one of his followers near him to invite me to meet and greet, and extended his hand to me and introduced himself as Shah Karim al-Hussaini. Everyone around us seemed astonished and looked upon me with an almost glazed admiration that at the time I could not understand. Karim asked me what I was doing in Islamabad, we chatted for no longer than a minute, when one of Karim's colleagues indicated that it was time to move on and, after exchanging Salaams, we departed their company. As they left, several of the men walking by me told me how blessed I was to have met and shaken the hand of His Holiness the Agha Khan.

From that point on, until this day, my friends and business associates that are Ismaili, always show special deference to me. If there is another Ismaili that just met me, when they hear I have met the Agha Khan, they immediately show respect towards me. I am very moved by their love and dedication to the Agha Khan. There is no doubt that he is a great man in the way he has touched so many hearts.

Visiting Taxila and Meeting Kala Baba

While living in Islamabad, I traveled to the town of Taxila. This town and the area around are known as the crossroads of the famous ancient trade routes, including the Silk Road.

Taxila is one of the most important archeological sites in the world. It is a city that is very well known for having strong ties and being the center of Buddhism in the country. Many statues of Buddha depicting the various stages of his life have been excavated and are currently present both at the Taxila museum as well as various stupas in the city; however, the best of these statues were plundered by various colonialists and taken abroad and displayed in museums around the world.

One of the oldest, and maybe the oldest recognized university in the world, is also present in Taxila. This university came into being in the Gandhara[15] period. At one stage, it had 10,500 students, including those from Babylon, Greece, Syria, and China. Experienced teachers from all over the world taught languages, Vedas, philosophy, medicine, politics, warfare, accounts, commerce, documentation, music, dance, and other performing arts including futurology, the occult and mystical sciences and complex mathematical calculations.

Taxila was in ancient times known in the local language, Pali, as *Takkasila*. The city's Sanskrit name, *Takshashila*, means "City of Cut Stone." The city's ancient Sanskrit name alternately means "Rock of *Taksha*" in reference to the Ramayana story that states the city was founded by Baharata, younger brother of the central Hindu deity Rama and named in honor of Bharata's son, Taksha.

The great Indian epic, the Mahabharata was, according to tradition, first recited at Taxila at the great snake sacrifice of King Janamejaya, one of the heroes of the story.

Buddhist literature, especially the *Jataka*s, mentions it as the capital of the kingdom of Gandhara and as a great center of learning.

---

[15] Historical region that encompassed Kabul, Peshawar, Swat, Texila and extended across the Indus River into other areas like Potohar, Punjab, Bamyan and Karakoram.

When Alexander the Great invaded India in 326 BCE, Ambhi (Omphis), the ruler of Taxila, surrendered the city and placed his resources at Alexander's disposal. Greek historians accompanying the Macedonian conqueror described Taxila as "wealthy, prosperous, and well governed."

I hired a taxi in Rawalpindi for the day to take me to Taxila, having in mind that I would visit all the historical sites and museums and return in the late evening but, as the Qur'an reminds in chapter 8, verse 30, "...[they] plan, and Allah plans. And Allah is the best of planners."

As we approached the outskirts of Taxila, I noticed the topography of the land in the near distance and found it unusual in that it appeared to have a series of mounds or small hillocks waving across the horizon of sight from the highway. It intrigued me at first, which was followed by a feeling of compulsion to explore this area by foot. I asked the taxi driver to pull over and let me out. I asked him to wait there on the road, assuring him that I would return soon and continue our journey. He showed me his stack of tins, full of food and a large bottle of water, and said that he had what he needed and told me to take my time.

I crossed into the open fields that meandered through the hillocks. Along the way, I came across a few shepherds tending their sheep and goats. One shepherd, in particular, stood out as he led his sheep away from the flat grassy areas where the other shepherds were grazing their flocks to the side of a large mound that had a peculiar array of what appeared to be pipes protruding from the top of the hill. I also thought, strangely enough, that I saw TV antennae as well. I followed the shepherd up the hill and discovered half way up that a stone path had been laid leading up and around the mound to the other side of the hill facing away from the road from where I had just come. I followed the path, coming around the bend of the hill. The path continued in front of me. Looking ahead, I noticed the path went up to the last third of the mound, where there was a door, framed in stone, set right into the mound itself. While getting closer to the door, I noticed that the protrusions from the top of the hill were, as I thought, pipes and there was a large TV antenna as well.

The shepherd had not yet seen me – he was well ahead of me. I saw him approach the door. He then pulled it open and led the sheep and goats through it. He looked back before entering the mound himself, which I guessed he did to check for strays. It was at that point he noticed me. He quickly closed the door and disappeared inside. My curiosity was by now in overdrive. What was in this mound? From the outside, one could presume that there was a dwelling there, which had to be quite a large space, maybe a cave and the pipes had to be ventilation; the TV antenna spoke for itself. I approached the door; it was made of hardwood, nailed together with black iron strips that indicated a sense of fortification. There was a knocker made of iron attached to the front of the door shaped like the sword, a *Dhulfiqar* (the double-bladed sword of Imam `Ali) that was given to Imam `Ali by the Prophet Muhammad. This gave me the needed courage to knock at the door and see what lies inside.

Yet, even before I knocked, I could hear voices coming from behind the door – some adults and others clearly children. I also heard and smelt animals; there was a slight hint of methane leaking through the cracks of the door.

Nevertheless, I lifted the *Dhulfiqar* and knocked three times.

The door opened and a man wearing a traditional Sindhi hat, vest and embroidered shirt was standing, warmly smiling at me, and welcomed me to enter.

As I walked in, the first thing I noticed were lines of shoes all through the periphery of this first space as well as pegs in the mud-packed walls, where shawls and jackets hung. The ground was packed with mud; the walls also appeared to be the same. Strung along the top curved ceiling was a line of dim lights; they circled around to a tunnel leading deeper into the mound. Once I was in, my host introduced himself as Abdul Rahim. He spoke fairly good English. He said that he was expecting me and that Kala Baba (literally meaning "Dark-Skinned Wise Old Man") was waiting to meet me. He asked me to follow him into the interior where Kala Baba was holding his daily *Majlis*.

I was led into a tunnel that meandered through one room after another. One of the first areas we passed through was a large carved out space where animals were kept in multiple adjacent caves and alcoves. As we passed through this area, I could hardly breathe as the smell of methane was overpowering. Looking up, I could see the array of air vents that lined the ceiling of the animal area. There were also some electric fans that were pulling the air up and out through the vents. Passing quickly through this area, the rooms and interconnecting halls and pathways all began to blend together, we turned right and left and back again, I could never find my way out without a guide through the labyrinth structure hidden in this mound. Looking ahead through the tunnel, I could see brighter lights in what appeared to be a large room up ahead.

We came to the *Majlis* of Kala Baba. The room was large, and the ceiling was domed. All the walls were a mosaic of mirrors, like what you might find in a tomb of a saint. There were several electric lights as well as many candles alight that sparkled in the mirrors. It created a mystical, otherworldly feeling almost breaking the sense of solidity and entering the presence of spirit and meaning as light bounced and played throughout the space.

There were many men sitting near what appeared to be a modified baby's crib, gilded in gold and silver, as well as more of the mirrors inlaid into the wooden frame. The crib was sitting in a slightly raised area where there were several women and children sitting close by. Incense filled the air and did a fairly good job in covering up the smell of methane as well as the odor of so many people jammed into a relatively small space. Tea and sweets were flowing and there was a general sense of community and family among those present. I was escorted to the front areas where the framed crib structure sat. I peered into the crib and there he was, laying on his back, legs thin, appearing like the broken branches of a fallen tree, arms the same, but even more wilted and a torso bent and twisted, but a face that shined like a rising sun over the blue expanse on a clear ocean view. His attendant lifted him up, leaning him against a stack of pillows so he could sit upright.

He was introduced to me as Kala Baba.

I found out that when he was a baby, he was left on this mound in what was once just a small cave. In the morning after he was abandoned there, a shepherd boy found him and alerted his parents to what he discovered who apparently did not want him. So, he was taken to their village where he was adopted by a family that looked after him. His deformed and broken body did not deter these most kind people from caring for him, lovingly looking after his needs. When he turned four, he started asking his adopted parents to bring him to the cave where he was first discovered. As the years passed, he frequented the cave and as he grew into puberty, he requested that his family increase the size of the cave by adding more space and dig deeper into the mound. From early on, his family noticed his deep insights and how even being so crippled, he excelled in the study of Islam and became *Hafiz* of the Qur'an – that is, he memorized the entire Qur'an – by the time he was nine. It was after he completed the memorization of the Qur'an that he started having visions of the future. This ability did not sit well with the local `Ulama (Scholars of Islam) and there was pressure put upon him to stop sharing his predictions with the public. He did not stop and explained to his family and friends that his visions were not from him and that he was compelled from within to share them. It was at this time, he retreated to the cave in which he was originally found. By this time, the cave had been expanded and, with the help of many of the villagers who supported him, they expanded the cave even more to accommodate him and the many followers that came later.

When I was brought to Kala Baba, he addressed me with a palpable sense of urgency. He began by insisting that I had a duty to share his vision of the signs yet to come, about the fate of the world, the Muslims and especially the West. He encouraged me to commit these signs to memory since they addressed the unfolding of the final collapse of the world as we knew it and the emergence of the Mahdi.

The first is that all the abuse, pillage and destruction that have been inflicted by the US and its partners, wherever they may be, would in turn be inflicted tenfold upon themselves. He underscored there was no way to escape this formula as it was a dynamic construct built into God's creation. However, it could be mitigated by immediately taking steps of ceasing these actions and making restitution. A sign that we reap what we sow will be that a black flag will rise from the ashes of places that have been inflicted. It will rise as a reactionary force bringing its own brand of misguided justification, perverting the teachings of Islam as a tool of chaos and destruction. Its fire will spread from the Euphrates in the East to the Pillars of Hercules in the West and beyond.

The second will be because of the abuse and disrespect for our Mother Earth. Kala Baba emphasized that we will soon reach a tipping point where, if nothing is done, it will be the end of life as we know it on Earth. Whoever survives will be driven into caves like this to survive as will all animal life – they too will adapt, forcing irreparable damage on their kind.

Thirdly, Islam will rise in the West in ways inconceivable and, to many Muslims in the East, unrecognizable. When Kala Baba began to speak about Islam in the West, his speech became soft and reflective. He looked at me with loving warmth beaming from his eyes as he said: "God's Mercy is vast beyond our ability to comprehend. His decree and the destiny that manifests His plan is uniquely His and only a few will recognize it while most will reject or remain confused. Nevertheless, it will happen as He is the best of planners."

He then advised me personally not to lose the vision of the big picture and purpose of my life, of all life, as His Mercy and Love to be known. He counseled me further that when I am down, disappointed and distracted, to remember the original decree that brought about the creation in the first place: that all relative issues in life will take their rightful place as passing weather encapsulated in the stillness of an all-encompassing sky.

I returned to my seat among the people in the cave. Tea and refreshments were served. I was not the only one to have a meeting with Kala Baba. There were many individuals who were waiting behind me for their turn to meet him and receive a message that is tailored uniquely and specifically for them. I watched their faces as they listened to Kala Baba talk directly to them; they were illuminated, refreshed, and moved on in joy and peace.

It had been about two hours since I left my taxi driver waiting. The shepherd boy guided me out of the cave I had followed originally and had led me to Kala Baba in the first place. I mused to myself, smiling that I too was one of his sheep guided, not to a coral but to the palace of a *Wali* of Allah.

Uch Sharif

Just outside of Dera Nawab Sharif was the ancient city of Uch Sharif.

Uch is known for its ancient history and as a city of knowledge. For centuries, Uch was the center of learning for all Islamic sciences, especially the most precious of all knowledge, which I refer to as *The Science of Awakening*. Sufi teachers from all over India and Central Asia migrated to this great capital of knowledge and established schools, universities, and Sufi lodges, making Uch a magnet for the best hearts and minds for centuries.

It was approximately 4000 BC when the Aryans arrived here. The Aryans named this city after one of their goddesses, "Ushas." Later, the city's name was changed from Ushas to Uch.

During the dynasty of the Achaemenid Empire of Persia, the Persian Empire governed the city of Uch through the 4th and 5th Centuries BC.

Their rule was succeeded by Alexander the Great, who built a new city on land near the joining point of the Indus and the Sutlej rivers and named that city as "Alexandria a-Ussa."

Over time, Uch was also controlled by the Greeks, Mauryans, the Parthian and later by the Kushans.

The city "Uch" had its golden era during the governorship of Nasir Ul Din Qabacha.

In this time, Feroza University was built in the city, which regularly accommodated more than 2500 students at a time from all over the ancient world.

The city saw many eras and rulers.

In the late 15th century, the Mughals took over and it was under their ruler beautiful monuments were erected that became the hallmark and symbols of "Uch" as a unique city unto itself with many shrines of Sufi saints built during the Mughals' rule over the upper Indus area.

In modern times, Uch remained a part of the Bahawalpur State until it joined Pakistan after the partition of the Indian Subcontinent.

Today, Uch Sharif is commonly accepted and regarded as a city of Sufi saints who spread the light of Islam. Although there were many established institutions of learning, most had an emphasis on teaching the core, inner meanings of the Qur'an and the transformative alchemy in emulation of the Prophetic example. Throughout their teachings they underscored love and service to humanity.

Some of Uch Sharif's more famous personalities include the following list of Sufi Saints whom are buried in Uch Sharif: Syed Jalal ud Din Surkhposh Bukhari, Syed Abdul Qadir Gilani Qadri Uchvi, Syed Jahanian Jahangashat Bukhari, Syed Rajan Qatal Bukhari, Syed Fazal ud Din Ladla Bukhari, Syed Jamal Dervish Khanda Rou, Syed Safi ud Din Gazarnavi and Bibi Jawindi of the Suhrawardiyyah Sufi order.

Dr. Khalid organized a visit to Uch Sharif that included Habib, one of the other American Sufis, and Dr. Khalid's driver. We started our journey early one morning to avoid the afternoon desert heat. The road from Dera Nawab Sahib to Uch was narrow and often became covered up by shifting sand. On our way we noticed several young children herding cattle along the roadway. All they had to control the beasts was a long pliable tree twig that they wiped about with stinging effect to keep their herds in line. One of the cows, a large beige Brahma got a fright, maybe from seeing a snake or just sensing danger, bolted towards the road and attempted to cross in front of our oncoming, speeding vehicle. The driver did his best to stop, all of us lunging forwards as the car crashed straight into the cow, nearly destroying, and overturning our car. We walked away unscathed; we were only slightly bruised and in shock from the whole encounter. The cow fared much worse – it was still alive, but all its legs were broken and it was bleeding. The young boy herder approached us in a clear panic, profusely apologizing as he broke into tears. The cow was moaning in pain but we couldn't do anything about it, except forgive the boy given the nature of the situation. We heard a man shouting as he ran towards us; he was the father of the young herder. He was also very upset and he admonished the boy, which we all thought was unfair. He insisted that we came to a mutually beneficial agreement for reparations for the damage of the car. I was very touched that in the heat of the moment cooler heads prevailed and, after finding a small withered tree that provided us some shade, we sat down to negotiate the damage and how to resolve it on amenable terms. After just a few minutes Dr. Khalid and the herder agreed that the damage to the front end of our car was equal to the value of the cow, i.e., what its meat could be valued in the market. The herder agreed that he would slaughter the cow, cut, and prepare and package the entire animal and bring it to Dr. Khalid's house in the next few days. All agreed and accepted the terms we had negotiated. In the meantime, our driver had pulled the car hood off along with both side panels and the front grill that were damaged in the accident. He placed everything in the trunk of the car and, within a few minutes, our stripped and steaming car was off to complete the rest of the journey to Uch Sharif. I was at first very concerned that we would not make it to Uch before the engine would seize, but the driver was a very experienced fellow and had been in circumstances similar to this. He assured us that all would be well and that we would make it to Uch where he would have the car repaired enough for our return journey. He was right. We prodded along, albeit driving much slower than before. We rolled into Uch, found a repair shop and went on to visit the Sufi shrines of Uch Sharif.

Great, Great Grandson of Imam Hussain / Indus River

We visited Uch Sharif on many other occasions to visit shrines and attend some of the many celebrations of *Urs* for the various saints that were interned in the city. On one of these return visits, the weather was quite hot, but also exceptionally dry with visibility for miles in every direction. Most of the time visibility was low due to something akin to "sand fog" that occurred when there was wind stirring up the sand. About three quarters along our way to Uch, we spotted a walled building; upon more detailed inspection, we also noticed a dome rising over the wall as well as what appeared to be a tall pole in which flags waved from the very top of the pole. It piqued our interest and we made our way through the sand towards the compound. We came to its gate, which was locked by an ancient iron padlock. It was the kind of lock that a large cast iron medieval type key would release. Looking through the gate we could clearly see it was a shrine, but neither Dr. Khalid nor any of our traveling companions knew anything about this place.

Upon inspection of the large flagpole, we had seen from the road, it appeared to be a very tall tree. One would see the places along its profile where there were once branches. This was very odd in that there were absolutely no trees for hundreds of miles. We called out to see if there was anybody attending this shrine that would let us in. An old man came out of the shrine's main doors. He was dressed in torn clothes wearing a red turban and packing a long-barreled rifle, which, as he came closer to the gate, he lifted to his elbow pointing it directly at us. We explained how we came to this place and asked about the history of this shrine. We talked at the gate for a few minutes until the shrine attendant felt comfortable to let us in. He unlocked the gate and guided us to a shady area under the entrance of the shrine. He told us this was the shrine of the great, great grandson of Imam Husain, who, having fled for his life from one of the Umayyad dynasties, took refuge near this spot along the Indus River. He went on to say that in the history of Uch and the surrounding areas, the Indus River, along with some of its tributaries, often shifted unpredictably. When the rivers shifted, it would cause havoc to the agriculture of the area, wiping away crops and even small villages. Over many years, the local people recognized the *Sayyid*[16] as being righteous, trustworthy, eventually considering him as a saint among them.

After a shift in the Indus, where the devastation was exceptionally bad, they turned to the *Sayyid* and asked him to pray for them and hoping that his prayers would intercede in Allah's decree and forever halt the shifting of the rivers and the destruction they caused. The descendent of the Imam accepted their request and, over a period of three days, he sat by the Indus in prayers and supplications. On the late afternoon of the third day, the Indus rose over its usual height and everyone with the *Sayyid* had to pull back from the banks of the Indus so as not to be washed away.

As the water climbed higher, the *Sayyid* noticed that a large dark object was flowing towards them in the river. As the object came close, it appeared to be a long, large tree stripped of its branches and barreling down the river like a ramrod. The *Sayyid* called out to the farmers and all the locals with him to capture the log and bring it safely to the banks of the river.

The *Sayyid* announced that this was a sign with conditions and an answer to the prayers of the people. He ordered the pole to be set upright, secured to the ground with 14 ropes evenly spaced and a flag noting the five *panjatan*[17] upon it. He said further that this pole was a metaphor of the Arch of Noah, which was made up of fourteen supporters and representing the fourteen *ma`suomeen*.[18] The *Sayyid* said that as long as this

---

[16] An honorific title denoting people accepted as descendants of the Prophet Muhammad and his cousin and son-in-law `Ali ibn Abi Talib through his grandsons, Hasan ibn `Ali and Husain ibn Ali.

[17] Meaning, "Five People" – The Prophet, Imam `Ali, Fatima, Hasan and Husain.

[18] Infallible – In Shi`a Islam, there are 14 people who are considered infallible: The

pole stood tall in this spot and people kept to the love and service of the *Ahlul Bayt[19]* of the Prophet, the river would not change course and their livelihoods as well as their spiritual well-being would be maintained. The old guardian told us that he was the direct descendent of this *Sayyid* and his family was tasked over the centuries to protect and guard this sanctuary and the pole from being interfered with. We remained at the shrine for the time it took to have tea and consume some sweets and took permission to move on.

During my stay in Pakistan there was no end to encountering similar situations, people, places and stories that fused the inner world with the outer. There is a special presence of the transcendent life and constant reference to the divine that permeates the landscape of this blessed country.

The Tomb of Great, Great Grandson of Imam Hussain

Prophet, Imam `Ali, Fatima, their sons, Hasan and Husain, and followed by Zain ul `Abideen, Baqar, Ja`far al Sadiq, Musa Kazim, `Ali Raza, Muhammad Taqi, `Ali Naqi, Hasan `Askari, Mahdi.

[19] The family of the Prophet through the lineage of Imam `Ali and his wife, and the Prophet's daughter, Fatima.

Urs of Bibi Jawindi

We arrived in Uch for the *Urs* of the great female saint and Sufi teacher, Bibi Jawindi, the great-granddaughter of the famous Sufi saint Jahaniyan Jahangasht whose spiritual legacy she embodied together with manifest wholesomeness. Jahaniyan Jahangasht literally means *one who wanders worldwide*. He was deserving of this title as he travelled widely and left a lasting impression wherever he visited especially in South Asia.

He implored people to follow and to read and absorb the Qur'an and the Prophet Muhammad's way of life in speech, conduct and action. He strongly recommended joining the Sufi path, as the Sufis were the hearts and souls of Islam and the maintainers of the path to Oneness. He often counseled in general to consume less meat, as that helped win over a person's lower self. Prayer, he said, could change one's destiny. He also held the soil of the Indian Subcontinent in great esteem, remarking that the feet of Adam touched this soil.

This manner of thinking, and more, became Bibi Jawindi's treasure, which she lived and shared generously with all who came to learn from her.

Today, the tomb of Bibi Jawindi is empty, partly washed away centuries ago, making her admonition and prediction infamously come true.

Over her lifetime, thousands of pilgrims visited Uch Sharif, to attend the regular celebrations of the *Urs* for the Saints that were buried there. They also came to sit in the *Majlis* of Bibi Jawindi, who was loved and regarded with the greatest esteem by locals as well as the visitors who came to hear her teach. During her presence in Uch Sharif, the city prospered. Many attributed the rise of Uch to the blessings of having Bibi Jawindi amongst them. When she felt the nearness of death, she warned and gave a stern prediction. She told them that as long as they remained faithful to the Qur'an and the Prophetic example, she would always remain with them and their city would continue to flourish. If they strayed from the Prophetic path, she would leave them, and the city would be ruined.

After some years past her departure from this world, the people of Uch abandoned their commitment to the Prophetic path and fell into gluttony, underhanded business practices, bribery, and other expressions of ignoble behavior. In one of the most unprecedented monsoon seasons ever recorded, the city of Uch and the tomb of Bibi Jawindi flooded, washing her remains away never to be found again.

After the word went out throughout Uch and the whole Bahawalpur District about what had happened, they all grieved for not only losing their beloved saintly mother Bibi Jawindi, but also for the loss of their way of life that she clearly warned and predicted. The loss of Bibi's presence among them inspired a revival of faith precipitating a ground-swell of reform and hope that pervaded throughout the district. The result was a revived community and reestablishment of the primacy of Islam as a guiding principle in their lives, a deep renewed love and appreciation for Bibi Jawindi and the eminence of all the Sufi Saints that blessed their city with their presence and legacy.

Bibi Jawindi Uch Sharif

Flashback to Our First Morning in Pakistan and *Jum`ah* in Uch Sharif

Although I have already talked about Uch Sharif and my experiences there, I'd like to go back and talk about my first morning in Pakistan after a long train ride from Karachi to Ahmedpur and my first visit to Uch Sharif.

Waking up in a new country for the first time seemed surreal. There were no usual sounds of the traffic piling up around our apartment building with people racing to work to meet a 9AM deadline that woke us up, but a canopy of voices filling the air with a proclamation of the oneness of *God and that Muhammad is His Messenger*. It was the *adhan*, the call to prayer! I woke up moments before my wife did, facing each other on the bed. When the *adhan* entered my consciousness, it brought a smile to my face. I looked over at Nafisa and a smile broke on hers as well. We were both delighted. We got up and walked over to the window as though to see where the *adhan* was coming from. It was impossible to tell; it seemed to be coming from everywhere at once, each line overlapping the next until it filled the sky as the daybreak filled it with light.

Each morning brings a new creation, each daybreak brings the good news. As the sun rose this morning, it spoke to us that today is a new day and for us it was the beginning of a new life.

We both offered our prayers, but today it was different because the feelings that permeated our bodies and minds were intoxicating. We were no longer this isolated couple doing this strange ritual – today the whole world around us was joining in our feast, and we in theirs.

I laid back in bed and began to listen to the sound of another world waking up. On this morning, car horns were replaced with the mooing of milk cows and traffic sounds were turned into the clatter of hooves on stone pavements. I remember slowly falling asleep to the sounds of children on the microphone of the mosque bestowing prayers on the Prophet and his family. I knew then we had arrived.

It was *Jum`ah* (Friday) today and our host Dr. Khalid came to our door and told us that breakfast was ready. We were filled with anticipation as we opened the door into our new world for the first time and I felt a mix of excitement and joy.

We were led into the house's main room, and there, on the floor, was a colorful spread laid out with fruits and foods that at first were unrecognizable to me. Where was my usual cup of coffee and the newspaper, I had become so accustomed to? I looked over to Dr. Khalid and found him peering at me as we sat at this unusual breakfast. I could tell that he knew *daal* (lentils) and *paratha* (fried flatbread) were not my usual morning repast.

After breakfast Dr. Khalid told us that we were going to offer *Jum`ah* (Friday's congregational prayer) in Uch Sharif, which is an ancient town about twenty-five kilometers from Ahmedpur East and about seventy-five kilometers from Bahawalpur in the southern Punjab, Pakistan.

Jum`ah means a gathering of people for the worship of God. As Muslims, we perform this once a week to confirm and experience the universal reality that each one of us holds in common. One people band together in the worship of the Creator, bringing strength and renewed confidence in ourselves as a community.

When it was time to go, a small Suzuki van pulled up at Dr. Khalid's, and we all squeezed in and off we went. I sat by the window, my eyes roaming uncontrollably, everything was so different. It was like watching a movie in which the climax scenes were being played out, but this time it was the whole time. As the van reached the road, we began being tossed up and down and back and forth in it as the road was filled with potholes, and unevenly laid asphalt. That, mixed with the fact that our van had no shocks, made for a most uncomfortable ride.

There was a moment there where I could have become irritated about it, but I broke into laughter on recalling what Shaykh Fadhlalla had said to me a few days before leaving as we rode around in his Mercedes. He told me he had me ride around with him in it so as to appreciate it, for where I was going there would be no such comfort. This experience now took on a meaning for me rather than just being a source of irritation. It became a lesson in being patient and humble and a way to appreciate what we have and not to become arrogant. Since everyone else here had to submit to it, so did I.

As we sped along this desert road, the sand spread out in every direction, and we were like a ship on a sea. The waves were now sand, and when the wind blew, it threw up the sand like the foam on the waves.

Along the road we could see villages and encampments of gypsies and the poor, their houses made of mud and the roofs of thatch. I remember thinking to myself how everything blended into the mud homes. There were also camels – so many camels! – with bells hung from their necks. It all made for an unimposing sight. It was easy to look at with no strain on the eyes. One didn't feel the sense of unbalance that one does when looking at a tall skyscraper from the ground. Life was humble there and nothing in the buildings indicated any arrogance. It was all at ground level.

Ahead, I could see a town coming up, and Dr. Khalid told us it was Uch Sharif. It was very crowded, for today it was not only *Jum`ah* but also the *Urs* of a famous saint. Our van headed in the direction of the bazaar and entered it and we became like a wedge into a mass of people. It was like a sea of people parting. My stomach ached with apprehension as we constantly came close to running several people over, but none were ever touched. At one point, there came in front of us a cart with oranges, and we hit it, thankfully not causing any damage. But where was the outrage on the face of the cart owner? Where was the remorse on the face of the driver who could have avoided the accident, but didn't try? The cart owner smiled and gestured for us to go through. I was touched by all of this and felt a great sense of appreciation for these simple, yet enlightened people.

The road began to climb up into a winding narrow street of walls and doors that led into the courtyard-like dwellings of the people of Uch Sharif. We went as far as we could and stopped and got out and started to walk the rest of the way. All around us were graves, mere lumps of mud piled up in irregular rows spread out over a continually rising area. We were now several hundred yards up on a hill. Later, I learned that once there was no hill at all and there were some graves. The hill was formed after many centuries of building on top of previous structures and graves.

As we walked further, a structure of unearthly appearance rose from amongst the graves. It shimmered in the sun, reflecting off its blue and black tiled walls. Its shape seemed organic as though it might have emerged from the ground. We came closer and its spaceship-like appearance awed us as it stood there as a reminder of a forgotten age. Now, we were at the summit of Uch Sharif and saw the whole of the hill was dotted with tombs of great saints.

Uch Sharif already existed as a city and trade center when the Prophet Muhammad was born. Soon thereafter, it became a great center for Islam, with universities and schools of Islamic knowledge. Sufis from all corners of the world came to teach and live in what was then definitely one of the most beautiful cities in the world. Now, there remain only small reminders of that time. The tombs of the great ones seemed to stand and call us to remember what had once existed, but now was crumbling into dust.

The *Jum`ah* was being held in the courtyard of a mosque built in honor of one of the great saints of Uch Sharif, Sayyed Bohari. We now were on a new road leading to the mosque. In front of us, there was an arched door and I could only see a little through the opening as there were many people stopping at its entrance and removing their shoes. But what I could see was fantastic: it appeared to be a courtyard built on the very top of the hill. As I removed my shoes and entered, my suspicions were confirmed: the entire tiled courtyard spread out over the hill and at one end was a mosque, covered in the same blue tiles we saw on the tombs. It was like a reminder that in life or death it is worship of Allah that is the same. As it says in the Qur'an in chapter 2, verse 156, *"From Allah we've come and to Allah we will return."* The courtyard was filled with men, women and children, who were all in their best clothes – a sea of turbans and *chadors* blowing in the wind.

I put my shoes down on the ground where they soon disappeared into the pile of shoes that grew at every moment. But I did not care as no one did. It was taken for granted that everyone would find their shoes. As we stepped over people to locate a spot before the *Jum`ah* began, hands stretched out from every direction assisting us in keeping our balance until we reached our spot.

I sat there enthralled. The mass of people itself was awesome. The faces of the people that surrounded me were timeless to the extent that if someone told me that the date was 1100 or 745 or even before this, I would've believed it. Time had stopped. It was a reminder that that which is true is timeless and only the absolute essence of a human being in their relation to their Creator exists at every moment. My sense of being a tourist or of being separate fell from me like a cheap Halloween mask, and in my heart, I knew I was being reborn.

After the *Jum`ah* prayer, Dr. Khalid said it was time to visit the saint in whose honor the mosque was built. Just across from the mosque, there was another building with an arched door at which many people were standing – some on their knees at its entrance, some crying and clinging to the door handles. I'd never been in a tomb before like this. Before entering I remembered what it was like at the Tomb of the Prophet Muhammad in Medina. There was a taste of similarity in it, but my reverence for the Prophet forbade me to compare the two.

I entered inside and the dark coolness of a mud-constructed building made me feel cold. I also felt a garden inside and felt that at any moment I would come to a waterfall or river or fountain. But, as I proceeded, there were only the graves of the saints and their *mureeds* that lined the path, welcoming me to the resting-place of the saint.

The tomb of the saint was lit up and covered by mounds of flowers that seemed to sparkle as they laid across the green cover of the tomb. I didn't know what to do, but I was compelled to touch the green cover. After touching it, I buried my face in it. The dark green color became darker as my face got closer and closer to it, and I felt as though I was being brought through a tunnel whose end was complete blackness. For a moment, there was nothing other than that blackness – that cool, uninterrupted peace. I remained in that position for what seemed to me only seconds; then tears came to my eyes, and I pulled back.

I could not speak. There was nothing to say. From darkness we come and to darkness we go.

Now, as we were travelling back in the van, the sights on the road lost their novelty for me: it's all life in one shape or another, and it's the same wherever we go. My Shaykh, may Allah bless him, always says, *"From the womb to the tomb."* What is it in between other than to realize our ultimate fate and, by that, our beginning? We returned to Dr. Khalid's house and after lunch we rested. The train ride from Karachi had caught up with me and I was fatigued. I slept very deeply that night. It was tough. I'd lived an entire lifetime in one day. Once a brother told me that sleep in terms of the Sufis was called "the little death." The meaning of it was abundantly clear to me as my eyes shut for the last time that day.

Shaykh Osman Beshir Osman

Photo Provided by Peter Sander Photography Limited

There is a great tradition within the teachings of Islam, and more particularly the Sufis, regarding the benefits of keeping the company of saints and teachers. For, although there is a great deal to learn from their books, writings and teachings, the knowledge and meaning of their teachings can be most effectively transmitted from being in their presence.

Human beings are mind and soul, heart and body. The mind learns by processing information, but it is the soul that refines information and comprehends its deeper meanings. When the heart is open, unfettered, empty, and present, it reflects these meanings and becomes the source of knowledge and enlightenment.

The best way to receive this transmission is by the physical proximity to the teacher in the acts of service. Service refines and promotes sensitivity and awareness. It requires alertness and attention away from yourself and directs it towards the needs of others. It makes possible moments where in the mundane routines of daily life the springs of light find their way to the surface, and the drink of transmission takes place.

Shaykh Osman Beshir Osman was one of these beings.

For many years, I had been visiting London, either passing through from travel to the east or to visit my teacher and guide Shaykh Fadhlalla Haeri. I'd stay at the center he had established there. Most of these visits coincided with the visits of Shaykh Beshir who'd also stay at that center. This gave me the privilege to serve him on many occasions and spend many days and nights in his blessed company. When I first met him, he was well into his seventies.

Shaykh Beshir was from Eritrea. He stood tall and straight, and when he walked, he leaned slightly forward as though walking downhill, always keeping a fast pace. He always covered his head with a turban and wore a *tasbih* around his neck. He loved a person instantly when presented to him as a fellow Muslim; though he never inquired about one's *Madhab*[20] or sect. One's presence and admission of faith were enough for him. Wherever he went, he brought with him the transmission of tasting the world beyond that of the senses. He lived his *Deen* as an example to others and gifted all whom he met with increase in *Iman* (faith; trust) for Allah's Domain of the *Ghayb* (The Unseen).

He often traveled with a special clay coffee pot. Many of his friends would visit him and bring special blends of coffee from their home country. They would prepare it in the traditional way by boiling the coffee over an open flame. They would huddle around the pot in a close circle and share its contents together. There was always a designated pourer, and he was sure not to let a cup go dry for too long. To attend these gatherings was like peering into a portal of timelessness. Regardless of modern-day conveniences, like a stove or kettle, the Shaykh and his friends would always bring a gas fire and set up the coffee-making wherever they were. When they passed the cups and tasted the coffee, it was clearly a medium of communion, not only with each other, but also with the Higher Presence.

Wherever he went, he saw the realms of the Unseen and with his unique gift, insight, and inspired heart, moved through the world like a sword through water. Whenever I looked into his eyes, I experienced him looking through me and through the materiality of this world, seeing beyond its temporal form into its essential meaning and unseen realities. At the same time, love and human concern were always present in his gaze, one inextricably linked to the other.

---

[20] Usually translated as "Religion". However, within Islamic jurisprudence, it also refers to a school of thought within Islam.

I'm now going to share with you some amazing stories about this great being to show the reader that there is more to our lives and this world than meets the outer senses. That, at any given moment, there is more influence by the Unseen than what we experience in the world we see, which is often only the shadow-show of a play whose breath and length are immeasurable. That the action of angels, prayers and decrees are more relevant, and that Allah is forever in charge.

The Medina Visit

In the spring of 1981, several members of our community in San Antonio, Texas set out to the *Hijaz* to perform *Umrah.²¹* Shaykh Beshir lived walking distance to the shrine, where the Prophet Muhammad is buried. While visiting the Prophet's Mosque in *Medina al-Munawara,²²* we had the honor to stay with him at his home.

Upon arrival in the great city of Medina, we were welcomed by the Shaykh to his family home. Inviting the guest and welcoming the stranger is regarded as one of the greatest acts and sources of *Barakah* within the teachings and cultures of Islam. We had hardly arrived at his home when I began to feel ill. Within one hour of the onset of that feeling, I was running a high fever and could only remain in my bed. My brother travelers had to leave me behind while they went to the *Masjid-un-Nabawi* (The Prophet's Mosque) to make their visit to the Prophet. I was very disappointed that I had come all this way and was not able to fulfill the intended purpose of my visit. Shaykh Beshir perceived my disappointment and, with his overflowing kindness, comforted me by reciting a tradition from the Prophet Muhammad on the virtues of becoming ill while in Medina. It was purification and I would benefit from this visit beyond what I could perceive at that moment. That night, as I laid ill in the house of Shaykh Beshir, I was taken over by a vision that began with the sound of a knock at the door. No one was home that evening, but the door was answered and four young men entered the room in which I was resting. They did not speak nor could I utter a word as they lifted me upon a wooden stretcher and carried me out of the

---

²¹ Pilgrimage to Mecca, which can be undertaken at any time of the year, in contrast to the Hajj, which has specific dates according to the Islamic lunar calendar. It's also known as "Minor Hajj."
²² Lit. The Enlightened City. Refers to the city of Medina where the Prophet Muhammad (PBUH) is buried in the mosque, which he had built when he migrated to that city from Mecca.

house onto the street. I felt as though I were being carried on the soft cushions of a celestial divan or a flying carpet. The only sound was the whispering of the night breeze as it wafted over me like a gentle hand cooling the burning of my raging fever. I remember thinking to myself that there were no sounds of traffic or the hustle of the Medina nights. Only the wind and its variety of tones whisking by, each one bringing a lovely tone like soft chimes on a midsummer's night. I raised my head and looked forward, gazing at what I had thought only a few hours before was denied to me. It was the Prophet's Mosque I was being taken to and headed for one of its magnificent entrance ways. As I was carried through the door, I noticed it had written on its entry arch the words in Arabic, *Bab ur-Rahman*, meaning, *The Door of Mercy*. I was awestruck by the entire thing. In and out of the Mosque we went like a weft through the warp of a fantastic tapestry, my bearers wove in and out of each entrance of the Prophet's Mosque. Each time, I could see the name of each door passing over my head. We circumambulated the entire Mosque, round and round, and I lost count and bearing, falling into a state of bewilderment. I no longer could make out the door names as we moved faster and faster through them. I did not know if we were in or out of the Mosque any more. I stopped trying to keep up and let myself go with the moment, all the tension of my body's confines had vanished and my fever was only a long-forgotten memory along with all my concerns about the journey that brought me there. I had experienced my intended purpose and was content with the gift of gratitude.

The next moment, I was being held in the arms of Shaykh Beshir on the floor of his home surrounded by his family and my travel companions. They all looked at me with deep concern, except for Shaykh Beshir. He then related to me a tradition of the Prophet Muhammad which states that whenever a traveler enters Medina for the sake of visiting the Prophet of Allah and becomes ill, the Prophet will come to visit him.

The Shroud

Once I was in London and staying at our center with Shaykh Beshir where I had the honor to attend to his needs. Towards the end of his stay in London after many nights of *dhikr* and gatherings had passed, I noticed that the Shaykh was more tired than usual. It was on the following morning of one of these last nights of gathering that I came to the Shaykh's room to deliver his breakfast; only this would not be a typical morning, but rather a morning of unveiling the depth of *Taqwa* – God-

Consciousness, and submission the Shaykh embodied.

As it was our routine, I knocked at Shaykh Beshir's door just after dawn, but this time there was no answer. I knocked again and again and still no answer. I began to grow very concerned since he was always up and ready at this time for his breakfast. I hesitated to open the door without his permission, but after considering his being noticeably exhausted the night before, I became concerned about his wellbeing and the possibility that something bad might have happened to the Shaykh in the night. I slowly opened the door, saying *Allahhu Akbar* (God is Great), over and over again, but there was no response. With heightened concern, I took the liberty to enter the Shaykh's room.

It was dark and the curtains were still closed. The room was dead quiet. I could see the Shaykh's bed – the covers had been lifted over his body like that of the dead. There was no movement. I thought to myself: had he died? I went over to the bed, and with my heart in my throat I slowly lifted the blanket off his face. His eyes were closed, his body still, and he looked as though he were dead. I pulled the covers off more and, to my utter surprise, I found his entire body was wrapped in a burial shroud and, around it, coiled like a snake around the trunk of a tree, was a 10,000 bead *Mashaha* (*tasbih*). My thoughts raced: had he died in the middle of the night and someone secretly came and prepared the body? While all these thoughts went through my mind, the Shaykh suddenly moved and opened his eyes. He smiled and greeted me, *As Salamu Alaikum!* He immediately perceived that I was distressed at what I saw. He asked me to leave his room and return in ten minutes at which time he would explain.

Upon returning to his room, he related to me that each night before he slept, he would take a *ghusl*, a ritual bath in the Prophetic way, in preparation for death. He would then wrap himself to the best of his abilities in a *coffin* and lie down upon his bed. As he fell asleep, he would recite his *wazifas* with a 10,000-bead *tasbih*. This *tasbih* would often become wrapped around him while he turned and shifted in his bed. He explained that it was his way of remembering death and that if he should die while asleep, those who would come after to wash and prepare him would have less work to do. Through all of this, the Shaykh asked me to forgive him for causing me any undue concern.

Walking the Streets of London

Another time it was an unusually bright, and sunny day in London and Shaykh Beshir suggested we went out for a walk, stopping later at a coffee house for refreshments. We were off that beautiful morning, setting our route through Kensington Gardens around to Kensington High Street and back down to Queensway where there was a lovely French patisserie. As we moved through the streets, the Shaykh chatted away to me in his native tongue of Arabic. I mostly guessed at what he was saying as I do not speak the language. I knew that he knew that, but it seemed all well and good to him. As for me, his being and glances made up for the deficit in understanding.

As we walked, I noticed that he began to have longer pauses in his conversation with me. Simultaneously, his grip on my arm became tighter, and he moved me closer to him, my side pressed against his. The sky also became bleaker and darker as though a shadow had moved across the sun. With his grip tightening, he began to tell me that nearly half of the people we were passing were possessed by the *Jinn*. He started to point out individuals to me. After some time, I could see what he was saying. I could see emptiness in them as though they were a shell occupied by something not human.

We soon found ourselves at the French patisserie and ordered coffee and some sweets. The Shaykh continued to tell me about how when people do not occupy themselves with the real purpose of life, they are susceptible to possession, especially those people who have no divine focus in life are easily taken over at the time they are watching television.

The conversation went on for about an hour. At one point I noticed the Shaykh had a smirk on his face that soon broke into a full smile. I was surprised that it came seemingly out of context and out of nowhere. I inquired what was so funny. He pointed out to me that we had been having a conversation and for someone who did not know or understood spoken Arabic, I had been doing very well. I was stunned. I had been completely unaware of this. I realized that I had carried on a conversation with him, understanding and answering him in Arabic. Seeing how awestruck I was, he said, *"Allah Kareem,"* (Allah is Generous and Giving), with his outstretched pointer finger pointing to the sky.

Passport to the Unseen

Once both Shaykh Beshir and I were staying at our Shaykh Fadhlalla's center in London. During his stay there Shaykh Beshir was invited by a local friend to attend his daughter's wedding in Morocco. He asked me to take his passport to the Home Affairs office in Croydon and obtain a multiple entry visa for him, which would allow him to re-enter England after his visit to Morocco.

With such a visa he could enter and leave the United Kingdom without any problems for at least 6 months. Although many friends informed him that obtaining such a visa was virtually impossible at such short notice, Shaykh Beshir insisted that all would be alright.

It serves to mention here that it is the policy of the Home Affairs not to issue this type of visa unless the application originates from the home country of the applicant.

Nonetheless, I went to the Home Affairs office as he instructed me to see what we could do.

As usual, the Croydon office was packed with people from everywhere in the world. London is the crossroads of the world, and the Croydon Home Affairs office is like the "Ellis Island" of England. Sprawled on the chairs, on the blankets and on the ground people of every color, custom and dress waited patiently for their numbers to be called to see what destiny might hold for them. One could not ignore the disdain marked on the overworked faces of the clerks as they listened one after another to stories of calamities, marriages, deaths and births, all legitimate reasons to stay a little longer in their already overburdened country.

There was a waiting system based on numbers. I took a number and, after three hours of waiting, it was finally my turn. I spoke to the already-tired and frustrated clerk about the Shaykh's request. As I was telling him, I could see that he had already made up his mind only moments into my plea. He was clearly unmoved by my request. He expressed his inability to give the visa that was requested. He cited all the policies and procedures, making it clear to me that, as far as he was concerned, there was no way, no how.

I returned to Shaykh Osman and reported what had happened. The Shaykh went suddenly silent. He soon asked for a piece of paper, writing down two of the names of Allah in Arabic and asked me to repeat them. I repeated the Divine Names in his presence, and he nodded to me in an affirmative manner. The two Names were *ya Sari`ru* (You are the Quickener) and *ya Qaribu* (You are the Nearer). He then instructed me to return immediately to the Home Affairs Office in Croydon, repeating these formulas again and again from the moment I set out and until the task is achieved. With my prayer beads in hand, I was off again to Croydon, all the while on the tube repeating the formula as instructed by the Shaykh.

I entered the Croydon office, noticing that the number I took from the queue was very high compared to what was being displayed on the board. It appeared that I was in for a long wait and possibly would have to return the next day. As I sat in the waiting area, I noticed the same clerk that served me earlier that morning. He looked over at me with more disdain. I could almost hear his inner voice saying, "Not him again!" After finishing serving the gentleman, he was with he went over to the number counter and pulled the string to call the next applicant in the queue. He shouted out number so and so. No one answered. He called again and again, and still, there was no response. He looked quite perplexed as most people who come here do not give up their place in the queue at the Home Affairs Office. Calling it up as a fluke, he pulled the string again, and again there was no response.

As this was going on, the *dhikr* I was instructed to repeat started to become more and more intense. I began feeling connected to what was happening around me and the numbers on the board were going by one after another with no response. I started experiencing a shift in my perception. It was like a tunnel vision effect in which I could only view what was between the clerk and I who was now racing through the numbers. I saw the clerk's face becoming more flushed and confused at this most improbable occurrence. I watched the numbers fly by until it reached my number. I called out, "Yes! That's me!"

I approached the agent who was noticeably in a state of shock. I politely reminded him of my request from earlier on in the day. I also communicated to him that I had been aware of what had just happened. I told him that these events were in connection to the saintly being that had sent me to Croydon. I implored him to consider the event as a proof of the legitimacy of his request. To my surprise and delight, he accepted what I was saying. He had been changed by the event, forced to depart from the norm and to look at things from a new and fresh perspective. He took the Shaykh's passport and disappeared into a back office. He was gone for only five minutes and returned with the passport stamped with the requested visas. He said that this was the one of only a few times that he had ever given a multiple visa on request from the counter. The last time was to a visitor whose wife had suddenly died and needed to return with the body and come back to England to visit his children. He said that the gentleman whose passport I had must certainly be a saint. I thanked him and turned walking straight out the door.

I was in a rush now because the Shaykh had already booked himself on a flight out that same evening. As I came to the street, I noticed a car speeding towards me and the back door opened as it approached. As it swung open, there was Shaykh Beshir sitting in the rear seat with several of his Eritrean friends. He signaled me to quickly get in. Without any inquiry regarding my efforts at Croydon, he immediately asked me for the passport. His friends told me they were on their way to the airport to drop off the Shaykh. I was overwhelmed. I felt the need to explain what had just happened, but before I could relate the story the Shaykh began to shake his head and laughed. He already knew, he already knew!

Just as the five senses act as windows to the world around us, there exist more subtle and unseen realities that are accessible by inner and subtler faculties of seeing. From time to time, we may experience glimpses of these realities. Intuition, premonitions, déjà vu and dreams often give us access to them. Shaykh Beshir had his inner sight so developed that seeing and interacting with these subtle realities was his constant state. He was blessed with knowledge of the unseen including the ability to communicate with the *Jinn*. I am in no position to comment any further, but what I can say is that he often provided me and others with keys and passports to the unseen in order to facilitate actions in this world for our mutual benefit.

The Farewell Kiss

After the event at the immigration office, Shaykh Beshir was off to Morocco to attend his friend's daughter's wedding. Upon his return to London, I continued to serve him and glean the gems of his being as they were so generously offered in his blessed company. Each day there was the ritual coffee drinking, and in the night gatherings of his friends and followers huddled together reminding their souls of the true purpose and meaning of their lives. They swayed like wheat in a gentle breeze, their lips moist with the remembrance of their Lord and the qualities of His messenger.

After an evening of prayer and meditation, Shaykh Beshir announced that it was time for him to leave and return to his home in Medina. That morning, like many others, I accompanied him to Victoria Railway Station en route to the airport. Everything went according to plan with no signs of anything out of the ordinary. While the last bag was put on the train, I stepped up onto the train to bid farewell to the Shaykh, kiss his hand and take his blessing. As I reached for his hand, he un-customarily quickly removed it from my grasp and placed his hands on both sides of my cheeks. He looked me in the eyes with a "high beam" stare whose light poured out living love and delights. I lost my sense of separation, disintegrating in the presence beyond both of us and heard utter silence. He then kissed me directly on my lips, like a father or mother would do to a beloved child. He had never done this before.

I was stunned, frozen. I could barely speak. From that moment, time and space were altered. As I stepped off the train my eyes again met with the Shaykh's eyes. He held me in his glance like a tractor beam on its catch. My perception was considerably altered, everything appearing to move in slow motion and in utter silence. The next thing I heard was the call by the conductor for "All aboard!" With that call everything changed. It was like changing the channel on the TV. The sounds of the train station emerged, and I became aware of people and activities around me. Out of my chest I felt a deep pain and fell to my knees in tears. I wept profusely, like a mother weeping for her child. It was clear to me beyond a doubt that the kiss he gave me on the train was my farewell kiss from the Shaykh: that this was the last time I had seen him. I don't know if he consciously knew or that it was all in some way preconceived.

That was the last time I saw Shaykh Beshir in this world. He passed away shortly after our visit into the next life in around 1984. Just before he passed away, he wrote a letter to my teacher and guide, Shaykh Fadhlalla Haeri. In it, he said that he loved me like a son and when a shadow passed across him from behind or to the side, he would think that it was me bringing some tea or food to share with him.

To this present day, although he has passed from this world, he remains very much a part of my life and alive. I often experience his presence around me and sometimes hear his voice or see him signaling me with his eyes and hands. These occasions are usually when I am about to travel or do something that pertains to official business. When I think of him, it is like he is only in the next room and soon I will go there and meet him.

Lady Shakura

In the fall of 1992, I was attending an Islamic conference at the Oklahoma City Conference in Oklahoma for Zahra Publications to introduce and sell our books. We had a booth in one of the conference halls where there were dozens of other book publishers, food importers and various Muslim wares on offer. The conference was over a three-day period. On the second day I was there, an Iraqi man came to chat with me several times. At first, the conversation was of a light nature, but as the day grew on his visits and words began to hint of something of greater importance that he wished to share with me, but was hesitant. I did not let on that I was aware of his subtle hints, wanting him to feel comfortable and not wanting to appear prying into his affairs. Towards the end of the day, he approached me and said that he had a problem that he wanted to discuss with me. He explained how he could not discuss this with most others, and how he felt comfortable with me. He sat down next to me and told me about the problems he was having with his wife.

Transformation of a Man / Recitation of *Surah Ya Seen*

He started his story by telling me that he had gone through a major transformation in the last few years. Being raised a Muslim in Iraq he admitted to not having much appreciation for Islam. It was for the most part a cultural aspect of his life. Regarding belief in God or in the practice of Islam, he had no belief and little inclination to the outer practices of Islam. He was educated in the UK, where he met his wife and after graduation took up a job in the USA where he remained to this day. His life was typically American, with the exclusion of diet to which he and his family remained loyal to Iraqi cuisine. His wife and he drank alcohol, and there was the occasional affair with other women. He was unhappy but could not ever put his finger on where the source of his discontent was coming from.

One day he was visiting a friend in a hospital in Michigan, when, over the public address system there was a call for anyone who could read Arabic. For some reason, he explained, when he heard that message, he suddenly felt overcome with a sense of urgency to answer that request. He immediately went to the information counter of the hospital and volunteered his services as an Arabic reader. Within minutes, a doctor and a nurse came to escort him to a room where there was a woman dying of cancer in her last moments of life.

When relating this part of the story, his eyes filled with tears. He dropped his head and under his breath he said: "I wish Allah had given me a wife like this woman."

He continued the story. The doctor explained that the woman dying was a Muslim and her last request was to hear the Qur'an being recited as she passed on to the next world. He could not believe what he was being asked to do. He had not picked up a Qur'an for the better part of his adult life; he didn't even believe in Allah let alone did he feel adequate to read it to someone as their last dying request. But all that consideration evaporated when he saw the face of the woman lying in the hospital bed. Her face shone with a golden light and there was a deep peace and joy in the room that could be seen reflected in the faces of all others present in the room. He put aside all considerations and all thoughts fell away. He knew in his heart that he was meant to be there. Hands shaking and heart trembling, he picked up the Qur'an and began to recite *Surah Ya Seen*. The words fell on his tongue like sweet drops of rain on earth long parched by drought. His eyes ran like rivers as he watched the last moments of life lift from her face. To this day, he said, he hears her last words like a mantra in his mind, *Allah, Allah, Allah*, into silence.

After finishing reciting *Surah Ya Seen* through, he greeted the family of the deceased and, with tears in his eyes and words choking in his throat, he expressed his gratitude to them for the honor of being witness to such an event. He could not fully explain to them or entirely understand what had really and fully happened that day, but his life was now changed forever. Upon returning to his home, he explained to his wife what had happened. She was quick to dismiss the entire episode as a fluke and criticized his weak character in the whole event. But he knew different. He made a pledge that night to make amends for all his bad behavior by memorizing the entire Qur'an and becoming a *Hafiz*. He would, from that day forward, do his prayers and fully adopt the teaching of Islam into his life. Although his pledge was not to impress his wife, it did not have a positive effect on her. She became more and more bitter about his new commitment to Islam. She refused to pray or do anything that had to do with Islam. She even went as far as to spill a glass of wine over the head of her husband while he was in prostration on his prayer mat. Soon, she was having affairs with other men and the writing was on the wall – it was a marriage that was coming to an end.

His reason for telling me all this was to ask for my advice in this matter. He felt that maybe he should not let her go in the hope that she would eventually come around and accept Islam for herself. I would have agreed, but this situation had been going on for the past four years, and it had just gotten worse. My suggestion was clear in my mind and heart: divorce the woman. I told him that there were plenty of women who would love to marry him. He agreed and said that he would act on it as soon as he returned home. He then said again how he would have loved to know that woman who died. That he would love to find someone like her to have as a life companion. I said, "You never told me her name." He answered that her name was Shakura. Upon hearing her name, I was overwhelmed. My hair stood up on end and my tears flowed out in awe. It was Shakura, a member of our community in San Antonio, Texas, whom I had personally known for the past seven years, until she had become ill with cancer and returned to her family for her last days. I could only say, *Subhan ALLAH!* How can this happen? Only by Allah's generous plot and design. He was shocked when I told him that I also knew her for many years. Allah is great. How this man was guided to pick me out of a crowd of thousands attending the conference, to tell me this amazing story, and I know her. *Subhan Allah!*

May Allah give us the honor of her company in the Garden of the next life!

May Allah protect us from the illusion that we are in-charge of our lives!

May we always look to His guidance in all things and fill our hearts with His light and nothing else!

May Allah bless Shakura, give her the ultimate station of witnessing and ease on the day of rising!

Amin!

The Play of Opposites

There are always dichotomies, opposites and contrasts that seem to follow along in every moment of life. It was on this visit to the Islamic conference in Oklahoma that I met a young redheaded man by the name of Steve Emerson, a so-called expert on what he referred to as "Islamic Terrorism," an oxymoronic term because killing the innocent is utterly un-Islamic.

He was the one to approach me at this conference and asked if he could interview me for a research project he was doing on Islam. I was eager to share with him what I could of the goodness of my path, but I soon realized that he was not really interested in a fair and balanced view of Islam. He was looking for the "inside dope." No matter what I tried to share with him about the beauty and benefits of our path, he would impatiently act as though he had heard what I was saying and then return to his pointed questioning about terrorism and the abuse of women. I was as patient and kind as I could be to him, even taking him out for lunch, and paying for it, because he had no money to eat. I soon ended our conversation after lunch as I realized he only wanted information that would confirm his predisposition and false assumptions. I later learned he wrote several books on Islam and terrorism and became famous in infamy after the tragedy of 911 as a paid consultant for the media, especially cable television.

There is a great tradition from the Prophet Muhammad, where he says: "The *Mo'min* (Believer) is the Mirror of the *Mo'min.*"

All human beings contain the divine message that Allah is in-charge of all things.

If we have the inward panorama of *Iman* and establish reliance on it, we will naturally reflect this inwardness to others, benefiting not only ourselves, but others as well. It is like the phenomena of sympathetic cords. When a cord is strung on a musical instrument, it vibrates other instruments of like nature with the same notes. In the same way, if we have illness and confusion within, we will reflect it to others, damaging not only ourselves, but also those around us.

Our lives and deaths are full of Allah's signs and messages, and often we give each other precious moments of reflection that change our lives and the lives of others forever.

In the ultimate picture of balance, humans are outwardly dependent upon each other and inwardly dependent exclusively on Allah. We need each other to see ourselves. The most precious secret of the path is to realize that the world around us, including all other beings, humans, animals, and vegetables, are aspects and signs of our own selves. This is clearly demonstrated in the first revelation from Allah, via the Angel Gabriel to the Prophet Muhammad, where Gabriel orders him, as it states in the Qur'an in chapter 96, as follows:

> *In the Name of Allah, the Beneficent, the Merciful.*
>
> *Read in the Name of your Lord who created. He created humans from a clot. Read, for your Lord is Most Bountiful. Who taught by the use of the pen. Taught humanity what they knew not.*

These first verses of the Qur'an were revealed to the Prophet Muhammad after he had spent many days, weeks and sometimes months in isolation in a cave on Mount Hira. This was the way of all prophets before him. In retreating from the outer world, one can inwardly expand the gift of awareness to its human limits and, through the grace of the Lord, break the bounds of the limited consciousness to realization and enlightenment of the one and only consciousness behind all created beings. The order to "read" was both a command and a statement of truth from Allah, revealing to the Prophet his divine station and purpose. He read what was before him: the ever generous and effulgent symphony of realities that indicate the one and only reality behind it all. The Prophet awoke to the true and ultimate purpose of humankind. But more so, and above others, he was charged to be the ultimate mirror and guide to others on this path of realization.

This process holds true for all of us, whether we are aware of it or not. The creation around us mirrors our lives and speaks to us relentlessly about ourselves. Either we are awake and "read" the message directed at us, or we remain asleep and the content while our life is wasted.

Shaykh Muzaffer Ozak al-Jerrahi

"It is easy to know God. But to find a way to God is painfully hard. You cannot find God without passing beyond your own being. A Sufi does not become a Sufi by sitting on a prayer mat. The dervish way is not just the donning of a special turban and a cloak. A Sufi is one who annihilates him-self in the truth, one whose heart is purified. The Sufi is someone who needs neither the sun by day or the moon by night. For the Sufi is one who walks day and night in the light of truth".

— Shaykh Muzaffer Ozark

In 1981, Shaykh Muzaffer wrote a brief autobiography titled, *The Unveiling of Love: Sufism and the Remembrance of God*. The following extract is reproduced here.[23]

---

[23] Editor's Note: The extracts are from Shaykh Muzaffer's book. We've added subchapter titles for the readers' convenience.

Dream About Imam `Ali Cutting My Head Off

During my early youth, while studying the Qur'an interpretation at the Aya Sofya Mosque in Istanbul, I dreamed one night of the Prophet Muhammad, on him be peace. He was riding his camel led by Imam `Ali, may God be pleased with him, who was holding in his other hand his famous sword, the two-edged Dhulfiqar. Addressing me, the Prophet asked if I had faith and if I was a Muslim. When I said yes, he asked me if I would give my head for Islam. Again, I said yes. Then the Prophet told Imam `Ali to cut my head off in the name of Islam. Imam `Ali asked me to stretch my neck out, then struck me with all his might, severing my head from my body. I awoke in terror. When I saw my Qur'an teacher next morning, I told him my dream and then told him who my father was. I knew he was a close friend of my late father, but I had never mentioned it before. He shook his head and said: "Ah, so you are the son of my fellow exile, are you?" My father and my teacher were among the seven hundred Shaykhs and theologians who were banished to the port of Sinop on the Black Sea by the revolutionaries of the Committee of Union and Progress, for having supported the Sultan. The exile of these religious dignitaries had continued until the First World War in 1914.

My teacher then interpreted my dream and said that I was going to join the Sufi path of `Ali and that I would become the Shaykh of a particular order.

Seeing Seyyid Shaykh Ahmed Tahir ul-Marashi in Dream

Many years after that incident, when I had opened my store of rare books near the Beyazit Mosque and become a well-known Imam and preacher, I had another dream. I was in the middle of the Bosporus between the Topkapi Palace and Uskudar, in a small sailing boat whose sails were torn and whose mast was broken. A terrible storm was raging. Someone handed me a sheet of paper and told me to read it so that I would be saved from the calamity. When I came back to my shop next morning, I saw the very person who had given me the paper in my dream, passing in front of my shop. I could not gather the courage to call him. A couple of days later I dreamed about the same person. He was walking on the other side of the street and beckoned to me with his walking stick. The next morning, in amazement, I again saw him passing in front of my shop. I felt that there was a spiritual meaning to these dreams, but I did nothing about it. A short while later I saw the same man again in a dream in which he hugged me so hard that I felt my bones about to break. Then he let me go, held up the crown of the Helveti Order, and put the turban on my head. I felt crushed under the weight of the turban. It was as if the seven heavens were sitting on my head.

As soon as I came to open my shop in the morning, I saw the man walking by with a stick in hand. I told myself: "There is a mystery and a spiritual message in this situation. I am not going to call this man. Let him come to me." He walked by, my eyes following him, then he stopped and came and stood in front of my shop, stuck his head through the door, and said: "You dogmatist, three times you have seen me. When are you going to start having faith?"

"Right now," I exclaimed, grabbing and kissing his hand. This holy person was Seyyid Shaykh Ahmed Tahir ul-Marashi, the Shaykh of the Halveti-Shabani order. I became his dervish, and he would come to my shop every day. Some days he would speak, on others remain silent, but in either case he would be teaching me. This continued for seven years.

Eventually, Shaykh Muzaffer became the nineteenth Shaykh and eight *Khalifah* of the Halveti-Jerrahi Sufi Order.

We will show them Our signs in the Universe and in their own selves, until it will become crystal clear to them that it is the truth. Is it not sufficient regarding your Lord that He is a witness over all things?

— Qur'an 41:53

Meeting Shaykh Muzaffer

Sometime in the spring of the early 1980's, Shaykh Muzaffer and a group of traveling Dervishes from both the Helveti-Jerrahi Order and the Mevlana Order of Sufism were visiting the United States. I was living in San Antonio, Texas when we were invited to attend a program organized for Shaykh Muzaffer by the Rothko Chapel in Houston. Many members from our community attended, including Shaykh Fadhlalla and some of his family members.

The program was held in the circular main event room, where Shaykh Muzaffer was invited to sit at center stage. When Shaykh Muzaffer sat down, he became the *"Ka`ba"* of the moment, metaphorically speaking, our hearts making *Tawaf* (circling around the Ka`ba) with the intoxicating love and welcoming that exuded from his being. He invited his guests as pilgrims of Love into his overflowing heart. Shaykh Muzaffer, who used to smoke, threw cigarettes at everyone, signaling to all that they were acknowledged and welcomed. Shaykh Muzaffer was a wide-open door of invitation to the path of Light, open for anyone, at any level or understanding.

This openness in his being was very familiar to me. I had met many teachers who came to America with the same or similar openness. It was loving openness and universality that initially attracted me to peruse many spiritual teachers and their teaching. I remember Shaykh Abdalqadir making a comment regarding his initial approach to his work in America. He said, "First I show them the ocean, then teach them to wear a swimming suit." Eventually this was the realization of many, including Shaykh Muzaffer.

After the welcoming and informal pleasantries and introductions, the program began. The lights were dimmed as several young men walked onto the stage in traditional Sufi lodge garb. In their hands were sheepskins that they placed under themselves as they formed a circle around Shaykh Muzaffer. The last of these men not only carried his own sheepskin, but another, larger and dyed red, which he placed in front of Shaykh Muzaffer.

The Dervishes continued entering the room, along with the musicians; all taking their place upon the sheepskin mats. Shaykh Muzaffer also took his place as the call to prayer was made from the stage echoing the eternal call. The room overflowed with its majestic presence, stilling everyone into silence, their hearts all responding to the timeless call of unity. Immediately after the call to prayer, the Dervishes stood up from their mats one by one and began rotating and whirling around the stage. Others remained sitting, chanting the beautiful names of Allah, while the musicians carried and blended all into a singular feast of the heart. Although we did not physically rise from our chairs, we all inwardly turned and twirled with the Dervishes as they spun along the edge of the stage and beyond.

Words fail to communicate when matters of heart have been offered. The program came to an end with the recitation of the Qur'an and the outer stage lights came on. There was an invitation to return to normal behavior, but few could hardly move. Like a top spun from the pull of a string, even when the string no longer influences the top, it continues to spin, turning its course until the natural forces take over; the memory, however, and the taste of turning remains.

On The "Sufi Magic Bus" / Day with Shaykh Muzaffer

The next day we were invited to attend an outing with Shaykh Muzaffer and his entourage. The plan was to attend another gathering later that afternoon and have lunch out at a local Texas restaurant. Accompanying me was a dear brother of mine, Hajj Daud Haroon (may he rest in peace!). We all met at the hotel where Shaykh Muzaffer was staying with other dervishes. There was a luxury bus waiting outside to transport us all to the next venue. It was just a delight to be on a bus with Shaykh Muzaffer and all the dervishes. As we traveled out, the Shaykh started chanting and everyone on board joined in. If there was ever a Sufi version of a "the magic bus" this was surely it.

After the morning gathering was over, we were taken to the restaurant for lunch. I was sitting directly across from Shaykh Muzaffer facing him at the table. Our hosts ordered food, Shaykh Muzaffer, giving carte blanche to our hosts to order for the whole group. When Shaykh Muzaffer's plate was placed in front of him, I saw him pause, staring at the oversized sausage sitting on a pile of Jamaican rice in front of him. I was close enough to get a whiff of it and knew that it was pork or a pork mixed sausage. I reached across the table with my fork in hand and stabbed his sausage, placing it on an empty plate on the table. I said to him, "*Hadha Khanzeer,*" meaning, "This is pork." I didn't speak Turkish, but I knew he would understand. Our host was very apologetic. He confessed he hadn't thought it through that the sausages (which this establishment was famous for) would be pork. Shaykh Muzaffer called me over to sit next to him, putting his arm around my shoulder and he hugged me saying (through a translator) that he would not travel in America unless I was at his side. We returned to the hotel on the bus and Shaykh Muzaffer asked me to accompany him to his room. He entered his room, asking me to remain in the hallway and wait for him. When he emerged from his room, he asked me to open my right hand, where he placed a medallion, decorated with Arabic calligraphy. He said it was the shield of the Helveti-Jerrahi and it would be a protection and blessing for me. I kissed his hand thanking him. We embraced. That was the last time I saw Shaykh Muzaffer, He died a few years later in 1985.

Shaykh Muzaffer Giving Shaykh Fadhlalla Permission to Recite the Jerrahi Diwans

Once Shaykh Fadhlalla visited Shaykh Muzaffer in New York, where at that time most of the Shaykh Muzaffer's community resided. I believe the gathering was held at one of his centers in upstate New York. Shaykh Fadhlalla requested Shaykh Muzaffer his permission to recite some of the litanies and songs from the Jerrahi Diwans. Shaykh Muzaffer immediately requested one of his students to present all copies and tapes of the Jerrahi Diwans to Shaykh Fadhlalla, authorizing him to recite them anytime and share them at his discretion. Many students present were shocked at this unprecedented move by their Shaykh to instantly authorize someone to control all the Jerrahi litanies at once. Traditionally, these songs and litanies are given in measure to students when they reach certain stations and milestones, as an acknowledgement of their progress and station on their path. Even some of the more experienced and accomplished students, some having the designation as a teaching Shaykh were surprised. It took some time for hearts and minds to settle in and recognize the veracity of Shaykh Muzaffer's decision.

Tosun Bayrak Becoming Shaykh of the Helveti-Jerrahi Order

Shaykh Muzaffer passed away while I was in California, where I had just moved to open a center for Shaykh Fadhlalla. I had been invited by some old acquaintances interested in Sufism. They had already rented a large house with this in mind; it was big enough to house several people. The house was in a beautiful area north of Sacramento, called Green Valley. It was in the foothills of the mountains and had easy access to the Bay Area as well as to Redwood City where Shaykh Muzaffer's community, now headed by Shaykh Ragip Frager, was centered.

I had heard about the authorization given to Shaykh Fadhlalla, mentioned earlier. It inspired me to contact Shaykh Ragip Frager for the purpose of forging closer ties of brotherhood and fraternity.

On one of our visits to the Helveti-Jerrahi center in Redwood City, we attended a gathering where Shaykh Tosun Bayrak (Shaykh Muzaffer's Khalifa and appointed Shaykh of the Helveti-Jarrahi order in America) was to make his first visit to the center after the death of Shaykh Muzaffer.

The center was overflowing with dervishes, students and friends. The meeting took place just after the sunset prayer, beginning with a short *dhikr*, and afterwards Shaykh Tosun addressed the gathering. With the utmost humility, he confirmed that he was appointed by Shaykh Muzaffer to take the primary office of Shaykh for the American branch of the Helveti-Jerrahi. He shared with us some of the last words spoken by Shaykh Muzaffer. Firstly, he acknowledged the work of everyone involved in representing and establishing centers for the teachings of Shaykh Muzaffer. He recalled that Shaykh Muzaffer's approach had historical emphasis on essential core universal themes and not as much on the structure of Islam, to which he, throughout his life, acknowledged as the source and foundations of his teachings. Shaykh Tosun acknowledged that over the years, there had been an evolution in Shaykh Muzaffer's approach in America that stood on its own merit. However, he was clear that he was not taking the same approach, underscoring that he was not Shaykh Muzaffer and had to proceed in a manner that is more genuine to who he was and what Shaykh Muzaffer's last instructions to him mandated.

He asked everyone to stand up. He then delivered his vision going forward, starting with an uncompromising condition. He said from now on, if they wanted to remain in the Helveti-Jerrahi and accept him as their Shaykh he required that they formally embrace Islam if they hadn't already. That was the first and only requirement he had. He continued, asking those present who agreed with this condition to please step forward and those who did not agree to step back. As people began to shuffle around the room, some moving back, some forward, some were also clearly perplexed and confused. It was a monumental change in the landscape of Shaykh Muzaffer's teaching approach and many were angered and felt betrayal and disappointment. When the room finally settled down, revealing that the split was roughly half and half, Shaykh Tosun addressed everyone with love and welcoming. He said that all could stay and have food and tea, reminding all present that they must remain friends, brothers, and sisters, but underscoring again that under his direction of the Helveti-Jarrahi, it must be with these conditions.

After a brief moment of silence, Shaykh Tosun turned and looked at me, asking me to stand up and introduce myself; after a brief introduction I sat down. Shaykh Tosun said to those present that I was to be considered a brother and friend of the Helveti-Jerrahi. That they must all embrace me and my teacher, Shaykh Fadhlalla Haeri, and declared that all Helveti-Jerrahi centers, welcome Shaykh Fadhlalla Haeri and his representative at their own centers as well. He further emphasized that they must put away any notion of bias towards *Madhab*, Sunni or Shi`a, and that we were all from the same tree whose root was the Light of Allah.

From that day forward, we would join in the Helveti-Jerrahi circle of *dhikr* nearly every week. Shaykh Raqip would begin the Jerrahi ceremonial *dhikr* in the style of their path and in-between, or just after, we would sing from the *Diwan* of Shaykh Muhammad ibn al-Habib and sometimes do the standing *Hadra*. I would sometimes be asked to do the talk at the end. This fusion of our traditions continued for some time.

The *Dargah* of the Helveti-Jerrahi Order in Istanbul

In 2017 I traveled to Istanbul, Turkey. It was my first visit and on the top of my agenda was to visit the burial site of Shaykh Muzaffer. One sunny bright morning, my wife and I set out to find the *Dargah*[24] of the Helveti-Jerrahi. We did not have any idea where it was, only that it was somewhere in an area of Istanbul called Fatih, which we learned was a vast borough on the outskirts of the city. We hailed a taxi, instructing the driver to take us to Fatih with no specific address. After entering the Fatih district, we came to a bridge that ran alongside a creek. There was a hill on the other side of the creek. I asked my heart if this was the place to get off and I asked the taxi driver to pull over. As soon as we got out of the car, standing on the bridge, was a tall handsome young man approximately in his thirties. His smile beamed at us as though he was happy to see us and had been anticipating our arrival. He wore a green turban on his head, the tail of which draped around his neck. On his shoulders was a long green cloak; one could see his prayer beads adorning his white, collarless shirt. His shoes were sandals, which were cut like those the Prophet Muhammad wore. I approached him with greetings of *Salaam* and he enthusiastically extended his hand and returned the greetings. I told him that we were looking for the *Dargah* of the Helveti-Jerrahi Sufi Center. He opened his arms and embraced me, taking me by the hand in a gesture to follow him. We walked hand in hand for some time om a road that went up the hill we had noticed from the taxi. Once at the crest of the hill, he pointed to the door of the Helveti-Jerrahi *Dargah*. He then asked his leave, bowed in humility and grace and walked away.

The *Dargah* was being remodeled by a department of the state that focused on upgrading spiritual and cultural buildings. The front door was blocked by wooden boards and a security guard stood near, attentively protecting the property. We walked around the side where workers had

---

[24] A shrine or tomb built over the grave of a revered religious figure, often a Sufi saint or dervish.

set flat boards along the ground that led into courtyard of the *Dargah*. I could see a room through a lattice of metal bars; just beyond the bars were the graves of the shaykhs adorned with their turbans. My heart leaped, urging me forward. As I entered the *Dargah*, I found the tomb of Shaykh Muzaffer. I raised my hands and recited *Surat ul Fatiha*, after which I paused in silent reflection and felt the immense presence of Shaykh Muzaffer; my eyes overflowed with tears, while I felt overwhelming love, majesty, and beauty all at the same time. At one point, the supervisor of the site approached me and asked us to leave immediately, explaining that no one was allowed until the property was fully renovated. Coming to our rescue, the security guard spoke on our behalf, asking the supervisor that we be allowed to stay and telling him that we had been invited by the Shaykh.

Libya Visit

In 1990, I was the host of a Canadian national cable television show called *"TV Islam International."* It was a weekly show, covering local and international issues pertaining to the Muslim community. After several months being on the air, the then Libyan government approached us to attend an Islamic conference in Libya. The highlight of our invitation was to include a personal, one-on-one interview with Muammar Gaddafi. I mused to myself that this could be a once-in-a-lifetime opportunity. No one at that time in the traditional media had interviewed Gaddafi. I imagined that this might be an opportunity for me to be seen by the mainstream media and open other opportunities.

There were problems right from the start. Firstly, due to United Nations sanctions and restrictions on travel by US citizens to Libya at that time, I had to travel with documents other than my US passport. Secondly, the flight arrangements to Libya were daunting! The first flight was from Toronto to London, then to Geneva, Athens, Malta and finally Libya. The entire journey was to be over 35 hours.

While in Malta, our passports were collected by a Libyan official. We were given special travel documents and were assured that our passports would be returned to us upon leaving Libya. It goes without saying that this made me very nervous. I resisted this move and argued over the reasons for holding our passports in such a way. My argument came to an abrupt halt when I was handed a firm ultimatum: either hand over the passport or go home. Being the positive person I am, I capitulated with the attitude that all would be fine and work out in the end.

Arrival in Libya

Upon our arrival in Libya, an official representative of the Libyan government met us at the airport. There was a line of black Mercedes cars and military vehicles waiting to take us to our hotel. I was very tired, and the whole journey and its build-up had been surreal.

We arrived at the hotel and were immediately escorted to the penthouse rooms at the very top. It was a huge building with crystal chandeliers and Persian carpets everywhere. I was later told that the entire hotel had been imported, brick by brick to Libya including all the plumbing, furniture, lighting, and other sundries involved in fitting out the hotel. All this added to the already surreal experience. All the glitz, however, did not impress me more than the thought of a bed and a good night's sleep. Finally, we were in our rooms. I collapsed on my bed and within moments I was asleep.

It wasn't even an hour later that there was a loud knock at my door. I stumbled, still half asleep, to the door and opened it. There were two military policemen who requested that I get ready to leave; *their leader*, as they put it, wanted to see us now. I tried in vain to tell them that I was in no state to conduct an interview, but it was met with a robot-like response: "Our leader wants you now" they repeated.

We were taken to the airport in the same limos that initially met us. Half my crew was still in their nightclothes. It was outrageous!

We were taken to the Tripoli Airport, and without going through security or the terminal building, we were taken directly onto the tarmac to the aircraft.

Several airport policemen led us up the ramp. The plane was a mess. It was dirty as though left unclean after an international flight. There were no stewards or stewardesses and no pilot. I tried to express my dissatisfaction about the whole thing to the police around us, but it fell on deaf ears. Soon a man in his pajamas was led up the ramp and taken to the cockpit. We soon found out that he was the poor pilot. After he arrived, the plane's engines started and within a few moments we were in the air.

Off to Benghazi

I cannot begin to express the feeling of despair and uncertainty that came over me on that flight. Here we were in the middle of the night, taken out of our hotel on a plane with one sleepy pilot, no crew and under guard and off to an unknown destination.

After some two hours, the plane started to descend. We were now told that we were approaching the city of Benghazi. As we got out of the plane a line of Mercedes cars and military police met us again. We were taken to a hotel in the middle of Benghazi. As we approached the hotel, I recognized it; it was an exact replica of the hotel in Tripoli. It was unreal. The security police took us to our rooms, identical in every way to the rooms at the other hotel, down to the smell. At this point I didn't care. All I wanted to do was sleep. I went to bed that evening with a real sense of dread that this ordeal was not over and that the worst was yet to come.

As dawn broke, I had been asleep barely three hours when there was another strong knock at the door. I opened it, and there were another two military officers instructing me to get up and get ready for the interview with the "leader."

We were taken to a domed building close to a conference center, where we were to conduct the interview. We set up our cameras and awaited the arrival of Muammar Gaddafi. The hours went by until we had been there for half the day. Suddenly, a group of Bedouins armed with automatic rifles rushed into the hall pointing their weapons at us and moving from side to side in an agitated fashion. They were yelling out to us. All we could do was freeze in our tracks. Soon, all the commotion settled down, and in walked the man himself.

Gaddafi's Speech

Flanked on either side by six Amazonian-like female bodyguards, each of whom had several weapons ranging from machetes to explosives, Gaddafi wore a long white silk robe, was barefoot and had his head tilted up in an arrogant fashion. He sat down at the table arranged for the interview and went right into a speech, part Arabic and part English.

A lot of Gaddafi's speech was about his being the only true "Islamic" leader in the Muslim world. He went on to say that most of the leadership today of the Muslims was subservient to Western powers. The talk went on for about an hour. Sitting near Gaddafi was a short man in civilian dress, scanning the area the entire time, closely watching everyone and everything that was going on. His sight soon became fixed on me. I felt more and more uncomfortable, as his stares became longer and more probing. After the last long stare, he stood up and started walking towards me.

The man looked at me like someone who was trying to remember a name, a place, or a person. As he came closer, I began to feel that I too had met him before. I searched my mind, but could recall nothing about this man. Yet, the closer he came the surer I felt that we had met.

"Don't we know each other?" he asked, standing in front of me.

"I don't think so," I replied hesitantly. My hesitation was because I had lied. There was indeed something familiar about this man.

"I am head of Muammar Gaddafi's personal security and I know you. I know you for sure," he continued. "I know you," he said repeatedly as I looked completely blank and nervous.

Arrested Due to Association with Shaykh Abdalqadir

"Tucson. Tucson. Arizona! Shaykh Abdalqadir's *Za`wiya*!" he blurted out, as something fell into place for him.

"I was there, yes! What is your name?" I asked as recognition began to dawn on me too.

231

Farooq, he replied, and went on to recall not only my name but those of others who were there.

It all came back to me then. He was one of the Libyan students who used to attend our gatherings of prayer and *dhikr*. He suddenly turned his back on me, walked over to several military police present and had me arrested for being a spy!

I was escorted to my room in the hotel, my keys taken away, my phone removed, and two guards placed at the door.

There, I remained for nearly three days. The interview was clearly off. I was under house arrest. I remained in good heart throughout, although I became more and more concerned about my welfare and what they were going to do with me next. After three days, not knowing my future, three security people came to my room and escorted me out for a walk in the garden of the hotel. They told me that I was to be taken somewhere else that day. This information made me very nervous. If they were to formally charge me, I would have little help from the State Department of the United States, as I was not supposed to be there in the first place. My family was in no position to help either.

As we walked through the garden area, I saw through the trees an old friend of mine, Dr. Mahmoud Ayub, a professor of Islamic Studies at Temple University. "Dr. Ayub!" I yelled, perhaps a bit hysterically.

"Mustafa!" he answered immediately. This was all the more remarkable an event in that Dr. Ayub is blind and recognized me only by my voice. He walked over and greeted me warmly. I didn't want to waste time in niceties as I didn't know how long I had left before being arrested and formally charged. I explained to Dr. Ayub what had happened and requested his help. Our encounter lasted about five minutes.

I was taken back to my room, and that evening, there was a loud knock at my door. When it opened, there were two security men and Farooq. I gasped, gripped with fear. But I didn't show my fear outwardly. Just as I was about to greet them warily, Farooq broke into a great smile and said, "Sorry, brother, I didn't realize you felt the same way about Shaykh Abdalqadir as I did. Come, let's take you out and show you Benghazi and get to know each other!"

What a turn around. I figured that Dr. Ayub must have talked to them and convinced them that I was not a spy-come-follower of Shaykh Abdalqadir.

Released / Shaykh Fadhlalla's Spiritual Formula

That night, I played along quietly listening to them boast about how they helped destroy Shaykh Abdalqadir's community in Norwich, England. They went on to say how they paid off people and had other Libyans help in fomenting dissent and spreading false rumors about the Shaykh. They even said they had their own operatives installed as leaders in the Shaykh's community, which, as they boasted further, resulted in the final split and downfall of that community.

I listened and, like an actor playing a role, agreed and nodded my head up and down. I couldn't wait until the evening was over. Finally, at the end, I requested my papers and passport back from the security people, which they obligingly returned to me. The next morning, I was at the airport and on the next flight out of there.

Shaykh Fadhlalla's *Dhikr* Formula / Shaykh Abdalqadir's Disapproval of My Libya Trip

Here, I should share with you that before leaving for Libya, I had visited Shaykh Fadhlalla at his home in Berkshire, England in part to film an interview with him as well as seek his advice and counsel on our visit to Libya and the proposed interview with Muammar Gaddafi. Shaykh Fadhlalla was very positive about me going; he even characterized the journey as being like a "*hajj*" for me, a pilgrimage of sorts. He also gave me a special practice to do while in Libya, and especially if I should encounter difficult or stressful circumstances while there. He could not have been more on the point. While kept under house arrest and later in lock-up at the Benghazi police station, that *dhikr* formula kept me in focus and balanced throughout the ordeal. Ironically, after receiving his blessing to go, he had called Shaykh Abdalqadir as-Sufi and shared the news that I was visiting Libya to interview Gaddafi. Shaykh Abdalqadir's response was to immediately stop me from going. He said it was potentially disastrous. Shaykh Fadhlalla later told me he tried to contact me and others to stop me, but it was too late. In the end, it all worked out for the best.

Shaykh Asaf Durakovic

Shaykh Asaf was born in the ancient city of Stolac, Herzegovina, on the River Bregava in the Balkan Mountains. He came from a family line of feudal landowners in Bosnia.

Early in his life, he was forced to flee to Croatia after the communist takeover of Yugoslavia, when their family lands were confiscated.

In his early years, he displayed extraordinary acumen along with a high level of inquisitiveness. His search for knowledge led him to attend many gatherings held in Sufi lodges, especially the Khalwati-Hayati *Tariqah*, of which he eventually was recognized and given permission as a teaching Shaykh of that order. Shaykh Asaf received his *Khilafatnamah* (a certificate given by a Shaykh to be his successor – *Khalifah*) from the late Shaykh Yahya of the Khalwati-Hayati *Tariqah* (a Sufi order) in Ohrid, Macedonia, and the late Shaykh Jemali of the Rifa`i *Tariqah* in Prizren, Kosovo.

Normally, when introducing the various personalities in this book, I have not mentioned or enumerated their individual academic achievements, but in the case of Shaykh Asaf, I feel compelled to mention his extraordinary achievements, as they speak to the rarity of his person and his unique contributions and engagements with the world of science and, in general, the world at large.

Extraordinary Academic Achievements

In his extensive studies, he earned four doctorate degrees in the field of Medicine, Veterinary Sciences, Natural Sciences and Mathematics at the University of Zagreb, Croatia, McMaster University, Canada, and an honorary doctorate from the Cosmopolitan University, USA. He served as a scientist at the Institute for Medical Research of the Yugoslavian Academy of Sciences and Arts and was subsequently awarded a scholarship by the British government to pursue postdoctoral medical studies at the Medical Research Council Harwell, Oxfordshire, UK. He continued his specialist studies and passed exams in the UK, USA and Canada. In 1991, he graduated from the Military Medical Academy in Fort Leavenworth, Missouri, and was promoted to the rank of Colonel of the Medical Corps, US Department of Defense. He authored over 220 scientific publications in recognized international journals. His corpus also included many studies and publications pertaining to Sufi contexts.

He spent several years at the King Faisal Specialist Hospital in Riyadh, Saudi Arabia, as director of the Institute of Nuclear Medicine. He spoke five languages fluently. In 2004, he was awarded the international Peace Prize in Jaipur, India, for his work on the medical and environmental consequences of nuclear warfare. He received numerous international honors including appointment as a Lifetime Fellow of the International Biographical Institute and Contemporary Men of Achievement, Cambridge, England. He held a position in the Department of Nuclear Medicine at the Walter Reed Hospital in Washington, D. C. and was appointed as a professor to four universities in the USA. As a visiting professor, he taught at many universities in North and South America, Australia, Europe, Asia, Israel, South Africa, the Soviet Union, Japan, the Middle East, and Far East. He also led the medical team at the USSR nuclear explosion test sites in Siberia and Kazakhstan.

The `Alami *Tariqah*

In the early 1960s, Shaykh Asaf established the `Alami *Tariqah* in America, with its main center in Waterport, New York. Later in the mid 90s, Shaykh Asaf underscored the primacy of his Sufi Order as the `Alami *Tariqah*. In Arabic, `Alami means: *that of the World/Universe/Whole of Creation.* The change reflected the focus of the Shaykh's mission and the subsequent work of its community members towards benefiting that which affects and impacts all of humankind.

During my first visit to Pakistan in 1980, news arrived that Shaykh Jamali, a master of the Rifa`i Sufi order from what was previously

Yugoslavia had visited *Bayt ud Deen* with an entourage of his followers, both local and from abroad. They had been visiting different Sufi centers along the east coast of the US, and one of these centers was represented by Shaykh Asaf. This was the first time I had heard about him.

Shaykh Jamali's visit to *Bayt ud Deen* had initiated a turning point for many members of the *Bayt ud Deen* community, especially with the acting Imam, Daood Abdul Haleem, who, during Shaykh Jamali's visit, publicly acknowledged Daood as a Shaykh (known as Shaykh Fattah) and began the process of initiating him into the Rifa`i order.

This event led to a great deal of upheaval and eventually a migration of many members associated with Shaykh Fadhlalla and his students at *Bayt ud Deen* to Shaykh Fattah's camp, eventually establishing his own independent center, separate and out from under Shaykh Fadhlalla's umbrella.

Sometime after I returned from Pakistan, I had a conversation with Shaykh Fadhlalla, where he mentioned to me that although I had not yet met Shaykh Asaf, he had an inspiration that I would have three encounters with Shaykh Asaf, all would be of a profound nature.

Tears to Visit Waterport

In the mid 80's I lived at *Bayt ud Deen*. I worked five days a week in San Antonio, half the time in a shopping mall, and the other was at an electronics super store.

One day, while at work, I received a call from Shaykh Asaf. I was quite surprised that he was calling me, let alone at my work. How did he get my work number? I learned later that Shaykh Fadhlalla had given him my contact numbers, and he tracked me down after speaking to my wife, Nafisa.

The manager of the store was an open critic of Islam, and Muslims in general. He was the one who answered the phone call. When I was called to the back to take the call, they commented in a questioning tone, while pointing at me, that the gentleman on the phone was asking for a Hajj Mustafa. That stirred up some concerns within me since I had enough of a difficult time to avoid exposing my association with Islam.

There were a lot of hijackings of airlines and other terror attacks being carried out by Muslim extremists, and Islam then didn't exactly enjoy good public opinion. Shaykh Asaf greeted me and apologized for the call at work. But he soon went right to the heart of his reason for calling me. He asked me if I could come immediately and leave for New York to meet him and address his community. I explained that with such short notice it would be out of the question to travel immediately. He argued with me and tried to convince me that if I acted upon his request, Allah would reward me with a greater provision than what I had now. I paused, thinking to myself that I really wanted to believe and be inspired by his call but could not see a practical way out of work, especially as it was a very busy season, and my employer would not let me go. Can you imagine telling your employer that you would like to have a week off to visit a spiritual community and spend time with their leader and mentor? I don't think that would fly!

While I was on the phone with the Shaykh, my manager walked by. It was at that very moment that Shaykh Asaf was telling me about the virtues of my teacher and his enthusiasm for Allah. I was heartily moved by his words and could not help the tears flowing from my eyes. My manager, seeing that I was crying, asked me with great concern if everything was alright. I nodded to her that all was well. She then asked me if there was a family issue or something that needed my attention. I again nodded in the affirmative.

While Shaykh Asaf was still on the line talking to me, she said to my delight and surprise, "Why don't you take a few days off and settle your situation?" I turned my attention to Shaykh Asaf, who was still on the line and did what was a complete 360-degree turn around. I agreed to come to New York, visit him and address his community.

Within a few days, I was off to Waterport, New York to meet Shaykh Asaf and visit his community.

I was picked up at the airport by one of the Shaykh's students and taken to their *Khanqah*[25] – a place where visitors stayed and guests were greeted and entertained.

On one of the three days I spent there, I was to address the Friday *Jum`ah* prayer at their community mosque. While addressing the community, a television production crew arrived from Canada. This was a cable network program called TV Islam International. They filmed my talk and the executive producer interviewed me.

I didn't know at the time that my encounter with TV Islam International would lead to my association with them later on and my experiences in Libya; though I have already discussed it in this book, the story of how I became its host is coming at the end of this chapter since it

---

[25] A building designed specifically for gatherings of a Sufi brotherhood or *tariqah* and is a place for spiritual retreat and character reformation.

is connected with Shaykh Asaf as you will see.

I remained in Waterport for nearly three days, but there was no sign of Shaykh Asaf. I became concerned that the time was growing short and that if I did not meet him soon then I would have to leave to go back home to my job. I called Shaykh Asaf from New York and his brother answered the phone. After I complained about the shortage of time, he asked me to be more patient. He reminded me that when Shaykh Asaf said he would meet me it did mean that he would meet me.

Well, the third and final day came, and it was still no show for Shaykh Asaf. I thought of calling again, but by this time I chalked it up to his "odd" behavior and gave up any expectation that we would meet.

That night, my last night at their community center, I had an extraordinary dream.

The Dream About Shaykh Asaf

I dreamt that I was standing in the middle of a city made of light. Every building, road and lamp post was composed of dew drops; like prisms, they each produced a rainbow, which all meshed together to produce a beautiful, brilliant white light. As I walked in amazement through the glimmering streets, I came to a courtyard where there was a great mansion that seemed to shine brighter than the others around it. The door of the mansion opened and a man in long robes and a turban appeared. He walked up to me and placed his hands upon my face.

"Thank you for visiting my community, it's time for you to go," he said. He then kissed me on my cheeks, right and left, and upon my forehead. On that last kiss I awoke with the call for the morning prayer.

I prayed and pondered this amazing dream. As the morning wore on, and the time for my departure was drawing near, I again called Shaykh Asaf's house to enquire about his whereabouts and whether he would show up here at possibly the last moment before I left. Again, his brother answered the telephone. I explained that I would be leaving today and expressed my disappointment that the Shaykh had not come as promised.

"Did you not see him last night?" he asked, with a perplexed tone in his voice. My mind leaped to the dream. Could he be referring to that? Is it possible that the dream was the promised visit and that it was somehow a miracle of the Shaykh in visiting me through a dream?

"Yes," I replied, equally perplexed.

"The Shaykh always keeps his appointments, one way or another," his brother reassured me.

1 left that afternoon returning to San Antonio, satisfied that I had fulfilled what the Shaykh had requested and felt more open to the expanded realities of this world – what is seen and unseen alike.

TV Islam International

I returned to San Antonio, feeling like a space-probe returning to earth. I even felt the burn of re-entry, especially when I returned to my mostly uninspiring job. This was partially due to the fact that, although I had been given permission to take leave, there was a resentful attitude permeating the atmosphere, especially coming from the owner of the business. This is what I had wanted to avoid when Shaykh Asaf had originally called me to visit his community. I did not want to jeopardize my position at work even though I did not care that much for the work I was doing. But given the critical financial needs of the time, it was sufficient. I soon saw the writing on the wall that I would not stay at this place for long.

After a few days, I received a most welcome and surprising call. Remember that interview I had had with the producer of TV Islam International? He was calling to offer me a job as the permanent host of their television program. He asked that I came up to Canada to discuss terms and he asked when I could begin. The Shaykh's words rang out in my mind and heart from the first phone call inviting me to visit his community in New York. He said that if I did this Allah would provide a better provision!

Within a few days, I was off to St. Catherine, Canada to take up the position of host for TV Islam International.

Shaykh Muhammad ibn al-Habib

In 1996, while I was living in South Africa, Shaykh Fadhlalla suggested that I visited Morocco to become acquainted with the unique architecture and building customs of North Africa. At the time, we were drawing up plans to create a model community of Sufis on a plot of land comprising approximately one thousand acres. The project was called Umdeni after the Zulu term for 'extended family.' I was to be accompanied on our journey by a local architect, an Afrikaner named Yusuf. Yusuf had been working closely with the Shaykh for some time on this project and other projects the Shaykh had involving his own home and farm. Yusuf had become fond of the Shaykh and, despite being a dedicated Christian, showed a deep appreciation of Islam and spirituality in general. The Shaykh thought that with exposure to Moroccan life and architecture, Yusuf and I could bring back with us valuable experiences to apply to the Umdeni project.

This was especially exciting for me because I had always wanted to visit Morocco.

Morocco held a special significance for me. It was there in Morocco that Shaykh Abdalqadir and the first members of his community met Shaykh Muhammad ibn al-Habib. Many had spent time living in the *Za`wiya* there. It was a place of pilgrimage that held a high rank in the cosmology of this community.

I had also always wanted to visit the place where Shaykh Muhammad ibn al-Habib taught and was buried. It was his collection of gnostic songs that became a nourishing spiritual staple for me through the years. His *Diwan* is filled with profound teachings, and the melodies used in its recitation have always moved my heart.

The *Diwan* was the very first book given to me when I embraced the path, and that very same one has been with me for over forty years.

Before embarking on our journey, I requested Shaykh Fadhlalla's blessing for the journey. I expressed my desire to visit the *Za`wiya* and shrine of Shaykh Muhammad ibn al-Habib while in Morocco. To my surprise he replied that he was unable to give me *idhn* to make that visit because he did not have the power to grant it to me. He remarked that there had been controversy and much *fitna* (trouble, conflict) around Shaykh Habib's shrine and didn't want me to become caught up in its wake. Although I accepted his guidance without hesitation, I was still very disappointed. It had been a long-standing dream to one-day travel to Meknes and visit the tomb of Shaykh Muhammad ibn al Habib.

Yusuf and I landed in the Moroccan city of Casa Blanca, remaining there for only a few days as we made plans and arrangements for our travel through the country.

After visiting Marrakech, our train was to pass through the great city of Meknes, where we were to remain overnight before continuing our journey. I visited many shrines and *Za`wiyas*, but I avoided the *Za`wiya* of Shaykh Muhammad ibn al-Habib, as I did not want to breach the warning of my Shaykh.

Meeting Shaykh Muhammad ibn al-Habib in a Vision

On the very first night while drifting asleep, I felt a presence of someone in the room, standing near my bed. I did not feel alarmed; on the contrary, I felt at ease, a cool sweet-scented breeze wafting over my face. I was compelled to look over my shoulder and see what or who had entered my room. There, appearing like a glimmer projected upon a flowing soft white silk screen was Shaykh Muhammad ibn al Habib, his face shinned, sparkling like that of a starry night in the desert sky. He waved his hand into the air, opening a space beyond the confines of the room; there appeared an archway, and written on the very top of the arch was *Babul Zaytun*, which means *Olive Door*.

Looking through the arch, I saw an old wooden door recessed within a niche of a Moroccan entryway. The door slowly opened and standing in the doorway was the smiling face of Sidi Muhammad, an old blind *faqir* of

Shaykh Muhammad ibn al-Habib. Although I had never actually met him in person, I recognized him from his photograph that was printed in the book *The Meaning of Man*. He smiled and beckoned me to enter the *Za`wiya*. As I entered the room, I saw that it was filled with a brilliant light that engulfed us all and its source was emanating from the shrouded tomb of Shaykh Muhammad ibn-al Habib. I then woke up.

I was infused with a deep sense of well-being and humbled for having been given such a vision. I felt that I did not have to visit the *Za`wiya* of Shaykh Muhammad ibn al-Habib, as I had been blessed with the vision of visitation from the unseen.

At the *Za`wiya* of Shaykh Muhammad ibn-al Habib

The next morning, we made visits to the many shrines and places of *dhikr*. While at one of these shrines, I became acutely aware of a man who had just entered. He was in striking contrast with all the others who had come to meditate or pay quiet respect to the saint buried here. He was dressed in what appeared to be rags, his turban was large and unruly and his hair peeked out like spikes in all directions from his head. He was yelling and demanding *"baksheesh, baksheesh, baksheesh!"* (Charitable Donation). I soon realized that he must have been a regular at this shrine as the people there did not seem to care and most compliantly reached in their purses and gave the rude gentleman some *baksheesh*.

Eventually, he was standing directly in line of sight of Yusuf and me. I could feel his radar focus on us and as soon as that thought popped in my mind, he, sure enough, made his way over to us. He approached me in a very agitated manner and grabbed my hand, insisting that I was in the wrong place and that I must go with him.

I recognized that this was an opening – an invitation I had to accept. I stood up while the man's hand was still grasping mine. He pulled me through the city streets of Meknes at a pace I struggled to match. I felt like a child whose shorter legs had to double in steps to keep up. We turned into a covered street. The entrance was marked with the words, *Babul Zaytun* (The Olive Door). At the end of the street there was a shaded area, which led to a doorway. My heart began to race and my legs became weak as I noticed that it was the very same doorway, I had seen in my dream the night before. The door suddenly opened and there, standing in the doorway, as in my dream, was Sidi Muhammad welcoming me into the *Za`wiya* of Shaykh Muhammad ibn-al Habib.

Sidi Muhammad

For many years, there had only been three places in this world I had wanted to visit. The first two were Mecca and Medina. The third was this *Za`wiya*. As I entered the *Za`wiya*, I could not speak. Tears ran down my cheeks flooding my eyes to the point of blindness. Sidi Muhammad, recognizing my state, grasped my hand and led me to the head of the shrine and sat me down. He sat next to me for nearly one hour as I remained unable to express in words my utter awe and gratitude.

I finally regained my composure and greeted Sidi Muhammad, both of us kissing each other's hand with the traditional greeting and recognition of the Sufis. Although we spoke different languages, we clearly communicated with the universal language of the heart. Light moved between us like a fragrant breeze wafting in a garden in full bloom and our hearts intertwined in the transcendent elixir of Love.

After some time, the wife of the late Shaykh entered the *Za`wiya* bringing a tray of hot couscous soup. Sidi Muhammad and I both ate. It was one of the most nourishing meals I had ever had. Before departing from the *Za`wiya*, I had the honor to sing from Shaykh Muhammad ibn al-Habib's *Diwan* alongside of Sidi Muhammad, listening carefully to the subtle inflection, soaking up the patterns of sound. I had no doubt that the Shaykh was present in our invocation.

The *Diwan* of Shaykh Muhammad ibn al-Habib is a treasure chest of knowledge and a transmitter of light. It must be recited with presence of heart and serious intention to raise one's state. It is a practice that resonates the eternal echo of true being-ness. It lifts the *Himma* (determination) of all who reflect on its meanings. I offer the following commentary of a Qasida, with the intention of sharing what I have discovered of its meaning. It is only a small glimpse into this song. The true and complete meaning is beyond anything I could possibly say.

The "Remembrance of My Lord" *Qasida*

I am ecstatic, alone, in the *dhikr* of my Lord. The *dhikr* of my Lord – it is the cure.

All expressions of life have come from One, Indivisible Source, One, Essential Divine Reality that is the origin and progenitor of the entire spectrum of existence.

Individual consciousness is a manifestation of Divine Consciousness, caught for a while within the womb of space and time.

We all have at the core and heart of our being a Soul or spirit that is seamlessly connected to Divine Consciousness that is beyond space and time.

The experience of separation from the Divine is a result of conditioned consciousness.

Conditioned consciousness naturally identifies itself as a unique and separate individual. As conditioned consciousness matures, higher consciousness rises and recognizes the transitory nature of its existence.

Experience itself implies duality.

The Shaykh is expressing in this *Qasida* that the key to realization of the United Reality is through *dhikr* (remembrance). The one who is in a constant state of *dhikr* sees only the One Actor in all actions. They witness the One Will behind the illusion of the many, and therefore becomes cured from the illusion of otherness.

I have loved a Lord – on Whom I can count in each single thing – it is He who decrees:

Love is the universal glue that binds and connects all that appears in time and space, yet the Source of that Love is beyond time and space. The awakened, simultaneously acknowledges the localization of Divine Consciousness and the transcendent Singularity. In this way, he or she acts out of a desired outcome and at the same time knows that any outcome is ultimately by decree.

And in each love for what is other-than-He, in it is pain – in it is grief.

Everything we claim, know, love or possess is vanishing. No sooner that we claim youth, it has slipped away. Wealth, position, family and friends are disappearing on the horizon of our lives. Whatever we are attached to in this world will be taken away whether we like it or not; this is the transitory nature of this life.

The Shaykh is counseling us not to abandon love, but to love with the Love of Allah. Embrace all that Allah has provided us in a way that leads us to seeing Him as the Owner and Sustainer of all things. If we see our lives and all that they contain as stepping-stones and signs leading to His throne, we will have achieved balance in this life and prepared ourselves for the next.

The Shaykh indicates the key to avoid overwhelming pain and grief is to abandon our will into His; to collapse our plan and stake our poles under the everlasting canopy of His Will. In this way, we will be spared the pain and grief of attachment that is born out of the illusion of other-than-Him.

Oh, the victory of the one annihilated beyond annihilation. He will have life and going-on!

Everything is already annihilated in Him. He is, was and will always be the One behind All. There is no reality but His Reality, and it is the illusion of other-than-Him which prevents the human being from experiencing true life and eternal bliss.

The victory of the one who is annihilated in annihilation is that they are no longer under the veil of the illusion of separation from the Unitive Reality. One constantly finds refuge in being present in the moment, in the now, until one no longer experiences oneself as the locus of perception and abandons identification with the conditioned self. They have died to themselves and born anew in having tasted the eternal reality. By it, they are gifted with True Life, in that they now know the One and Only Giver and Source of life itself. They are given *Baqa* (ongoingness), and, by that Life Giver, take their place as true reflectors of the Divine Light.

Oh Lord, bless Muhammad! From his essence light! Radiance too!

The Prophet Muhammad was both *Abdahu wa Rasuluhu*, slave *and* messenger. His great being reflected the balance of both divinity and humanity at the same time. He was the pure conduit to which divine guidance flowed, and he exemplified the highest form of its expression. His inner light was evident to all and was made perceptible by his human qualities. Through him we know the extent of Allah's mercy, and by him we can come to know ourselves by emulating him in his way of being.

His Family and noble Companions. They make the trusts! They keep them too!

Allah says in His book of revelation:

> *Allah only desires to keep away the uncleanness from you, O people of the House, and to purify you with a [thorough] purifying. (33:33)*

The Messenger of Allah said, *"Oh people! I have left amongst you two things, and if you take hold of them, you will never go astray: they are the Book of Allah and my progeny."*

Shaykh Muhammad ibn al Habib was a descendent of the Prophetic lineage on both sides of his family. He was both Hasani and Husayni. His love and predisposition towards the Prophet's family is evident throughout his great collection of *Qasidas*.

In the *Qasida*, '*The Minor Song*,' the Shaykh ends with a prayer:

> *"May Allah's blessings be upon him [the Prophet Muhammad] and his family and whoever follows them, give them Ihsan[26] to the day of rising."*

Access to the Prophetic light is through transmission. One heart to the other, as it has been throughout time, forms the unbroken chain of light to this day. It has taken many routes as it has flowed through the hearts and hands of the *Awliya*.

All of the Sufi *Tariqahs* are conduits of that light. Within each lineage, there is the presence of the Prophet's enlightened family. At the head of all, with the possible exception of the *Naqhbandi Tariqah*, believed to be headed by the Prophet's companion and the first Caliph, Abu Bakr, is the king of the Sufis, `Ali ibn abi Talib, the nephew and son-in-law of the Prophet Muhammad. He was the first male to accept the Prophetic revelation and was the appointed leader of the *Ummah* (Community of Muslims) after the Prophet.

Imam `Ali and the descendants of our lady of light, Fatima Zahra bint Muhammad, along with the "noble companions" made the foundation of the house of Islam. They were as the Shaykh describes:

> *"They make the trusts! They keep them too."*

---

[26] Beautification, Perfection, Excellence.

Shaykh Sidi Fudhul al Huwari

During my visit to Morocco, I had the opportunity to visit Fez, where Shaykh Sidi Fudhul al Huwari was born sometime around the turn of the twentieth century and grew up. It was one of the places I had always wanted to see and spend time. I had heard of its stature as the city of *Awliya* as well as being a World Heritage site, containing the Qarawiyyin Mosque and *madrasah* and for the presence of countless scholars, teachers, and exemplars of Sufi lineages.

While visiting Fez I was blessed with the honor of meeting Shaykh Sidi Fudhul al Huwari, who was given the mantle of the Habibiyya Sufi *Tariqah* by Shaykh Muhammad ibn al Habib, along with Shaykh Muhammad Bel Kurshi.

He earned his living as an artisan and craftsman and was known to have a highly developed sense of empathy for his fellow human beings. He participated in local politics, always standing for justice and social responsibility.

His First Encounter with Shaykh Muhammad ibn al-Habib

He first encountered Shaykh Muhammad ibn al-Habib outside a shop where he was employed in his late teens. Shaykh Habib would pause in front of the shop while on his way to the mosque, glancing at Sidi Fudhul. He recalled how his "look" touched his heart and left with him a strong attraction towards the Shaykh, as well as an impression of the depth and stature of the man.

From time to time, he had also seen the Shaykh walking towards the Qarawiyyin Mosque.

After a short while, Shaykh Muhammad ibn al-Habib asked the owner of the shop if he could take Sidi Fudhul with him to the mosque.

The shopkeeper obliged and Sidi Fudhul made his way to the mosque with Shaykh Muhammad ibn al-Habib. When they arrived, several of the Shaykh's *mureeds* were already gathered, waiting for the arrival of their Shaykh. It was in this circle that Sidi Fudhul began his education in the Sufi way. One of the Shaykh's first instructions to Sidi Fudhul was regarding being present in the moment, to sit and observe, advising him that things might not seem clear at first, but by practicing being awake and fully present in the moment would result in seeing that everything was clear.

Sidi Fudhul committed to attend the gatherings with Shaykh Muhammad ibn al-Habib. His love for the Shaykh and his fellow students grew. It wasn't long that he came to realize what the Shaykh had originally indicated to him. He came to know himself and the divine treasure that laid at the center of his being.

In time, he went on to become a scholar in his own right and was also recognized as the leading disciple of Shaykh Muhammad ibn al-Habib.

During his life, he served as an Imam in the large mosque near *Bab Boujloud*. He also taught Ibn Ashir and other texts in the Bou Inania Mosque. His lectures on Ibn Ashir were some of the most well-attended and popular lectures in Fez among common people.

He was also the main commentator of the *Diwan* of Shaykh Muhammad ibn al-Habib, as well as a poet of some reputation himself.

He was a man of great humility; even though he had been authorized by Shaykh Muhammad ibn al-Habib with the mantle of the *Tariqah*, he did not feel himself worthy of filling the shoes of his Master. Due to the vast knowledge Sidi Fudhul possessed, many people recognized him as a saint and a scholar. He was known for his commentary on the Qur'an and also possessed many *ijazah* (permission to transmit knowledge) in the various areas of sacred knowledge.

Shaykh Bennani, a scholar and *qadi* (a judge) from Fez said of him:

> *"Sidi Fudul knows what most of the great scholars do not. He knows his Lord."*

Whenever Shaykh Muhammad al-Alawi al-Maliki visited Morocco, he would take time out to visit Sidi Fudhul al-Huwari.

Sidi Fudul al-Huwari was a beautiful man, a true gentleman, erudite, learned, forbearing, and above all, he was in a constant state of submission to his Lord. He had a gentle character and an illuminated presence; it is said his face would remind people of Allah.

His tongue was always moist with the remembrance of God and he always had time for anyone who came to him. Later in life, he owned a spice shop where he would spend time reciting the Qur'an and absorbed in his many litanies.

Towards the end of his life, he lost sight in both his eyes as well as major loss of hearing. Even with these disabilities he still opened his heart and home to visitors who came for his blessings and *Barakah*.

Receiving *Idhn* from Shaykh Muhammad ibn al-Habib

At the time of Shaykh Muhammad ibn Al Habib's death, he gave unlimited permission, referred to as *Ijaz al-Mutlaq* in the Sufi circles, to just Shaykh Muhammad Bel Kurshi and Shaykh Muhammad Fudhul al-Huwari to teach and spiritually train. Shaykh Fudhul al-Huwari, being an individual of great humbleness, considered the idea of himself as a *Murshid* (a Sufi Teacher/Shaykh) as preposterous and would respond to requests for spiritual guidance with the exclamation, *"I know my limits, and I could never fill the shoes of Shaykh ibn al-Habib."*

Eventually, after two decades, he finally relented and accepted Shaykh Hashim al-Balghiti as a *mureed* who became the only person to receive *idhn* from Shaykh Fudhul al-Huwari, becoming his successor as well as the first and only *Murshid* in the Habibi Shadhili Darqawi *Tariqah* since the death of Shaykh Muhammad ibn al-Habib.

Visiting Sidi Fudhul al Huwari

Within the walls of the old city of Fez, we entered the house of Sidi Fudhul al Huwari. His wife had answered the door and, when we shared our intentions for arriving unannounced, she happily welcomed us in informing us that there had not been many visitors of late, especially those connected to Shaykh Muhammad ibn al Habib. She said the Shaykh would be delighted to visit with us and counseled us to not linger too long as he grows tired quickly due to his advanced age.

It was a simple traditional Moroccan home, with little decoration or carpets. His *Majlis* (Sitting Place) was whitewashed with simple tiles and a woven straw rug beneath our feet. The only decoration in the *Majlis* was a picture hanging on the wall of Shaykh Habib and other black & white photos of his family in a small built-in glass shelving unit in the wall. Sidi Fudhul entered the room on the arm of his wife, wrapped in a white winter cloak of rough goat hair, yellow pointed leather slippers and black felt Turkish style hat crowning his head. His eyes were beaming with light, warmly welcoming us enthusiastically and affectionately like one would act towards a beloved family not seen for some time. My Moroccan guide introduced me to the Shaykh and my connection to Shaykh Muhammad ibn al Habib. He especially lit up when I mentioned my love for the Diwan. After the formal introductions were made, Sidi Fudhul spoke to us, expounding upon the times we were living and the need to discover the Light within and hold firmly to love of the Prophet and his inheritors. He elaborated on the need to spend time in retreat whenever we could and keep company with the people of *Zauq*.[27]

---

27 Taste. "People of *Zauq*" commonly means, "People of good taste and discrimination."

Initiation Into the Habibiyya *Tariqah* / Singing the Diwan

He asked how I had come to the Shadhili-Habibiyya path. I shared with him my original exposure through meeting the *Fuqara* of Shaykh Abdalqadir as-Sufi, spending the better part of two years with Shaykh Abdalqadir and a year in Norwich, England. Upon hearing this, he asked me to sit close to him. He asked for my hand and said that Allah had preserved me from error and, through sincerity, protected my heart from deception. He said, "From this day forward, from my hand to yours, I fully initiate you into the Habibiyya *Tariqah.*" He recited many prayers and evoked many of God's names and attributes. I became lost in the overflowing heart-fullness, remembering only that I kissed his hand, and he kissed my head.

In an act of spontaneous celebration of this moment, I sang from the *Diwan* of Shaykh Muhammad ibn al Habib. Shaykh Sidi Fudhul, joined in the singing, as well as his wife and some young family members of his household. After we finished, his wife turned to me and said it had been many years since he sat and sang in a public way and thanked me for taking the initiative to sing, pointing out how pleased Sidi Fudhul was to sing along.

Upon leaving Sidi Fudhul's home, I felt hollowed out and, at the same time, the fullness of emptiness. Upon returning to our hotel, I could not speak or eat for some time.

Shaykh Abd al-Aziz bin Muhammad bin al-Siddiq al-Ghumari

During the last few days of my journey through Morocco, I was visiting Tangiers doing some last-minute shopping before returning to South Africa. Tangiers is famous for tailoring traditional Moroccan clothing; there are at least half a dozen tailors in Tangiers that provide the royal family with such clothing. I had commissioned one of these tailors to design and tailor two traditional Moroccan *Jalabiya*, one for myself and another for Shaykh Fadhlalla. This particular tailor had a wide variety of the finest embossed cotton cloth from Egypt and Nigeria. It would be a three-day wait for the order to be filled. During that time, I searched the old markets for prayer beads, *tasbih*, or *subha*, as they are called locally.

Prayer Beads (*Tasbihs*)

My interest in prayer beads goes back many years way before I took to the Sufi path. Sufis wearing a *tasbih* around their necks seemed to be a common hallmark in their dress, especially in Morocco.

I had always been intrigued by prayer beads. Lama Kunga Rinpoche, a Tibetan Lama from the Sakya lineage of Tibetan Buddhism who was my first meditation teacher and gave me my first set of prayer beads.

I once asked him about the nature and significance of prayer beads. He shared three meanings of wearing and using prayer beads. The first is that it's a simple tool to count and keep track of how many times you have repeated a certain formula. When you know the number and use your prayer beads, you are less likely to skip or forget how many repetitions are required. Most formulas prescribed in Tibetan Buddhism have what one may call an "effective dose" number; too little may not work and too many may have the opposite effect. The second was that no matter what state you might enter, the passing of the beads through your fingers grounds you to the earth and, by extension, the body. He said this helps your intellect to connect higher reflections to their mirror counterpart, which is the manifest experience of the world. The realm of meaning and the realm of form are seamlessly connected, each having their own place in perfection. The third, and maybe the most important, benefit in wearing your prayer beads, is a reminder to be humble; to bear the presence and weight of the beads is a metaphor of carrying the burden of *Samsara*[28] and, at the same time, a useful tool towards higher realms of contemplation.

While still living in the Bay Area, I had become good friends with the owner of the Jerusalem Shop in the Castro district of San Francisco. Sitara, the owner, carried a wide variety of clothing, jewelry, and textiles from the Middle East. I knew Sitara and her husband Iqbal through The Sufi Ruhaniat Society or SIRS for short. SIRS was established by Samuel L. Lewis, also known as Murshid Samuel Lewis and Sufi Ahmed Murad Chisti (October 18, 1896 – January 15, 1971).

I regularly attended their gatherings, especially the Dances of Universal Peace. On a visit to her store, I spotted a prayer necklace made of Ussr (black coral); some of its beads were inlaid with silver and accented with natural red coral spacer beads. Sitara gave them to me as a gift. It was my first set of "Sufi" prayer beads. I still have them to this day.

Before heading out into the Tangier markets I had a roll of camera film that needed to be processed. I found a one-hour processing shop near my hotel. I'm mentioning this here because the building in which the photo shop was located had a stunning wooden dome in the main area, where the processing machine was, and the walls had mosaic arches rivaling the

---

[28] The concept of Samsara in Buddhism refers to the cycle of life, which includes birth, living, death and returning to life – "continuous movement" through six realms of existence, similar to the ideas of Karma and Nirvana.

many historic shrines and mosques that I had visited earlier on my trip throughout Morocco. I was left impressed with a sense of *"Barakah"* about the place, which remained with me from that moment on. It was only later that this inner sense revealed its secret.

I left the film to be processed returning later that afternoon.

While searching the Souks of Tangiers for *tasbihs*, I wandered into an alley that was lined with craftsmen making the very *tasbihs* I was seeking. Each craftsman sat on the ground using his feet to peddle a mechanical gear attached to rudimentary lathe, freeing his hands to guide the carving tools over the spinning wood into the desired shapes. I was especially drawn to one of them who was markedly different than the others. The space around him was exceptionally organized; his work hung on pegs behind him around the opening of his shop where they displayed the fine quality of his work. Centered on the back wall was a beautiful calligraphy of the name of Allah in the fashion common to the Shadhili Sufis. He wore a large beautiful *tasbih* around his neck along with several talismans sown into pieces of green and red cloth that draped down his chest. I complimented him on his work and asked about some of his readymade pieces displayed on the threshold of his shop. He explained that he ordinarily would have some to sell, but all the ones displayed and the one he was currently working on was pre-commissioned by his *Murshid*. I asked about his Shaykh, inquiring if he had any public gatherings of *dhikr*, or if he could find time to meet a guest. Immediately upon my request, he stopped working and began closing his shop. He asked me to sit on the stool he used for working until he finished closing and that he would take me to see his Shaykh. After he closed everything up, he escorted me down a dizzying maze of streets, pathways, and stairways until we reached a green door set into a wall of succeeding doors in a narrow, cobblestone walkway. The door had large wrought iron straps holding the weathered hardwood together. In the middle of the door was a knocker in the shape of a *Hamsa* (a palm-shaped amulet). My guide tapped the knocker on the door and called out, *"Allahu Akbar"* three times. While waiting for an answer, a warm and earthly scent seeped through the cracks in the door. It was the familiar scent of aloes wood, also known as *Oudh*. The scent always surprises me in that, no matter when and where I encounter it and no matter what condition, the powerful oil affects my body and mind producing a sense of calm and relaxation. I even sometimes feel intoxicated by it.

Meeting Shaykh Abd al-Aziz al-Ghumari

A voice emerged, although muffled, from the other side of the door. It opened, revealing a lovely smiling young man, *tasbih* in hand, welcoming us and inviting us to enter. The first steps through the door opened into a tiled courtyard, lined with palm-like plants complimented by rich clusters of Bougainvillea, their vines, climbing the walls like color streamers, shimmering in the breeze. There was a water feature that echoed throughout the inner courtyard and seemed to grow louder as we were led to a side stair leading to the *Majlis* where the Shaykh was waiting for us.

The *Majlis* was in a large room, carpeted with Berber and Persian rugs, all in traditional colors of red and orange. The walls were lined with bookshelves, housing thousands of books, plaques, pictures, and ornaments. We were invited to sit and told that the Shaykh would be right in. I remember sitting in wonder about how anybody could read so many books in one single lifetime, some of which I was sure were as deep as the ocean itself? It seemed quite an unbelievable feat!

But when Shaykh Abd al-Aziz al-Ghumari entered the room, such thoughts quickly vanished.

We were greeted and warmly welcomed by the Shaykh. He was like a lion, a large man with large hands and shoulders; yet with one twinkle of his eye he disarmed you, making you feel embraced in heartfelt welcoming. The young man who led us to the Shaykh remained with us as he spoke English and acted as a translator. Upon hearing that I was a new convert to Islam and that I came to the *Deen* through the door of the Sufis, he was delighted and inquired in some detail as to how I made that transition and through whom. I underscored introduction to Shaykh Muhammad ibn al-Habib, which elicited a response from him of joy and excitement.

I told him how the *Diwan* of Shaykh Habib was and continued to be a great influence upon my life and every time I sang from it, new meanings came to my heart and mind, often with a sense of thrill and thunder. As I spoke about this, he kept saying, *"Huwa Bihar al Anwar"* (He is a Sea of Light).

We didn't have long as the Shaykh had a previous appointment, but during the gracious hour he afforded me, I absorbed a great deal from him regarding what he represented in not only his *Tariqah*, but also in the Sufi lineages themselves as well as in the heritage of Islam in Morocco.

He was from the *Idrisi* branch of Moroccan *Sayyids* that trace themselves back to Idris – the first to lead a Shi`a revolt against the Abbasid dynasty.

Although Shaykh al-Ghumari studied in a Sunni Islamic university, he made known his own critical thinking often to the chagrin of his teachers, especially when he attended Al Azhar University. His views were based on his own research, much of which he sourced from scholarship outside his school of thought and the influence of popular religious culture. Among some of his most unpopular views was his rejection of venerating all the companions of the Prophet Muhammad. Shaykh Ghumari only saluted six of those companions and disregarded the rest because they fought against Imam `Ali. The Shaykh also was of the view that it was obligatory to celebrate the Prophet's birthday, even if the tradition originated from outside of traditional Islamic culture. The Shaykh also came under extreme pressure from the Sunni scholars throughout the Muslim world regarding his stand on Imam `Ali. He believed in the supremacy of the Imam's stature and spiritual station. He openly criticized the validity of the narrations put forth under both Umayyad and Abbasid rule concerning Imam `Ali, accusing some narrators to be manipulated by the political ruling institutions of that time.

Although we did not get deeply into these issues, I found him to be exceptional in my experience of scholars, not because I emphatically agreed with his conclusions regarding Imam `Ali, but for his openness and courage to speak out and engage outside his circle of followers to the risk of his reputation and career. As we stood up to leave, he embraced me and recited prayers over both my right and left shoulders. His final words to me were to always love and honor the family of the Prophet, for they are the Ark of Noah in this time and throughout time.

He walked us to the entrance door down the stairs and opened it to see us out. Just as we were walking through the threshold, I asked him if he knew where I could find an old Shadhili *Subha*? He answered, "you don't look for them, they look for you!"

What You Seek is Seeking You

It was now late afternoon and I needed to pick up my photos at the one-hour photo shop. As I made it to the shop, they had just pulled the open sign as I entered to close the shop. My photos were ready. I sifted through them, making sure they were all acceptable. Since I knew they were closing I felt the pressure to leave. I thanked them and headed out the door. Just as I was passing under the thick threshold of the door, my eyes fell upon what appeared to be a single bead, stuck to the wall, positioned direct center above the doorway. I was stopped in my tracks. I could not leave the shop. I looked closer at what I now was sure was a wooden bead and it seemed to have small spaces on the left and right of it, indicating that it was attached to something behind the stucco wall. I turned to the attendant and asked for a chair to stand upon and get a closer look. There were two attendants working and I noticed that they were both questioning what this "crazy" American man was doing. I asked the older of the two attendants about the history of this building and especially this room. He did not know for sure but suggested that it was once a place where people met for prayer and teaching. I asked them to please be patient with me. I requested a hammer and a screwdriver to chisel the wall around the bead to see what was behind the wall. I wanted to see if there was more to this one bead. They were trying so hard to be polite. They said they would call the owner since they could not make that decision on their own. The owner lived upstairs in the same building and arrived within a few minutes. I explained that I wanted to chisel the wall open to see what was behind it. He paused and then asked me how much I would pay him for the damages and whatever repair had to be made. We came to a fair number and agreement. I asked him also about the history of this building, and he explained that it had always been in his family for many generations. Passed on from father to son, each opened a new business as they took possession of the property. He said that this was originally a Sufi Za`wiya over one hundred years ago.

I started to break through after hammering away at layers upon layers of stucco. I commented to the owner about all the layers that I was cutting through. He mentioned that his grandfather had seen the beads hanging over the door on the wall. In his days they could still see most of the beads. I asked why they did not remove them? He said that it was left in place for the *Barakah* of their presence and the ones that used them so long ago. He continued to say that instead of taking them down, they just placed stucco over them until they were forgotten. It took about an hour to carefully remove the beads from under the stucco. What emerged was a large necklace of hand carved ancient hard wood prayer beads. The spacers, separating the ninety-nine beads into groups of thirty-three beads, were expertly carved, and in the place of the Imam Bead was a large *Alif*, as it is commonly known. It was covered in stucco and paint, but I knew this was the *tasbih* I had hoped to discover. The words of the Shaykh echoed in my heart and mind, instantly correcting me; ***it was the beads that found me, not the other way around.***

That which is not meant, the hand cannot reach

And that which is allotted you will find wherever you may be.

— *Saadi*

Shaykh Fadhlalla Haeri and *Barakah* of Surah *al-Mulk*

أَلَا إِنَّ أَوْلِيَاءَ اللَّهِ لَا خَوْفٌ عَلَيْهِمْ وَلَا هُمْ يَحْزَنُونَ ﴿٦٢﴾

But for those who are on God's side there is no fear, nor shall they grieve.

— Qur'an, 10:62

No doubt!

Also, the Messenger of Allah has said:

> *"Truly, there are among my people men who rejoice openly at the Mercy of God and weep in secret for fear of His punishment. They live on the earth but their hearts are in the garden; they themselves are in this world but their minds are focused on the next world. They live in tranquility and draw near to God through the means of His Grace."*

It is rare in life to be blessed with meeting and acknowledging another human being that mirrors and reflects one's own true nature and, with love, trust, and compassion, facilitates the discovery and path to aligning conditioned consciousness (aka the individual self/consciousness, or limited consciousness, which gives a person their identity) with the representative of the Absolute, the Soul (or *Ruh*/Spirit) within.

Meeting Shaykh Fadhlalla is the living metaphor of meeting my authentic self. If one has the fortune to meet someone like that, know that you have now met the door to your soul. From that point on, one has either to move toward that inner Light or digress in avoidance and covering up.

Everything, including everyone whom one meets, is a sign, verse and mirror, communicating directly to your consciousness, who and what you are. Everyone is a "book," unfolding in the Eternal pages of The Author, lovingly wanting you to awaken and read, just as the first word revealed of the Qur'an to the Prophet Muhammad was *"Iqra,"* meaning *Read*: *"Read in The Name of your Lord, Who created you from a single, hanging piece of flesh."*

No one can read, live and breathe for you. No Shaykh, teacher, Prophet, or friend can give you what is already living and abiding within, directly connected, seamlessly to The Source of Life itself. Relative Life or conditioned consciousness is an echo, albeit toned down and expressed through the limited senses as a matrix of dualities. It is designed as such to *dis-cover*, that which is forever, the representative of the Absolute within; the spark of which is the eternal Light that is your soul.

The best one can expect from anyone is to be a mirror, a discernable example of someone that has yielded to that Light within. He or she points to the way so that you recognize the stepping-stones of that path and, with courage and honesty, traverse it with enduring and consistent commitment.

There is no way I can adequately express my gratitude or repay my debt to Shaykh Fadhlalla. I can only come close to repayment by realizing, and fully actualizing the true purpose of my existence and live in a way that harmoniously transmits the knowledge of the true purpose of this creation and source from which all emanates.

During the forty plus years of his mentoring, companionship and friendship, there have been several outstanding moments and situations that are concentrated capsules of teaching that contained direct, shareable knowledge and wisdom.

I have endeavored to account here but a few, to celebrate the eminence of this great being and hope to share with all that read their content a "taste" of their living wisdom and the potential that lies within each one of us.

My engagement with Shaykh Fadhlalla began several years before settling in San Antonio and officially accepting his invitation to formally commit to him as my teacher, mentor and Shaykh. In the Sufi tradition, this is called taking *Bayat*, commonly referred to as "taking the hand of a Shaykh." It was only months after I had embraced Islam and made the same commitment to Shaykh Abdalqadir as Sufi that Shaykh Fadhlalla appeared on the scene where I had the opportunity to develop a meaningful relationship that grew and developed over a period of more than forty-five years. Even before Shaykh Fadhlalla had openly revealed his certification as a teaching Shaykh, I was destined to take his hand, being informed by him many years later that during our journey to California, Shaykh Abdalqadir told Shaykh Fadhlalla that he was only "holding" me until Shaykh Fadhlalla was ready, or until I was ready to accept it.

If you have read through the previous chapters, you will notice my mention of Shaykh Fadhlalla throughout the book. My connection to him is woven in my journey as a Sufi Muslim, playing key roles in my own personal evolution in life.

I offer here some encounters with Shaykh Fadhlalla; although these are stories with plots, twists and turns, the truest encounter with Shaykh Fadhlalla cannot be described or shared in any one story – it is from the realm of non-time, beyond describable incidents or circumstance – it is the *Mihrab* (niche) of meanings and Light.

A Brief Encounter with the *Kiraman Katibin*[29]

Around 1979 I was invited by Shaykh Fadhlalla to move to the *Dar al Hikma* (Door of Wisdom and Healing) hill compound northwest of San Antonio, Texas, where he and his family lived. It was also the US residence of Shaykh Hosam Raouf, who had built a home on the opposite side of the hill. There were also Shaykh Fadhlalla's offices and a laboratory where his wife Muneera produced Aromatherapy oils; she specialized in procuring the best oils and extracts from all over the world. One of her projects was a line of men and women's perfumes uniquely formulated for commercial distribution. Shaykh Fadhlalla asked that I come on board with the perfume company, heading the sales and distribution of these perfumes and following products that Muneera had in the pipeline. Being at *Dar al Hikma* afforded me the unique opportunity to be near to Shaykh Fadhlalla and to spend time with him, not only discussing business, but also for afternoon tea, prayers and shopping with and for him. There also was a large pavilion built, nestled in between the houses with its own separate pathway leading from the road to its entrance.

Nearly every week, gatherings were held there for the study of the Qur'an and in the evenings for *dhikr* and meditation. It was around this time that Shaykh Fadhlalla was visited by the exiled daughter of the Shah of Iran, Princess Shahnaz Pahlavi, along with her husband, Khosrow Jahanbani, introduced to us by his new name Muhammad Ibrahim. In a very short time, Muhammad and Shahnaz grew close to Shaykh Fadhlalla and his family, eventually moving to a home just behind the *Dar al Hikma* compound. Also, at this time *Bayt ud Deen* was being constructed and Muhammad Ibrahim was given various tasks in the overall planning and execution of the project. By matter of circumstance, I became close to Muhammad Ibrahim and his family. I would often visit them several times a week for coffee and meals. Even though we came from about as different backgrounds as one could imagine, there were many areas of similarity. We both had an interest for spiritual matters early on in life. We enjoyed some of the same music and appreciated the culture of the hippies. But all through our relationship I felt a distance; an air of superiority of status punctuated our interactions. At first, I overlooked

---

[29] In Islamic tradition the two *kiraman katibin* (honorable scribes) are two angels who record a person's every action. One angel figuratively sits on the right shoulder and records all good deeds, while the other sits on the left shoulder and records all bad deeds.

these as aberrations of a past life as a royal being pandered to as such and having anything you wanted provided for you. In retrospect, truly one does not have to be raised as a Prince of Persia to acquire these characteristics – one could be a spoiled pampered child who grew up in a working-class neighborhood without the Lamborghinis, palaces, servants and best foods as well as clothing from the world's most renowned designers. I think, in the end, I also shared some of these very same traits that led to strains on our relationship. At one point our transactions irritated me so much that I stepped back from our being more familiar, to only public or business meetings. It was at the height of our estrangement that one morning Shaykh Fadhlalla asked me to meet him in his office. He shared with me how Muhammad Ibrahim was not happy with my behavior; he cited a few incidents that, from my perspective, were represented far from how I perceived those circumstances. Nevertheless, I kept an open mind and presence of heart, my experience informing me that when it rose to the level of Shaykh addressing me, it was something I had to pay attention to as almost always there was more than just the recounting of an outer event or circumstance. There was often something for me to grasp and take to heart.

Shaykh Fadhlalla pointed out in a lengthy critique that I was not aware of what came out of my mouth, that I spoke too often without presence and without foundation in the appropriate reality of the moment.

He ordered me to record everything I said, without exception, morning till night for the next seven days. Once I had completed this task, I was to make a copy to be given to Muhammad Ibrahim for his review. He further underscored that Muhammad Ibrahim was to listen to all the tapes and then meet with me for his evaluation and comments.

I felt as though I was going to implode right in front of Shaykh Fadhlalla. Recording myself for seven days was a monumental task, but the idea of giving the recordings to Muhammad Ibrahim was like swallowing a hot burning coal. I kept my composure, trying my best to at least appear centered, but I had no doubt that the Shaykh sensed my anxiety and repulsion by the task at hand. Thankfully, good sense prevailed and stepping forward and with love and trust, I agreed.

I immediately set out to purchase a cassette recorder and a whole case of cassettes and started my seven-day journey of discovery, reflection and witnessing.

It was one of the most powerful and difficult tasks I had ever had handed to me. Each word that came from my lips had to pass the guardian of humiliation, waste, and ego. From the get-go, I was challenged to be always present, watchful in what was forming in my mind and about to escape through my lips. Almost instantly I spoke less and listened more. The first days were the most difficult as I fought the inertia of habit. After some days it became easier. I thought less about the coming humiliation of these tapes being dissected by another whom even at this point I felt could not do justice in his review, let alone his comments.

The weight of this task shifted to the everyday, nearly every moment, to be present and watchful. It was a sobering remedy that overflowed with insights into the inner workings and impulses of my mind. It was an education born out of restricting the self so that the inner light of awareness made itself known.

By the seventh day I was in the zone. I no longer cared about who would listen to these tapes, the journey was what mattered, and the gifts had already been distributed.

I met with Shaykh Fadhlalla in the late morning of the seventh day. In my hands, were the stack of cassette tapes, each marked with a date in sequence of the seven days. I handed them over to him and he placed them on the side of his desk. He expressed that he was pleased that I had completed this task, saying that there was no doubt that good had come from it. Then, in a surprising move, he handed the tapes back to me, saying there was no reason for anyone to listen to these recordings, but that I should review them myself and brand the lessons learned deep into my heart and mind and let them be a reminder of the treachery of the tongue.

Estes Park Mercedes Debacle

In the early 1980's Shaykh Fadhlalla and his family had purchased a mountaintop home just above Estes Park, Colorado, perched on a hillside with views stretching miles across the tree line and beyond into the majestic cascading Rocky Mountains on the horizon. At the back of the house were patios that led to a circular stonewall enclosure. We would often gather inside this space, which we later referred to as the Eagle's Nest. From there, one would enjoy a 360-degree panoramic view of our mountaintop retreat.

Shaykh Fadhlalla would often invite his students and guests to accompany him there as it provided the perfect ambiance that inspired the Shaykh to work on his book projects as well as have impromptu talks, especially while we were gathered at the Eagles Nest.

On one of these occasions, the Shaykh asked us to ask him questions pertaining to the most pressing issues of our time, drawing from our own personal and universal inquiries. We would record each session, later to be transcribed and edited. Here are some samples. "The Seeker," "The Chase," "The Veil," "Emotions, Mental Attitudes," "Time and Non-Time," and "Decree & Destiny,"

Over several months, these inquiries became distilled into chapter headings and addressed by Shaykh Fadhlalla. All in all, these became three chapters, with thirteen sub-chapters. Compiled together they became the book called *Beginning's End*.

Almost every afternoon, I would join Shaykh Fadhlalla for tea on the balcony outside his office. I looked forward every day to these precious meetings with him. By this time in his life there were so many people wanting to talk and engage with him, notwithstanding all his personal and business activities. I savored these moments that were full of deep reflection, overflowing in Presence of the Eternal Now. I relished these times so much, not wanting them to end, but as all things must pass as a rumbling and disturbing sound in the distance began to encroach upon our little corner of the garden. The rumbling became louder, accompanied with the sound of clanging metal and the smell of burning oil wafting over the balcony. Shaykh Fadhlalla sent me out to see what was happening and report back immediately. Going swiftly to the driveway that was just outside the front door of the house, I saw Shaykh Fadhlalla's brand new Mercedes pull up in shambles. The sides, roof and hood were crumpled, smoke poured out of the tail pipe and most of the windows were either broken or unable to function. Coming out of the car were three men who were students of Shaykh Fadhlalla. I learned later that they were given the task to deliver Shaykh Fadhlalla's new car to him at his home. They then were to stay over, while some of us were to return to Texas. I asked the one student who was the *Amir* of the journey and what had happened. He related that they were traveling too fast, wanting to make good time because they were late starting out. He fell asleep at the wheel, driving into a ditch and rolling the Mercedes several times before it came to a stop. It just so happened that it landed on its four wheels, and they were able to drive, albeit slowly, arriving late and in this condition. They were all very remorseful and feeling very guilty.

I returned to Shaykh Fadhlalla, and told him what had happened.

Living in the Moment

As I related the story in detail to him, I witnessed something so special: it did not change his state. He did not get angry or express any rancor whatsoever. There was not even a blip in his eyes, and I was very sensitive at this moment observing him carefully. There was nothing but total acceptance. He then asked me to see that the men who came had something to eat and a place to stay in the outbuildings. He also asked me to tell their *Amir* that he wanted his car returned to him in the exact condition it was before wrecking it. Shaykh Fadhlalla also added a second condition that he would not see or talk to him until this was done.

He then asked me to immediately book the first flight out of Denver to San Antonio, Texas. He asked that I wait for him outside while he packed his belongings and drive him to the airport. Although I resonated as much as I could with the Shaykh's state at that moment, his nonattachment and unshakableness eluded me. I expressed my disappointment to him. I reminisced how we were all having such a wonderful time and that we should not let this intrusion stand in the way. He generously accepted my disappointment and said, "Yes, but we are not in charge of our own affairs, this is Allah's business. I can't stay here; I don't want to be around the energy they brought with them."

Time was of the essence. The first flight from Denver was in about an hour and half and the drive to the airport was at least 45 minutes to an hour. Shaykh Fadhlalla quickly came down to where I was parked, and we were off to the airport. For most of the journey down the mountain, we sat in silence. Although my silence was that of my tongue only, my thoughts and emotions were in high gear. I was clearly feeling agitated by these events and still very upset that my time with Shaykh Fadhlalla had been taken away by such foolishness. I knew the Shaykh was aware of my state that made it sometimes hard to contain. So, about three quarters of the way, I again expressed my disappointment to him. He addressed it, admonishing me that there is good in what happens. He said that if I do not see the present in every situation then I am not living the moment to its fullness. At that very moment my stomach sank and panic struck as I realized while listening to him counsel me on basically being present and seeing the goodness in each moment, I was not paying attention to the off ramps for the airport and passed them miles back. I was so anxious that I could hardly muster up the courage to get the words out of my mouth, that we had overshot the off ramp for the airport and that we had to take the next exit and turn around and go back. Shaykh Fadhlalla immediately shouted at me to stop the car and pull over on the shoulder and stop. I followed his request. Once stopped, he got out of the car, removed his bags from the trunk and asked me to leave, while he tried to flag down a taxi on the freeway to take him to the airport. I was beside myself (in more ways than one) and could not conceive that he would be able to flag down a taxi, and even if he did, considering the time and everything, he would not make it to the airport to meet his flight. But this was no ordinary man; he is *Abdul Waqt*,[30] and with that at his core within seconds a taxi pulled over that was already going to the airport. Shaykh Fadhlalla jumped in and he was gone. I learned later from his wife back at the Estes Park house that Shaykh Fadhlalla had called, letting her know that he had caught the flight and was now at his home in San Antonio.

Instructions to Recite Surah *al Mulk* for Forty Days

In 1993, there was a Sufi gathering in Hamburg, Germany. It was organized by a group of new German Muslims who had sponsored Shaykh Fadhlalla to lead a seminar during a weekend retreat. During the time we were there, I had an opportunity to sit with Shaykh Fadhlalla privately and we discussed the future potential of activates in Germany, as well as the United States and Europe. During that conversation, Shaykh Fadhlalla informed me that he was interested in South Africa, and that he felt that it might very well be the place where he would like to live and work on his books and teachings.

While Shaykh Fadhlalla spoke about his vision of South Africa, I felt a gradually increasing otherworldly presence surrounding us. The defining outline and material cohesion of everything was fluctuating between its normal appearance and form and its non-material energetic reality as shimmering light. Within the wholeness of that moment, there was a communication, a command, if you will, that I would be part of Shaykh Fadhlalla's new venture in South Africa. I exclaimed with heart-felt certainty that I would join him. The intensity of Presence grew until there was nothing but silence. It was like the description of the "Night of Power," "*Laylatul Qadr*," peace until the rising of the dawn. Shaykh Fadhlalla's eyes tearing, mine too, we both said simultaneously, "*Hadha min Fadhle Allah*" (the overflowing Grace of Allah).

---

[30] Lit. Slave/Servant of Time; metaphorically, it means a person who lives in the moment.

Shaykh Fadhlalla instructed me to recite Surah *al-Mulk* for forty days upon my return to the U.S., between *Maghrib* and *'Isha* prayers. He added that, with Allah's permission, performing this would open the way for me to join him in South Africa. He did not know how or when, only that this came to his heart from the Grace of the moment.

3D Posters / Visit to California

Within days of returning to the U.S., my family and I set off by car to visit my mother, brother and sister who lived in California. I did, however, make a brief stop at our local shopping mall to purchase some clothes for my children before departing. As is the case in most malls, there were kiosks lining the walkway between the shops. Some of these spaces were fixed and others were temporary. One particular kiosk caught my eye. There were two teenage boys sitting at computers printing images on a dot matrix computer. The images were simple dots printed in an artistic pattern in various sizes as well as shifting patterns. There was a great deal of excitement surrounding these prints. The boys who were printing these images joined in on asking those looking at them if "they could see it." Many answered, "Yes! I can see it," and those who could not were being helped by others, including the two boys, to learn the technique of seeing what others were getting excited about. These were Stereogram prints, created by an algorithm designed to overlay two images, which when looked at in a certain way, the brain responds by creating an illusion of a three-dimensional image. All the images were already embedded in the patterns and after some struggle learning the technique, the image popped out in 3D. The whole idea of seeing with the brain and not exclusively with the eyes was intriguing.

I was drawn to these images. I instinctively felt that there was a strong potential to make these available to a larger audience and to improve the quality of images, possibly applying the concept further afield. Time was short for me as I was leaving that afternoon. I bought several copies of each design, got their contact information and in all of five minutes shared with them a vision I had to make their product successful. We all hugged and made plans to see each other upon my return. I rolled the prints up tied with rubber bands inside a black garbage bag and placed it in the trunk of my car before loading my family's luggage.

Al-Baz Publishing House

In those days, I had been working as a sales and marketing representative for Al-Baz Publishing House, founded by Ruslan Moore in 1991.

In 1986, after acquiring manuscripts of some of Shaykh Fadhlalla's works and finding that there were almost no English translations available, Ruslan turned to an old friend of more than 30 years, Muhtar Holland, one of the foremost contemporary translators of classical Arabic and enlisted him to make translations for his own personal use. On reading these translations and being struck by the beauty and wisdom found in them, it became apparent that it would be selfish indeed to keep these for himself, and the idea of a publishing company which would be a means of sharing these gems was born.

Al-Baz was set up almost as a hobby, owing its existence not to the principal notion of publishing books to make money, but rather for the purpose of supporting the Muslim community with books of truly worthy content in an age where the pressures of the world were very great, and Muslims were hard-pressed to find support for their faith.

After some mutual friends introduced us, Ruslan asked me to help in the sales and marketing of the newly formed company. In 1991 I accepted to help in any way possible. I was already engaged in sales and marketing with Zahra Publications, which at the time was the sole publisher of Shaykh Fadhlalla's books, pamphlets and community magazines.

I had spent most of my savings on my trip to Hamburg and had very little money left in the bank. I was relying on my next monthly salary from Al-Baz Publishing, which was to be deposited in my account within a few days. When I arrived in Modesto, California I called Ruslan, concerned that my check was not deposited in my bank account. He regretfully informed me that the company was unexpectedly low on funds, and he could not pay me.

Here I was with my family, newly arrived in Modesto with less than fifty dollars in my bank account. It was not enough to sustain me in the short-term during my visit with family, let alone to fund my way back to our home in San Antonio, Texas.

I called Ruslan from a phone booth outside of a local mall in Modesto.

I went out and sat in my car in the parking lot thinking what I was going to do.

Bella Vista Publications – Selling 3D Posters

I recalled having those posters in the trunk of my car. In a moment of inspiration, I retrieved the posters and walked into the mall with the idea that I would find a poster shop with the hope that I would interest the manager or owner into purchasing duplicates for sale in their shop.

I went to the trunk of my car and retrieved the posters I had placed in a trash bag. I unfolded them and prepared them to show to the poster and art shops in the mall. As I walked towards the mall, I noticed two people, a man and a woman getting out of a car. I immediately recognized them, and they recognized me. This was the couple to whom, seven years ago, I had sold the restaurant that I owned and operated in Berkley, California. They walked eagerly towards me, embracing me with tears in their eyes. They told me how happy they were to meet me after all these years. They both shared with me how they wished that one day we would meet again and share the story of success they had with the restaurant I had sold them. They explained to me that it was through that restaurant they funded both their medical college expenses, eventually graduating with medical degrees and later specializing as anesthesiologists.

I took meeting with them was a harbinger of good news and a sign that something special was happening at that moment, as though I was being reminded by meeting them that whatever goodness that you had sowed in the past meets you in the now. We embraced again, exchanged phone numbers, and promised that we would be in touch more often. I headed towards the mall and there was a poster shop. I walked in with my trash bag and posters and asked to speak to the manager. I showed him the 3D stereograms and explained to him the technique to visualize and see the 3D images appearing on the prints. He was so excited to be able to do it. When he saw the 3D images hovering above the paper, he showed it to all of his employees, and everyone became very excited about this new printing technology. He immediately turned to me and said, "How much are they?" I said to him, "Well, we sell them in different sizes." I was completely unprepared going into this and I had no idea how much I wanted to charge for them. I hadn't thought this through yet, so right off the cuff I said the small ones were 2 dollars each and the large ones were 4 dollars each. He put in an order that equaled 120 dollars. We exchanged phone numbers and I told him that they would be delivered within 14 working days. At that point I knew I had something special, and this was the end of the 40th day of reciting Surah *al Mulk*. I took the samples and went to another poster shop and got a similar order. From there, I took my family and stopped at every town and city from Los Angeles to San

Antonio, Texas stopping at every mall where there was a poster or art shop. By the time we reached San Antonio, I had over $20,000 dollars in orders. The day after I arrived back in San Antonio, I went back to the mall where I met the two young men, who had originally printed the posters and were responsible for their designs. I told them that I wanted to become their marketing and licensing agent and that I would immediately pay them to start working for me producing various novel images. I formed a company named after my mother called Bella Vista publications and began to print posters with these 3D images. By that time orders began coming in from all over the United States, and 3D stereograms were well on their way to becoming the new pet rock. Everybody wanted them.

Enough Money to Stay with Shaykh Fadhlalla in South Africa

With the help of my family, late nights rolling posters in tubes, running between the post office and UPS deliveries, after the first six months we had over $100,000 dollars in orders. Publishing companies from all over the world were contacting me, and I began to license the images for producing calendars, storybooks, coffee table books, and posters. Within one year, I had committed sales and collected royalties of nearly half a million dollars. Shortly after this explosion of good fortune, Shaykh Fadhlalla informed me that he was moving to South Africa. This was in 1994. I traveled with him to South Africa that year to visit the provinces and cities in which we would eventually live.

This was a culmination of that original intention in 1993 when we were in Hamburg, Germany and Shaykh Fadhlalla had given me the instruction to recite Surah *al Mulk* for 40 days in which he said that at the end of those 40 days Allah would make a way for me to join him in South Africa, and it all came to pass. So, at the end of 1994 and the beginning of 1995, I had enough money and resources to travel with my family to South Africa, and that was the beginning of our five-year stay with Shaykh Fadhlalla there.

Sitting on a Pile of Gemstones

One morning I was visiting Shaykh Fadhlalla at his home in South Africa. I found him pruning and digging around his covered vegetable garden up to his ankles in dirt. He invited me to join him in weeding out the unwanted plants and clearing the way for his vegetables to grow. While digging away, he mentioned to me that the previous night he had a vision of me. He said he saw me sitting upon a vast pile of gemstones, mentioning rubies in particular. He went on to say that if in the near future I was still performing the five ritual prayers, my future and provision might be involved in gemstones. He made it clear that he could not give any details but encouraged me to be awake and alert to opportunities in this direction.

In the past Shaykh Fadhlalla had these types of insights that he shared with me, and mostly out of small mindedness I ignored him or, in some cases, made some effort, but soon gave up any intention in time. In hindsight, had I followed his insights, time proved him right and I had missed an opportunity. When this gemstone vision came, I was acutely aware of my past ignorance and was committed to follow through this time.

Within a few weeks after Shaykh's vision, a traveling stranger visited me from Mozambique. He had heard that an American businessman was in White River, South Africa, who was interested in gemstone materials. I had shared my interest with various people in White River, the dentist, real estate agents, and friends. The word was out, and an answer came to my door. I do not remember the traveler's name, but he explained to me that he was an independent miner specializing in aquamarine. He brought a kilo of aquamarine rough to show me before heading to Johannesburg where he had a regular aquamarine buyer. I was very impressed with his materials, although at that time I did not know much about identifying and evaluating gemstones, let alone any specific stone. I still could see that these were clear, in good color and useful sizes for cutting and polishing. I explained that I was not able to offer him anything for his materials, but that soon, once I was educated more, I would welcome him back to review what he might bring for consideration.

After a week or so, we had planned a visit to Johannesburg. Shaykh Fadhlalla was often invited to give a talk or accept invitations for *dhikr* and other socially relevant events. It was on one of these occasions I traveled with him. While in Johannesburg, I saw a signboard on the road about the GIA starting fall classes. The GIA is the Gemstone Institute of America. There was a phone number and address which I wrote down, and then I went to visit them. It turned out that their fall classes were just beginning for a Certification Program in gemstone identification and evaluation. It was a six-to-eight-week course, longer if you included diamonds. I immediately signed up for the classes, beginning a few days later. The classes ran Monday through Friday. I remained in Johannesburg during the week, returning on the weekends to White River. After the eight-week course, I was certified in both Gemstone and Diamond

Identification and Evaluation, certifying in the top five percent of my class. Within a day or two of finishing my certification, I was having a coffee at Sandton Shopping Center, where just one table away from where I was sitting there was a group of men discussing gemstones from Mozambique. They had carts on wheels, with trays full of rough and cut stones. I was compelled to walk over and introduce myself to them and communicate my interest in gemstones. This began a long relationship between two of the men, one a local gemstone, fossil, and mineral dealer, the other a gemstone procurer traveling to mines all over Southern Africa and bringing materials to Johannesburg where most of the buyers and exporters were established.

The procurer's name was Jeff. He and I began working together.

Jeff would travel to Mozambique in search of semi-precious gemstones, with an emphasis on high grade aquamarine. We focused on aquamarine as there was a constant demand and we had established buyers already known to us both here and in the US. During this time, we connected with a local gem and mineral businessman who had a two-tiered business in gemstones. The first was common materials from Southern Africa and the other rare materials from mines such as Tsumeb, Brandberg and the Wessel mine in the Kuruman Desert of southwestern South Africa. He also was a partner in a new find of quartz that was referred to locally as "Spirit Quartz." In the West this name lent itself to a "spiritual" connotation, but in fact it was called this locally because of the way it was first discovered by local farmers. While tilling their fields, they would hit a vane or outcrop of these crystals; initially these crystals were purple, like the color of amethyst. When the tilling blades hit the quartz, it would throw a plum of purple dust into the air. The name "Spirit" was given to this new type of quartz, because it resembled Methylated Spirits, a cheap and commonly used purple, liquid cleaner.

Jeff and I worked together for the better part of the year, and then parted ways due to our very different approach to business and a divergent direction to where we envisioned the business going forward.

The gem dealer from Mozambique continued to visit me with partials of various grades of aquamarine. I regularly purchased his materials and encouraged him to bring me the best quality. When I mentioned my parting with Jeff to him, he acted stressed and uncomfortable. This was a mystery to me until after many months of buying and selling aquamarine when I was in Pretoria meeting a buyer from Briton.

Blue Beryl Mafia

I had been staying in a Bed & Breakfast hotel when I received a call from a gentleman requesting a meeting to discuss the aquamarine business. He said that he would send a car around to pick me up and take me to his home just outside Pretoria. At the time, I did not suspect anything untoward, but I would soon discover there was an entirely different purpose to this meeting invitation. The car and driver came to pick me up. We drove for about an hour on the main road and then a turn on a gravel road for another two to three kilometers. It was on the gravel road I started to feel a pit and pain in my stomach. This got worse when I saw up ahead a gated home flanked by two armed guards brandishing very large and menacing automatic military style rifles. The guards looked into the car, I waved, and we were escorted into what was a compound. There were several checkpoints, many armed guards and a horde of Rhodesian Ridgebacks roaming the spaces in between the building and the perimeter of the compound. We pulled up to a domed building that looked more like a mausoleum than an office. But as the door opened to my ride, I was welcomed by one of the guards to their office. This was an office designed to intimidate any non-initiated person to this rarely seen world in the gemstone business. I was asked into the center room where the dome loomed above us. It was mostly marble and gilded with hieroglyphics, mathematical shapes and formulas and some strange iconography. Underneath the dome was a marble table made from pure white stone. It was shaped as a hexagon – each side had a chair in front of it. At the edge of the table that framed the hexagon was an indentation. At first, I had no idea what that was all about, but I was soon to have a demonstration of its use. I was offered tea and cakes as well. As the tea became ready, several men walked into the room along with my host, who promptly introduced himself to me and informed me that he was the one who had invited me there today. Everyone took their seat at the hexagon; it was almost ritualistic in the way they sat down, knowing where their specific place was.

My host began to talk to me about aquamarines. He explained that his family had been in the aquamarine business in South Africa for over 400 years. He went on a bit, covering some historical events and how no matter what changed, i.e., whoever ruled Southern Africa, be it kings, queens, pirates or governments, they have not been interfered with in the mining, procurement, and export of aquamarine. He saw that I had been listening attentively; I think I slightly, ever so slightly, endeared myself to him. He asked me if I would be interested in seeing some of the best aquamarine available in Southern Africa. I was very eager and answered him in the affirmative. Just behind the hexagon table were shelving units made from hardwood that contained a series of drawers, each marked with a number and symbol. My host reached behind and pulled out a drawer, which was a tray slotted in sections filled with the most dazzling aquamarine I had ever seen. The cuts and the luster of the variety of sizes were mind boggling, but most of all the color. They were what are called Santa Maria blue. If you were to imagine the bluest of eyes, they would not come near the radiance of the Santa Maria aquamarine. He laid the tray in front of me. He pulled out from the tray one of the larger individual containers within the box and poured the stones onto the white marble table in front of me. After a few moments, everyone in the room was commenting on the quality and how they exclusively represented these stones and comparable quality. Then, with one swoop of his hand, he pushed the stones into the indentation in front of me that I have mentioned earlier. After pressing a button underneath, the table, the indentation slightly rose and became removable from the table like a sleeve. At the end of the sleeve was a cap, which he opened revealing a spout, from which he poured the stones back into the container and then into the drawer, replacing them all back into the shelving unit they originally came in.

My host asked what I thought of the materials. I naively answered that I would love to find these and others to sell them to buyers in the States and Europe. At that point there was a heavy pause of silence that encompassed the room. I realized at that point why they had brought me here. The pit in my stomach tightened. I looked around directly at the faces of everyone in the room, all making sure that I had no doubt that what I shared with them regarding my interest in the aquamarine business was a non-starter, but to what extent was still unclear. My host broke the silence ominously stating that I was called here today to see what I would never have, not now or in the future, and that if I knew what was good for me, I would immediately cease buying or selling aquamarine.

At this point, he and everyone stood up. The driver was called in and asked to take me back to my lodging in Pretoria.

I later recounted this event to my GIA professor, and he was shocked that they invited me to one of their main compounds. Dangerous as it was, many people he knew in the past just disappeared when they made even a small incursion into what they considered their exclusive right to the aquamarine business. He explained, with the pretext that what he was about to tell me is nowhere to be found in any historical account of the gem trade in sub-Saharan Africa. He conceded that there was much more regarding the DeBeers mafia, but little on the trade of colored semi-precious gemstones. He went on to say that there were four family dynasties that controlled over seventy-five percent of Sub-Saharan gemstone production. Twenty-five percent was mined through government agencies or leased by gemstone producing states to private industry; however, seventy-five percent of total production were small mines, thousands spread out over dozens of countries in villages, small towns and no-man's lands, where local bosses, chiefs and warlords controlled the production and sales of the materials. Most of this material fed into the four families that made sure it flowed to them and to them only.

Over the next few weeks after that encounter, I divested from aquamarine. Strangely enough, after this meeting, no one ever came again to my home from Mozambique or anywhere peddling aquamarine.

No Aquamarine, Spirit Quartz

Although aquamarine was now out of the picture, I focused on the new find mentioned earlier, called Spirit Quartz. I had several meetings with the suppliers that had already contracted with the local villagers and farmers to excavate the gem material from the land. They had hired a warehouse, and through a hands-on selection process separated the qualities of the Spirit Quartz into "flats," white cardboard boxes that held a series of smaller boxes inside where the materials were placed by size and quality. I negotiated with them exclusive rights to sell wholesale into the States. I had to commit to large quantities, but it was worth the investment as this new find became the entrée into the gem and mineral market in the U.S. After returning to the U.S., I already had a growing market for quartz.

The US gemstone market in 2001 was a niche market, mostly made up of collectors and curious buyers. The spiritual and energetic appreciation of gemstones was still in its infancy, but clearly growing fast. It was into this stream I focused my efforts.

Back in the United States Selling Gemstones

After returning to the States from South Africa in 2001, I began attending Gem & Mineral Shows around the North and Southeast part of the US. I discovered wholesale rock dealers and acquired most of what I would sell from the Tucson Gem & Minerals Shows. Over one million people attended the Tucson shows with vendors from all over the world.

There were usually over 35 venues, each with a minimum of 35 vendors to larger shows with over 300 vendors. It literally became the "Mecca" for gemstone enthusiasts over a two-week period.

In late 2004, I started carrying semi-precious gemstone beads; this was just before beads became very popular. Within six months of adding beads to our show, it wasn't long before they took over my tables at the shows, leaving the heavy rocks and minerals in storage.

In February 2005, I was offered a room in a used men's clothing shop on an up-and-coming street to open a bead shop. In 2006, we expanded into half the clothing store space and, by the middle of the third year, we had taken over the entire shop. To this day, almost 18 years later, it has been a successful endeavor, not only supporting myself and family, but a group of artisans providing a natural and creative medium to easily enter with little expense and lots of potential to showcase their creativity.

From Shaykh Fadhlalla's garden to the Gem-Garden, we rode on the wave of his inspiration. The success of the business was born out of an acknowledgment that we are not the managers of our affairs. When we are fortunate to be presented a wave of inspiration from one whose heart and mind is resonating with the soul consciousness, you can be assured that goodness will follow. In the end and in the beginning, intention is born of trust and the acknowledgment of love; regardless of outcome, its road will always lead to goodness.

Since Shaykh Fadhlalla shared his inspiration with me, and gemstones have not only provided me with a livelihood as he predicted, but they have been a medium to meet many people who were ready to embrace the path of Love and Light.

Spiritual Significance of Gemstones

I want to mention here the ancient traditions of gemstone healing and traditional use of gemstones as an enhancement or amplifier of energy expressed in many traits of human behavior and psychology. There is a rich prophetic tradition for the use of gemstones, reaching back to the Prophet Muhammad, Imam 'Ali and the Imams of his progeny and beyond.

Gemstones represent hidden qualities metaphorically buried in the earth, the same as contained within the heart's core, i.e., the Soul. Their beauty can be fully revealed when they are brought out from the darkness into the light.

They are cleaned, polished and, when cut by the hand of a master gemstone cutter, their true inner beauty emerges. The light of life refracts through them, giving off a radiance that for most of humankind we have always been compelled to value, display and use as an adornment. They represent the qualities of the soul expressed in the facets of God's creation. They reflect Beauty, Strength, Majesty and Awesomeness, Joy, Generosity and so much more.

> *Christian, Jew, Muslim, shaman, Zoroastrian, stone, ground, mountain, river, each has a secret way of being with the mystery, unique and not to be judged.*

— Rumi

In a garden, stones communicate and instill a feeling of rest, repose and induce reflection of spiritual thought.

Fountains in which stones are used reflect polar opposites in nature. Witnessing a fountain like this brings one to recognize and sense the singular harmony that is beyond the opposites.

We find the echo of permanence in "writing things in stone" – they communicate, in gravestones, statues, and other monuments, the perpetuity or the transcendent nature of time.

Gemstones have had an important place in many prophetic teachings. In the Judeo-Christian tradition, the Bible refers to twelve stones set in the breastplate of the high priest, symbolizing the twelve tribes of Israel. In Hinduism, nine gemstones are associated with the nine planetary gods in Vedic Astrological traditions.

In Islam, the practice of wearing gemstones developed from legends associated with the Prophet Muhammad, Imam `Ali, and their progeny.

Tradition relates that Imam `Ali wore four rings on his hand each containing a different gemstone. The Arabic names for these four are: *Aqeeq*, or Agate/Carnelian, *Yaqut*, or Ruby, *Feruz*, or Turquoise and *Hadid Theen*, or Hematite.

Aqeeq is generally regarded as the most important gemstone in Islam. The Prophet was said to have worn a silver ring on his right hand with an Abyssinian or Yemeni stone. It was his habit to wear the stone turned inwards towards his palm. Imam `Ali was also said to wear an Agate or carnelian ring, commonly attributed to ward off enemies and general misfortune.

Sometimes, the word *Yaqut* is translated as Opal, and it is said that Imam `Ali wore *Yaqut* for "beauty and dignity." But most scholars who are followers of Imam `Ali believe it refers to Ruby.

Feruz is unanimously accepted as Turquoise.

It is said that Imam `Ali wore turquoise "for obtaining divine help and victory." There is also a tradition from Imam Ja`far as-Sadiq that a person wearing *Feruz* will never be poor. In another tradition of the Prophet Muhammad, wearing Turquoise is a remedy for melancholy.

Hadid Theen is understood to be Hematite. It is said that Imam `Ali wore this gem for strength and fortitude. There also is a caution to wearing Hematite constantly or for long periods of time as its effect may cause one to be overconfident, making one subject to error especially when facing adversaries or oppressors.

There is also a fifth stone of significance known as *Dur-e-Najaf.*

Dur-e-Najaf is generally considered to be a type of clear or water Quartz, even possibly a rock crystal found in and around Najaf al-Ashraf area of Iraq, hence, its name. Quartz is known as a magnifier. It is known to enhance the energetic quality and intensity of vibration of other stones.

The Black Stone is the cornerstone of the *Ka`ba*, which is kissed. Kissing is the most intimate metaphor representing an act of love that leads to the yielding and disappearance in the love of the beloved.

The Black Stone is the most significant stone in all of Islam. It is the key to the *Ka`ba*.

After Thoughts

When I first embraced Islam, my family's reaction was that I had either lost my mind or that I had been abducted and brainwashed into joining an Islamic cult. My friends' reactions, old and new, were more nuanced: most of them thought that I was going through a phase that I might or might not recover from. All in all, it was a very emotionally trying period for me, especially regarding the estrangement that followed with my close family members and the betrayal I felt from the reactions of my friends.

For me, becoming a Muslim came out of a deep recognition and acceptance of the obvious: that Islam was not "like" other religions, but the all-encompassing inclusive updated message from The Source of all "other" messages. It was all the prophetic teachings throughout history contained within one wisdom teaching.

I take responsibility for some of my family and friends' responses in that when I returned from Sufi Boot Camp to the commune in Albany, California, I was not only visibly changed but my attitude was a borderline, classic zealot like that of a born-again Christian or a very enthusiastic Krishna devotee, trying to save your soul and get a donation at the same time.

Looking back, it was a process like so much in life. There are always "honeymoon" periods in almost any endeavor; some love affairs can take on an appearance of madness. I was certainly lovesick with being a Muslim and especially exuberant towards having and maintaining my new life.

My priorities at that time were not entirely formed regarding my friends, and I felt confident that those who really knew me would come to accept and understand that it was all for the best. As for my family, I was even more confident that one day God would surely open their hearts and minds in a way that would be in His wisdom and at the appropriate time and place.

This brings me to the story of my uncle Jay.

My Uncle Jay

I had been a Muslim going on approximately two years still estranged from my family and most of my old friends. Just shortly after I returned to the commune, several members of our ISHK (Institute for the Study of Human Knowledge) embraced Islam, including Jerry Patterson, whom I mentioned earlier in this book. All in all, there were nine who journeyed

285

to Monterey to make their acceptance of this path to Light. Many have become steadfast friends to this day and some have passed.

In the late seventies, my uncle Jay was diagnosed with cancer. It had metastasized throughout his body, giving him only a few months to live. My mother broke her silence towards me to inform me that my uncle was in hospital and invited me to come visit him in his last few days. Although I felt an inclination to see him, I was not compelled enough to endure meeting his wife and family, who had been especially mean and critical of me for becoming a Muslim. I thought long and hard about how my refusal to come would affect my mother, compounding the already existing hard feelings that she felt along with other members of my family. After searching my heart, an inspiration emerged to write him a letter:

> *Dear Uncle Jay*
>
> *I greet you with a hope and prayer that this letter finds you in peace, trusting in God's wisdom that His Love and Mercy encompasses us, and that He is the best manager of our affairs.*
>
> *I regret that I will not come in person to visit you, hoping that you will understand and forgive me, especially in the light of our recent strain in our relationship. I felt in consideration of our recent estrangement, I would prefer to share with you in writing what is from my heart and mind.*
>
> *There is an account of our Prophet Abraham. I put this to you humbly for your immediate reflection; whether or not you believe in God, you are facing the inevitable visit of death.*
>
> **So also, did We show Ibrahim the power and the laws of the heavens and the earth, that he might (with understanding) have certitude. When the night covered him over, He saw a star: He said: "This is my Lord." But when it set, He said: "I love not those that set." When he saw the moon rising in splendor, he said: "This is my Lord." But when the moon set, he said: "Unless my Lord guides me, I shall surely be among those who go astray." When he saw the sun rising in splendor, he said: "This is my Lord; this is the greatest (of all)." But when the sun, set, he said: "O my people! I am**

indeed free from your (guilt) of giving partners to Allah. For me, I have set my face, firmly and truly, towards Him Who created the heavens and the earth, and never shall I give partners to Allah."

This recollection regarding our Prophet Abraham is from the Qur'an 6:75-79 and, as you know, it is also found in our Hebrew traditions.

Dear Uncle, you are witnessing everything fading away. Your life and all that you have accomplished are vanishing. Your wife, children, work, hopes and dreams are irrelevant to this moment of passage into the next life. Like our Prophet Abraham, who he let go of everything relative and ephemeral, take this as your sword to cut through attachments and pierce this veil of worldly existence and prepare yourself for the hereafter.

With Loving embrace, your nephew

David

My mother read this letter to my uncle in the hospital while he was in the last few moments of his life. After hearing the content of my letter, uncle Jay asked that everyone leave his room; his wife, family and nurses all left, except he asked that my mother stay behind. He took the letter from my mother's hands and placed it upon his chest. He told my mother that we all had misjudged her son. He said that from this point on, he did not want to see or hear anything more of this world, but this letter. On saying that, within a few minutes, my uncle Jay passed.

My mother called me immediately after his passing, crying and asking me to forgive her wrongful judgments she assumed about me. From that moment on, I had a rapprochement not only with her, but reconciliation with my entire family.

I share this story as an encouragement to many who have had monumental changes in their lives – religious or otherwise – that if you are acting in response to truth, with clear and pure intention, eventually it will shine and be acknowledged by those whom you love. If it does not, be resigned that only God brings the hearts together.

Witnessing Perfection

After returning to the States from South Africa in 2001, I made it a habit to visit Shaykh Fadhlalla every year, mostly at the time when the Rasooli Community would hold its annual International Gathering. I tried to split my time between visiting him at his home in White River and Pretoria as well as Johannesburg, where many of his students and community members were based.

On one of these occasions, I believe it was about 2005, I stayed for some days at Shaykh Fadhlalla's farm.

During my visit he told me about a book that he was writing called *Witnessing Perfection*, and that he would like me to read through the manuscript. Later that day, he brought it by my room. From the very first words of the introduction, I was drawn into what can only be described as a vortex of lights, seamlessly linked in a cascading fractal of unfolding acknowledgement directly absorbed and reflected within the heart and mind. Even though I obviously was not the writer of these words, the experience of reading *Witnessing Perfection* was as though it was already written within me. It was like a rose bud rooted in my heart. It began to unfold its beauty and scent as the meaning of each word alighted upon it. I read through most of the manuscript only putting it aside to test its premise that it should be used as a manual for the seeker. Shaykh Fadhlalla suggested using it similar to the I Ch'ing, referring to it from time to time, opening it at any page and reading where one's eyes fell. I tested this premise, and it always perfectly synchronized with every present moment.

I have found no end of the giving this book provides. Of all of Shaykh Fadhlalla's books, I found this one the most useful, second only to the *Four Journeys* that in some way mirrors *Witnessing Perfection*, but in a more allegorical, poetic way.

Shaykh Fadhlalla kindly gave me a copy of the manuscript for my own personal use. It became my daily reader and I referred to it spontaneously as well as with specific intention on a regular basis. I also used it as part of a series of lectures mostly after a session of *dhikr* and meditation.

The book had a life of its own, and one day its generous and magical power transformed an unlikely encounter to unexpected sweet openings of body, mind and spirit.

I was out shopping one afternoon at a specialty gourmet food shop called Southern Seasons in Chapel Hill, North Carolina. They were well-known for their imported cheeses, deli foods and specialty items from all over the world. After completing my shopping, it was my habit to buy some of their Turkish delights or other sweets at their sweets counter with a cup of coffee and to savor both before moving on.

While standing at the counter deciding what I was going to have that day, a man moved close. I noticed he was bobbing his head slightly up and down as though he was experiencing some sort of inner delight. He addressed me saying, "Witnessing perfection," followed by, "Are you witnessing perfection?" I was taken by his question. I viewed this moment as something in the realm of the unseen, even of the miraculous. I asked myself: *how does he know that I am filtering nearly everything through the reflections of Shaykh Fadhlalla's book?* I felt as though the angels had brought him to inquire about my own state. Was I really witnessing perfection?

I turned to him and said, "There is nothing other than perfection and I am striving to see it in every moment." His answer to me was, "Come, sit with me and taste true perfection." Wow! I was even more struck by this invitation. I thought: *who is this man and what is this all about?* We found a table; he kindly bought me a cup of coffee and picked out a selection of chocolates to share. Our conversation took off on the subject of perfection. We spoke for hours, covering the universal to the mundane, both agreeing that there is a seamless connection between the two. We dived into science and religion and how these two disciplines intersect. We floated the idea that they both are ascending on a curve of evolution toward an inevitable meeting place and that place is the human heart and its ability to witness perfection in all things. He was very interested in Islam and why I had become a Muslim. He admitted humbly to me how he had never thought of Islam in the light of our conversation. He was so excited about discovering the depth and breadth of these teachings that he proposed we met on a regular basis to discuss Islam. As the time came for us to depart, I still was bewildered about what had inspired him to approach me in the first place. I asked him, "Why did you approach me, inquiring whether or not I was witnessing perfection?" His answer: "Chocolate! You were standing in front of the chocolate counter, where my handmade chocolates are displayed and offered to the public. I'm a confectioner specializing in handmade organic chocolates. When I saw you standing looking at my creations, I asked if you are witnessing perfection." This was truly a moment of *witnessing perfection.*

Over the coming months we met on a regular basis until he had become ill and succumbed to his illness. Before he passed away, he thanked me for our friendship and all the times we spent together. His last words to me were in gratitude that he had the opportunity to expand his vision of perfection from what he and humankind attribute to themselves, to acknowledging that all humanity, and the universe at large, is predicated from the only original and truly One source of perfection.

Glossary of Terms

A

Adab – Courtesies
Adhan – Muslim call to obligatory prayer
Allahu Akbar – God is great, or the greatest
Amir – Leader
Awliya (plural of *Wali*) – Friends. Plural of *Wali*. Full term is *Wali u'lla* (Friend of Allah)

B

Barakah – Blessing
Bismillah – In the name of God

D

Dargah – A shrine or tomb built over the grave of a revered religious figure, often a Sufi saint or dervish
Darqawi (or *Darqawiyya*) – Sufi order that is a revivalist branch of the *Shadhiliyah* brotherhood which originated in Morocco
Deen – Way of life; a path, but commonly translated as "religion"
Dervish – A spiritual wayfarer – a *Faqir*, in Arabic
Dhikr – Remembrance (of God)
Diwan – A collection of songs praising God or the Prophet Muhammad
Du`a – A supplication

F

Faqir – A wayfarer to a spiritual path, mostly used in Sufism
Fuqara – Plural of *Faqir*

H

Hadra – Presence, or Dance of the Sufis: A form of *dhikr*, usually performed standing up in a circle with some movements
Hafiz – Someone who has memorized the entire Qur'an by heart
Haram – Forbidden
Hijrah – Migration

I

Idhn – Permission to transmit spiritual knowledge to others as a Sufi teacher

Iman – Faith / Trust

J

Jalabiya – A traditional robe worn by many Arab men

Jirga (or *Jirgah*) – A council of tribal elders

K

Karamat – Supernatural wonders performed by Muslim saints.

Khalifa (or *Khalifah*) – A successor, especially of a Sufi master

L

Laylat ul Fuqara – Night of the Wayfarers

M

Madhab – Usually translated as "Religion". However, within Islamic jurisprudence, it also refers to a school of thought within Islam

Madrasah – School

Majlis – A gathering / A sitting place

Masjid – Mosque

Muqaddim – A Sufi designation given to one who represents a Shaykh

Mureed – A disciple of a Sufi master, upon whom the person has taken an oath to obey him as the teacher and guide to the spiritual path the Sufi master follows

Murshid – A Sufi teacher / Shaykh

P

Pir – A Sufi spiritual guide. Also called, Shaykh

Q

Qasida – An Ode, often praising God

S

Sayyid – An honorific title denoting people accepted as descendants of the Prophet Muhammad and his cousin and son-in-law `Ali ibn Abi Talib through his grandsons, Hasan ibn `Ali and Husain ibn Ali

Shahada – Profession of faith, to revert to Islam

Shaktipat or Saktipata – (Sanskrit, from shakti "(psychic) energy" and pata, "to fall") refers in Hinduism to the transmission (or conferring) of spiritual energy upon one person by another

Shaykh – A Sufi spiritual guide

Shaytan – Arabic for Satan

Subhan Allah – Glory be to God

T

Tariqa (or *Tariqah*) – A school or order of Sufism, or specifically a concept for the mystical teaching and spiritual practices of such an order with the aim of seeking *haqiqa* (or *haqiqah*), which translates as "ultimate truth"

Tasbih – Prayer beads

U

Umrah (aka *Minor Hajj*) – Pilgrimage to Mecca, which can be undertaken at any time of the year, in contrast to the Hajj, which has specific dates according to the Islamic lunar calendar

Urs (from Arabic `Urs) or `Urus (literal meaning 'wedding') – The death anniversary of a Sufi saint, usually held at the saint's shrine

W

Wali (pl. *Awliya*) – A friend of God

Wudhu – Washing before performing the Muslim prayer

Z

Za`wiya – A Sufi Center

Made in the USA
Columbia, SC
05 November 2022

70500332R00176